The Practical Guide to Corpc Responsibility

Corporate social responsibility has gained substantial traction in recent decades but many still struggle with conveying the importance of integrating ethics and environmental and social values within the demands of a business world understandably concerned with making profit. First published in 2009 as 'Do the Right Thing', *The Practical Guide to Corporate Social Responsibility* guides you through the basics, teaching how to recognise CSR benefits and put principles into practice in a business-focussed way.

This new edition helps readers get to grips with improving their organisation's environmental management, sustainability, health and safety and trading ethics with straightforward guidance and tips. A new 'Do the Right Thing' Model assists organisations with identifying risks and frames corporate social responsibility in a business context accessible to all. Features include:

- An updated 'Do the Right Thing' Model aligned to the new ISO high level structure for management system standards.
- 20 global case studies to demonstrate how the model can impact performance.
- A corporate social responsibility policy template for your organisation's use.
- Helpful 'Test your thinking' exercises to check your understanding and stretch your working knowledge.
- 100 practical actions for you to start implementing today.

This is an essential introduction to the complex areas of corporate social responsibility that affect health and safety practitioners, environmental managers, human resources personnel and those working with quality and business assurance. It will also be critical reading for those looking to understand how CSR fits into the new high level structure of ISO 9001, ISO 14001 and ISO 45001.

Stephen Asbury is the HSE Technical Discipline Manager at PetroSkills LLC, the world's largest provider of competency-based training. In a career extending over 30 years, Stephen worked in a variety of risk management roles with

Rugby Group plc, BTR plc and GKN plc, before moving into consultancy in 1996 as head of liability consulting with Royal and Sun Alliance Insurance Group. After a short spell as a director of Aon, he founded Corporate Risk Systems Ltd in 1999 where he was Managing Director until 2015.

Stephen was a RoSPA Safety Professional of the Year in 1995. He was presented with the IOSH President's Distinguished Service Award in 2010, and with the PetroSkills Top of Class Award for 'innovation and excellence in instructional performance' in 2014.

Stephen is a Chartered Fellow of IOSH and a Chartered Environmentalist. From 1998 to 2012, he was a member of the IOSH Council of Management, and chaired several IOSH committees over this time.

In his recreational time, he enjoys theatre, scuba diving and F1 motor sport. This is Stephen's fifth book.

Follow Stephen on Twitter @Stephen_Asbury

Richard Ball is Health and Safety Systems Manager at High Speed Two (HS2) Limited. He has worked on corporate social responsibility (CSR) projects in a wide range of sectors. Richard graduated in environmental management, before starting work in the automotive industry. He then moved into the public sector, working for a statutory organization supporting young people, charities and voluntary organizations with facilities management and risk management responsibilities. Since moving into the consultancy sector over ten years ago, Richard has developed and delivered health and safety, environmental and CSR training courses for organizations including Astra Zeneca, Merlin Entertainments and Police forces. As a Head of Environment he has a global perspective, working internationally with delegates from over twenty countries for the oil and gas sector. Richard developed CIEH's Environmental Protection qualifications and developed IEMA's applied learning route to Associate Membership and Pathway to MIEMA routes, and on a variety of consultancy and auditing projects, including CSR. In his leisure time he enjoys running and spending time with his family. He is also a Vice-Chair of school governors.

www.routledge.com/9781138901841

Health and Safety, Environment and Quality Audits
Stephen Asbury

'A most welcome addition to the library of any manager active in this field and ought to be the standard work in HSEQ auditing. This [is] the 'go to' handbook for those who aspire to drive a prosperous and thriving business and I highly recommend it' – Dr. Andrew Rankine, University of Glasgow

'This is a refreshing publication and all auditors would benefit by reflecting on the advice and tips contained' – *SHP* Magazine, January 2014

Dynamic Risk Assessment
The Practical Guide to Making Risk-based Decisions with The 3-Level Risk Management Model
Stephen Asbury and Edmund Jacobs

'It will become the classic work on the subject' – Dr. Stephen Vickers (former Chief Executive, NEBOSH)

Health and Safety, Environment and Quality Audits
A Risk-based Approach
Stephen Asbury and Peter Ashwell

'An excellent read, brilliantly written by two authors who clearly know their subject . . . it deserves to become the standard work in this area' – *SHP* magazine, July 2007
'An excellent book by two authors who are among the best in the world at both auditing and training auditors' – *Health & Safety At Work* magazine, August 2007

Environmental Management
Richard Ball and Anna-Lisa Kelso

Environmental Principles and Best Practice
Richard Ball and M Gavin A

The Practical Guide to Corporate Social Responsibility

Do the Right Thing

Stephen Asbury and Richard Ball

Routledge
Taylor & Francis Group

LONDON AND NEW YORK

First published 2016
by Routledge
2 Park Square, Milton Park, Abingdon, Oxon OX14 4RN

and by Routledge
711 Third Avenue, New York, NY 10017

Routledge is an imprint of the Taylor & Francis Group, an informa business

© 2016 Stephen Asbury and Richard Ball

British Library Cataloguing-in-Publication Data
A catalogue record for this book is available from the British Library

Library of Congress Cataloging in Publication Data
The practical guide to corporate social responsibility: do the right thing /
Stephen Asbury and Richard Ball.
pages cm
Includes bibliographical references.
ISBN 978-1-138-90184-1 (pbk.: alk. paper) – ISBN 978-1-315-69765-9 (ebook)
1. Social responsibility of business. I. Asbury, Stephen, author. II. Ball, Richard
(Environmental management consultant), author.
HD60.P725 2016
658.4'08 – dc23
2015031327

ISBN: 978-1-138-90184-1 (pbk)
ISBN: 978-1-315-69765-9 (ebk)

Typeset in Sabon
By Swales & Willis Ltd, Exeter, Devon, UK

Contents

List of figures   ix
List of tables   xii
List of case studies   xiii
Foreword   xiv
Endorsements   xv
Preface   xvi
Acknowledgements   xxv

Introduction   1

1 Business control and risk management   4

2 The evolution of CSR   45

3 The appetite for CSR and the triple bottom line   70

4 Stakeholder expectations   84

5 Opportunities for organizations   106

6 Reporting and verifying   126

7 The case against CSR   149

8 Opportunities in the supply chain   169

9 Personal social responsibility   189

10 Learning from London   219

Appendix 1: 100 CSR actions   249
Appendix 2: sample CSR policy   256
References   258
Glossary of acronyms   268
Index   269

Figures

0.1   The DTRT Model: the six core elements of doing the
      right thing   xvii
0.2   A prokaryote, c. 3.5 billion years ago   xix
0.3   *Australopithecus africanus*   xxi
0.4   A proportional view of the history of the world. Innovated
      by Stephen Asbury, created by IOSH   xxii
0.5   World human population 1800–2020   xxiv
1.1   The main pillars of management systems thinking from the
      4th to the 20th century   6
1.2   William Edwards Deming in the 1950s. Photo courtesy of
      The W. Edwards Deming Institute®   7
1.3   The PDCA cycle, commonly known as the Deming Wheel   9
1.4   ILO-OSH, 2001   12
1.5   Asbury & Ball original CSR model, 2009   14
1.6   Mapping of control frameworks to the Deming Wheel/PDCA   15
1.7   The five stakeholder groups   22
1.8   The DTRT Model: the six core elements of doing the
      right thing   23
1.9   Look at the horizon to see factors impacting the mission   24
1.10 Business environment – vision – mission – business
      objectives cascade   29
1.11 JCB's vision statement   30
1.12 Shell's vision statement   30
1.13 H.J. Heinz's vision statement   30
1.14 Achieving success by aligning objectives   31
1.15 Examples of risks in an organization's 'risk universe'   32
1.16 The 4Ts   37
1.17 The essence of enterprise   39
1.18 A simple risk-ranking matrix   40
1.19 The DTRT Model: the six core elements of doing the
      right thing   43
1.20 The Asbury & Ball CSR MSS, The DTRT Model ©, 2016   44

2.1	Spoof job advertisement for nineteenth-century chimney sweeps	52
2.2	An audience of 72,000 attended the Live Aid concert at Wembley Stadium in 1985.	54
2.3	Map showing the 178 states (at April 2008) which have ratified the Kyoto Protocol to the United Nations Framework Convention on Climate Change	57
2.4	Changes in greenhouse gas emissions by Kyoto signatory countries since 1990	58
3.1	Michael Wright (Director – Executive Board), Danielle Roe (Marketing Manager), Megan Turner (Events Coordinator), Lily Proctor (HR/Training Apprentice) and Tanya Parker (Receptionist) spent a day helping staff at the facility to paint fences, tend to the hospice garden, bake with some of the patients and help sort through clothing at the Shop and Drop Donation Centre	74
4.1	The business in society	93
4.2	Good stakeholder engagement	95
4.3	Reducing water consumption and carbon footprint	100
4.4	Promoting hotel-room recycling	100
4.5	Encouraging us to replace our towels on the rail, instead of on the floor	101
4.6	Materiality scatter matrix	104
5.1	Added value from CSR	108
5.2	Construction of Terminal 5 at Heathrow Airport, London	113
5.3	The tip of the iceberg: the relationship between insured and uninsured costs	119
6.1	High-level structure for ISO 14001:2015, showing the improvement cycle	136
6.2	Tariq, aged 12, stitching Nike footballs in Pakistan.	147
7.1	Macondo Well Disaster	161
8.1	Would you want your brand showing here?	171
8.2	Sustainable procurement guide adapted from the Environment Agency	184
9.1	Seven steps to PSR change	191
9.2	Fair trade logo	197
9.3	Soil Association Organic Standard logo	198
9.4	Rainforest Alliance Certified logo	199
9.5	The 'Möbius loop'	200
9.6	'Möbius loop' with markings to show the item is made from recycled materials	200
9.7	'Crossed-out wheelie bin' symbol for recyclable electrical products complying with EN 50419	201
9.8	Forest Stewardship Council logo	201
9.9	PEFC Certified and PEFC Recycled logos	201

9.10	Plastic recycling classifications	202
9.11	The green dot (*der grüne Punkt*)	203
9.12	An energy rating label for a washing machine	203
9.13	Fuel savings from reduced speed	206
10.1	The ODA legacy plan for London, 2012	222
10.2	The Carbon Trust three-stage approach to developing robust offsetting strategy	230
10.3	The waste hierarchy	231
10.4	The Formula E racing car	236
10.5	Spaces for charging electric vehicles at the Marriott/NCP car park in Bristol, UK	238
10.6	Labourer deaths in sports big builds 2000–2022	244

Tables

0.1 Extinction events   xxiii
6.1 'I have reconsidered using a company's products
    and services that has avoided paying tax in this country'   130
7.1 BP's payments related to Gulf Coast recovery   167
8.1 A summary of the principles of the UN Global Compact   178
8.2 The Carbon Fix Foundation four-phase certification scheme   181
9.1 The value chain benefits of a CSR programme through
    a framework of 'creating shared value'   195

Case studies

1.1   Hon Hai Precision Industry Co., Ltd (Foxconn),
      Taiwan and Catcher Technologies, Jiangsu, China   16
1.2   Collapse of the Grand Banks Fisheries, Canada   25
2.1   Cadbury pioneers CSR, UK   47
2.2   The evolution of CSR at Unilever, International   61
3.1   Donate-a-day at Henderson Insurance Brokers, UK   73
3.2   Pearson plc. wins global health and safety award,
      International   75
4.1   Prohibition and American college football, USA   86
4.2   200 thousand hotels and 17.5 million hotel rooms,
      International   98
5.1   Heathrow Airport Terminal 5, London, UK   112
5.2   Two views of Coca-Cola, International   120
6.1   Corporation tax dodgers, International   128
6.2   Can certification save our forests? Brazil and International   140
7.1   The Saudi Arabian Oil Company, Saudi Arabia   155
7.2   When risk and reward fall out of balance, Macondo,
      Gulf of Mexico   163
8.1   Rani Plaza disaster, Bangladesh   171
8.2   Carbon management within a supply chain, UK   179
9.1   Coffee bean links consumers to growers, Latin and
      Central America   192
9.2   Ethics Adviser resigns over 25,000 deaths, India   208
10.1 Electric sport sells electric cars, China, Malaysia,
      Uruguay, Argentina, USA, Monaco, Germany, Russia, UK   235
10.2 FIFA Soccer World Cup 2022, Qatar   244

Foreword

Corporate social responsibility can seem a baffling concept to some, combining as it does ethics and environmental and social values with the business world, understandably concerned with making profit and sustaining its enterprise into the future. But 'sustainability' applies happily to both society and business. The best work in corporate social responsibility recognizes that these two needs can be balanced, and mutually beneficial. My own work at Age Concern, the Equality and Human Rights Commission and the International Longevity Centre – UK shows that valuing people and their place in society isn't just about 'doing the right thing' – it's about maximizing potential for individuals and business.

I welcome this new book from Stephen Asbury and Richard Ball, designed to bring clarity and understanding to a subject that's critical today, and will become increasingly important in the decades ahead.

Baroness Greengross OBE Chair,
All Party Parliamentary Group on
Corporate Responsibility

Endorsements

'Corporate sustainability has rapidly become central to all successful organisations.

A growing world population with increasing demands for water, energy, food and materials places enhanced pressures on environmental and social systems. Steering a course through these sustainability challenges requires short-term action based on long-term thinking, a critical skill needed of professionals working in this space and this book provides much needed support.

It is essential reading for people wanting to create long-term social and economic value and protect and enhance natural capital'.

Tim Balcon, Chief Executive,
Institute of Environmental
Management and Assessment

'Corporate social responsibility continues to evolve as a mainstream business activity with standards and transparency aspiring to the same professionalism as financial reporting. Yet the rate of change remains slow with regard to the continuing and increasing urgency upon society and business. The window of opportunity for long-term sustainable development remains relatively small, as the "time to act now" was many years ago. However, the advantage of organizations and industry collaboration remains strong leadership, coordination and change management. I was delighted to read and endorse this inspiring and knowledgeable book, which aptly demonstrates the value of CSR and how to continue to 'actually do the right thing'. I am certain it will inform, educate and enable professionals to get and stay ahead of the curve'.

Colin Parry, CEnv MIEMA
Environmental Manager, Diageo plc

Preface

The highest courage is to dare to be yourself in the face of adversity. Choosing right over wrong, ethics over convenience, and truth over popularity . . . these are the choices that measure your life. Travel the path of integrity without looking back, for there is never a wrong time to do the right thing.

–Attributed to Michael Moore, American filmmaker

On reflection, when we researched and published our first book about corporate social responsibility (CSR) in 2009, I think we saw the theme as a little bit 'pink and fluffy'. Wouldn't it be nice to save the world, so to say? You'll notice that our thinking on CSR has moved on in the intervening years, and we now see – and commend to you – CSR as a positive choice for treating identified business risks, and a component of overall corporate responsibility; using CSR as a means of treating or mitigating foreseeable and significant risks to lower, more tolerable levels.

Organizations indulging in CSR-like behaviours and implementations are those that successfully integrate sustainable behaviours throughout their activities, products and services. Leading companies can demonstrate responsible concern for both the environment, with regard to sustainable sourcing of raw materials, and communities, including the safety and well being of their employees, right through the supply chain or value chain, as ISO 14001:2015 will reframe relationships upstream and downstream. And, they make it relevant to the business context within which their organizations operate. This book provides our advice to organizations in every industry and every sector on how to think about and respond to CSR-related risks.

Later in this Preface, you'll enjoy a short history about the creation of the universe and of our Earth. Whatever you believe, first there was (probably) nothing. And this is where the business context evolved over the last couple-of-hundred years (and continues to evolve). The need and the opportunity for CSR is now gigantic – we (the passengers of spaceship Earth) need to find the new products, services and business models for a world that needs to be able support nine billion sustainable lifestyles by the year 2050.

Doing the right thing

Chapter 1 provides a review of the history and evolution of modern business control, risk management and management systems thinking, and introduces you to our 'DTRT Model', a part of which – the core elements – is shown below.

In each of our twenty-or-so case studies, we'll use this model of core elements to pick out the CSR-related themes within the study so you can decide whether proportionate preventive or control actions had been taken to mitigate the risks – where the approach taken 'pushes the buttons' (or not), so to say. We call this our DTRT Model Core Theme Indicator.

In Chapter 2, we'll explain the evolution of CSR so you can see its origins, present, and likely future. In Chapter 3, we'll describe the growing appetite for CSR in organizations of all types. Many organizations illustrated in the case studies presented in this book have adopted our principles and, using our DTRT Model©, others can repeat our process and achieve similar or even better results.

Chapter 4 is all about stakeholders, and you'll be introduced to the significance of each of the five groups of these for the first time in Chapter 1. For now, suffice to say, each will likely be passionate about your organization and its performance. We'll contrast their often-conflicting views, and explain how you/your management team can use CSR to meet, moderate, and mitigate excesses in stakeholders' opinions and expectations.

By this point, we'll be ready in Chapter 5 to bring all of our learning so far together by highlighting the benefits of a CSR/DTRT risk management approach by all types of organizations. As we've said, we'll bring a range of selected examples of these behaviors to life as case studies based in organizations and sectors.

Chapter 6 explains reporting and verifying claimed performance, and the importance of transparency. There is so much more to CSR than planting a few trees and preparing a report about it!

In Chapter 7, we turn 180 degrees and argue the case against CSR. There has been much hype and unsubstantiated claims and counter-claims (especially

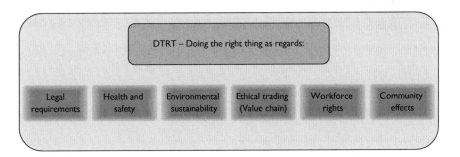

Figure 0.1 The DTRT Model: the six core elements of doing the right thing.

on the internet), and we want to rigorously test our DTRT Model against these arguments. Our conclusion is interesting, to say the least!

As we move towards the concluding chapters, Chapter 8 looks at the supply chain from suppliers to customers, and we look for opportunities to apply our DTRT Model and CSR principles in your value chain.

Chapter 9 can (almost) be read as a stand-alone. It highlights how you can contribute to social responsibilities in a personal, individual way. We do not see this as a choice between CSR and PSR, but approaches that when blended can provide the best engagement and results for the organization and for all of us – the dwellers of plant Earth.

Chapter 10 analyses the approach taken to CSR at the 2012 London Olympic Games, which were judged to be the most sustainable Games ever, and shows you how you might deliver this in your own organization. You'll learn how LOCOG and ODA envisioned, planned, built and successfully delivered a safe, low-impact, legacy-positive, memory-making event on time and on budget.

> One small step for man, one giant leap for mankind.
> –NASA Astronaut, Neil Armstrong,
> speaking from the surface of the Moon, 20 July 1969

In just 0.004% of the time...

Our home, the planet we call Earth, is billions of years old: 4.6 billion for those who can handle BIG numbers. It took a very long time for it to become just right for life to thrive. In the course of just a few generations, we are causing a lot of damage to it, consuming more than our fair share of its resources and exploiting too many of its people.

To put this into context, and to simplify the impossibly huge numbers, earth has been around for about 60 million human lifetimes, while modern humans have been around for about 2500 human lifetimes. This represents a human occupation of about 0.004% of the total time Earth has been here. Not much.

While most of the Earth's life extinction has been a natural phenomenon, we may be at the brink of substantial change. Some experts have estimated that up to half of presently existing species may become extinct by 2100 (Wilson, 2002). We have a lot to cover and little space and time in which to do it. Let's get started....

A short history of the universe and the earth

Everything we know, and possibly everything we'll ever know, started 13.7 billion years ago with an event that has become universally known as the 'Big Bang'. The first stars were formed from the hydrogen and helium created at this time. As a result of nuclear reactions, heavier elements were generated that resulted, around 5 billion years ago, in the creation of stars such as our Sun.

Around 4.6 billion years ago, the earth began to form from a cloud of dust, rocks and gas. As it grew, its gravitational field allowed it to retain an atmosphere, including water. A mixture of volcanic activity and bombardment by objects from space altered the atmosphere, creating a mixture of mainly ammonia, methane, water vapor, carbon dioxide and nitrogen.

Life on earth

We can only speculate about how and when life began on earth – perhaps around 4 billion years ago. In the energetic chemistry of the early earth, a molecule (or something else) gained the ability to make copies of itself. This 'magic' molecule is widely known as the 'Original Replicator'. The nature of this molecule is unknown; its function having long since been superseded by life's current replicator, deoxyribonucleic acid (DNA).

Current evidence suggests that the last universal common ancestor lived during the early Archean Eon, perhaps 3.5 billion years ago, or earlier. This cell is the ancestor of all cells, and hence of all life on earth. It was probably an early prokaryote, possessing a cell membrane and probably ribosomes, but lacking a nucleus or membrane-bound organelles such as mitochondria or chloroplasts. Like all modern cells, it used DNA as its genetic code, RNA for information transfer and protein synthesis, and enzymes to catalyze reactions.

Life remained unicellular for up to 2.5 billion years. Around 1 billion years ago, the first multi-cellular plants emerged, probably green algae in the oceans. Possibly by around 100 million years later, multi-cellularity had also evolved in animals, probably sponges.

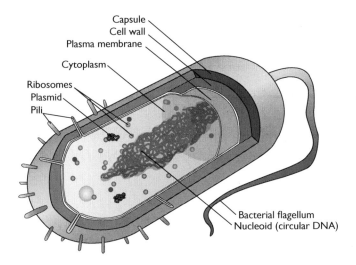

Figure 0.2 A prokaryote, c. 3.5 billion years ago.

For most of the earth's history, there has been no life on land. The oldest fossils of land fungi and plants date to 480–460 million years ago, though molecular evidence suggests they may have colonized the land earlier than this. The process will have started with plants (probably resembling algae) and fungi growing first at the edges of the water and then out of it. Although these organisms initially stayed close to the water's edge, mutations and variations resulted in further colonization of this new land environment. When the first animals left the oceans is not precisely known: the oldest clear evidence is of arthropods on land dates back to around 450 million years ago, perhaps thriving and becoming better adapted as a result of the vast food source provided by the terrestrial plants.

Four-legged animals evolved from fish around 380–375 million years ago, and by 360 million years ago they were spreading across the land. Around 310 million years ago the synapsids (including mammals) diverged from birds and reptiles.

The most severe extinction event to date took place 250 million years ago, at the boundary of the Permian and Triassic Periods, known as the P–T extinction event. Around 95 per cent of life on earth died out, possibly due to the Siberian Traps volcanic event, the largest eruptions known. But life persevered, and around 230 million years ago dinosaurs split off from their reptilian ancestors. Another extinction event occurred 200 million years ago, though this spared many of the dinosaurs and they soon became dominant among the vertebrates. Though some of the mammalian lines began to separate during this period, the mammals at this time were probably all small animals resembling shrews.

The first birds lived around 150 million years ago. Competition with the new birds drove many non-avian birds, such as pterosaurs, to extinction. The dinosaurs were probably already in decline for various reasons when, 65 million years ago, an asteroid nine miles wide struck earth just off the Yucatán Peninsula in Mexico, ejecting vast quantities of particulate matter and vapor into the air that occluded sunlight, inhibiting photosynthesis. Most large animals – including the non-avian dinosaurs – became extinct, marking the end of the Cretaceous Period and Mesozoic Era. In the Paleocene Epoch, mammals rapidly diversified, grew larger and became the dominant vertebrates. A small African ape, *Australopithecus africanus*, which lived around 6 million years ago, was perhaps the last animal whose descendants would include both modern humans and their closest relatives, the chimpanzees (Archeologyinfo, 2015).

Human history

Humanoid apes of the genus *Homo* have been around for only a tiny fraction of the history of the world that we've just outlined. And of that tiny fraction – around 2 million years – 99 per cent is classified as the Stone Age, during which *Homo sapiens* and other, now extinct, *Homo* species developed stone tools and the use of fire.

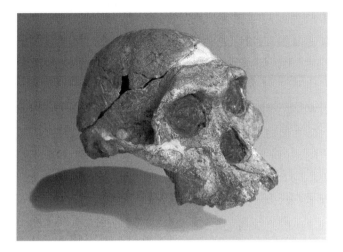

Figure 0.3 Australopithecus africanus.

The first humans to show evidence of spirituality were the Neanderthals (generally classified as a separate species, *Homo neanderthalensis*, and with no surviving descendants). Neanderthals buried their dead, often with food or tools beside them. Evidence of more sophisticated beliefs, for example in early cave paintings, appeared 32,000 years ago.

Anatomically modern humans – *Homo sapiens* – are believed to have originated around 200,000–250,000 years ago in Africa. The oldest human fossils date back to around 160,000 years ago, and humans had spread as far as Borneo by 40,000 years ago. By 11,000 years ago, *Homo sapiens* had reached the southern tip of South America, the last of the uninhabited continents apart from Antarctica. Tool use and language continued to improve; interpersonal relationships became more complex.

Throughout more than 90 per cent of its history, *Homo sapiens* lived in small bands as nomadic hunter-gatherers. Language became more complex, the ability to remember and transmit information increased, and ideas could be exchanged and passed down through the generations. Cultural evolution outpaced biological evolution, and history properly began.

The history of the last 10,000 years or so is one of continuous cultural, social and technological development. Yet it wasn't until the end of the 18th century that humans began to develop the technology that allows us to lead our modern lives – and affect the entire planet, for good or ill. Today, we have the power to alter the world's climate and annihilate ourselves with immensely powerful weapons. The figure on the next page lays out the earth's history proportionally – it shows how short humanity's time on earth has been, yet how disproportionate our effects on the planet are.

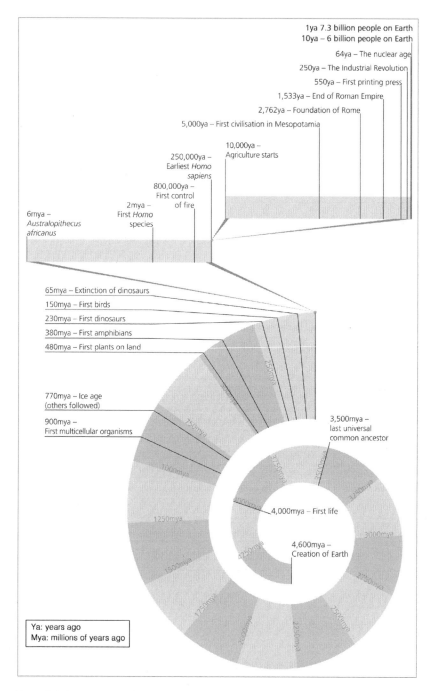

1ya 7.3 billion people on Earth
10ya – 6 billion people on Earth

64ya – The nuclear age

250ya – The Industrial Revolution

550ya – First printing press

1,533ya – End of Roman Empire

2,762ya – Foundation of Rome

5,000ya – First civilisation in Mesopotamia

10,000ya –
Agriculture starts

250,000ya –
Earliest *Homo
sapiens*

800,000ya –
First control
of fire

2mya –
First *Homo*
species

6mya –
*Australopithecus
africanus*

65mya – Extinction of dinosaurs

150mya – First birds

230mya – First dinosaurs

380mya – First amphibians

480mya – First plants on land

770mya – Ice age
(others followed)

900mya –
First multicellular organisms

3,500mya –
last universal
common ancestor

4,000mya – First life

4,600mya –
Creation of Earth

250mya
750mya
1000mya
1250mya
1500mya
1750mya
2000mya
2250mya
2500mya
2750mya
3000mya
3250mya
3500mya
3750mya
4000mya
4250mya

Ya: years ago
Mya: millions of years ago

Figure 0.4 A proportional view of the history of the world. Innovated by Stephen
Asbury, created by IOSH.

Table 0.1 Extinction events.

Date	Extinction event
770 million years ago	Ice age caused all the oceans to freeze
488 million years ago	Ice age
440 million years ago	Ice age
365 million years ago	Ice age
250 million years ago	Siberian Traps volcanic event: the largest eruptions in history; known as the P–T extinction event
65 million years ago	An asteroid nine miles wide hits Mexico; credited with extinction of dinosaurs; the K–T extinction event
Biblical flood legend	Noah and his family the only human survivors of 150 days of flooding, finally found dry land on the Mountains of Ararat in Turkey
1991	99.9 per cent of all species that have ever lived are now extinct
2100	Half of presently existing species extinct?

We mentioned extinction events early in the planet's history – the major known and likely ones are listed in Table 0.1. Worrying, isn't it?

Over 250 years since the start of this growth in knowledge, technology, commerce and consumption, and the destructiveness of war, development on so many fronts has accelerated, creating the opportunities and perils that now confront the human communities that together inhabit Earth. Change has continued, and still continues, at a near exponential pace. We have seen the development (and destruction) of nuclear weapons, stem cell research, mapping the human genome and early endeavors in sustainable energy. At the same time, we have developed huge capacity computers, big advances in medical care and nanotechnology. Economic globalization spurred by advances in communication and transport technology has influenced everyday life in many parts of the world. Political, cultural and institutional systems, such as democracy, capitalism and environmentalism have all played a part in shaping life on earth as it is today. Major concerns and problems such as disease, war, poverty, consumption and climate change have become more pressing, and the world population is increasing. By 2015, the global population had reached 7.3 billion (Worldometers, 2015). Figure I.5 shows the growth from 1 billion in the 215 years since 1800 and a forecast for the year 2020. Imagine too the growth in per-capita consumption of resources – land, food, fuels, plastics, precious metals and so on....

The economies, political affairs and defense of nations around the world have become increasingly intertwined. This globalization has often produced discord, although increased collaboration is also noted, such as the

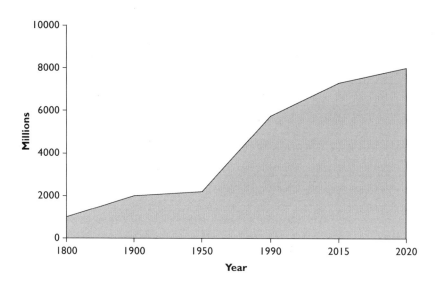

Figure 0.5 World human population 1800–2020.

CFC-control agreements made by 196 countries and en-block the European Union under the terms of the Montreal Protocol, 1989–2008 (UNEP, 2015).

Going forward in time from here, we'll need the highest level of collaboration we've ever seen if humans are to overcome the current environmental and other challenges. But with diminishing resources, increasing populations, climate change, epidemic diseases, regional wars and terrorism this goal seems distant. Is it possible that humans could ever bring life on earth to an end?

Four and a half billion years after the planet's formation, one of earth's life forms broke free of the biosphere. For the first time in history, earth was viewed first-hand from space. Yuri Gagarin was the first human to orbit the earth in 1957, and 12 years later Neil Armstrong was the first person to step onto the surface of the moon – yet we still can't feed the earth's population.

We urge you, like Neil Armstrong, to take the first 'small step' on this new journey for the human race.

> The current generation has the opportunity to affect the destiny of the human race.
>
> – Professor Michio Kaku,
> American theoretical physicist

We have relied on a broad number of sources for our summary presented here, but recommend Wells (1920), Parker (1997) and Spodek (2001) for the main chronology.

Acknowledgements

Stephen Asbury

Ten years after writing my first book, I have come to realize that I really like thinking about a subject, researching it and sharing it with you, the reader. Thank you for your continued confidence in me, enabling me to bring fresh ideas and new concepts to the world of risk management and risk control. I have enjoyed writing for you, and I that hope you enjoy and find useful this new book, my fifth.

Speaking around the world as I do, I enjoy meeting with Sustainability/HSEQ/CSR/Insurance/Audit/Risk Managers and responding to their questions, checks and challenges. Everyone who has ever attended one or more of my training classes (and there are over 15,000 of you from over 70 countries on six continents) has shaped my thinking, and I thank you all for this.

Thank you to Richard, my co-author for the second time, for sharing his intellect and ideas. Once again, he you have been a pleasure to write with. Thank you too to Sade Lee and our editorial team at Taylor & Francis for their support in helping develop our script into something that we hope is of value to you, our readers.

Joe Henderson, Andy and Mandy Wood and Lewis Hamilton have helped to make the last twelve months amazing – thank you. As ever, I thank my late parents Alan and Betty for helping to make me who I am. My wonderful wife Susan tells me that they would be proud of me.

This book is dedicated to my daughter Kimberley. She is my personal hope for, and contribution to, the future.

Richard Ball

My family is always my centre. Macey and Harrison, you always make me strive to look at the world with open eyes, questioning everything and considering what legacy I leave for you. I hope in some small way that my work makes the Earth a better place to live for all. To my parents I say no charge, even though I owe them much. Whilst my wife clears the mist and steadies me in the storm, this book is dedicated to you, Tasha. This would not have happened without any of them.

On a practical note thank you to all at Routledge, Anna-Lisa Mills for her contribution to the case studies and my co-author Stephen for your hard work, challenge and ideas.

We both send our thanks to the amazing John Haslam for providing his fantastic illustrations to complement our text. You'll find more about John at http://www.johnhaslamillustration.com/.

Introduction

千里之行，始于足下

(Even the longest journey begins with a single step)
                    –*Tao Te Ching, 6th century BCE*

Our planet, the Earth, seems incredibly durable. For the last 4.6 billion years, it has apparently handled everything the universe has thrown at it. Occasional catastrophes have punctuated long periods of stable conditions that are ideal for life, but each time the planet has recovered and continues to support a wealth of life. Today, it provides an ideal home for two million or so catalogued species – it's still the only place in the universe where life is known to exist, despite NASA's powerful telescopes and the journeys of its long-haul exploration spacecraft.

There are now over 7 billion human beings on earth and the population is growing at a rate of about 80 million per year. No species has previously dominated our planet in the way that we now do. Are our behaviors, our consumption and our emissions changing the conditions we need to survive? Is it sustainable?

Driven by our desire for wealth and to feed the needs of our expanding population, we've plundered the earth for its resources – ores, coal, oil, gas and wood. Our hydrocarbon fuels will probably run out in the next 100 years. We know this, and have been investing in wind, wave, solar and biofuel alternatives, as well as nuclear power. But these aren't without their problems. The Chernobyl disaster – so far the only level 7 release on the International Nuclear Event Scale – caused 56 immediate deaths, an estimated 9,000 additional cancer cases and the evacuation and resettlement of over 300,000 people. Biofuels, once hailed as the answer to both climate change and a shortage of fossil fuels, are now implicated in the recent rises in food prices. Can we grow enough crops for food *and* fuel? Or is it a question of distributing wealth more equitably between the continents?

Carbon dioxide levels in the atmosphere are increasing at alarming levels. After years of debate, the environmentalists seem to have won this argument, and we all know that we should reduce our waste, recycle more and cut down on our driving. So far, the world's forests have absorbed 25 per cent of man-made carbon emissions. But these natural lungs are threatened by the same man-made processes – the need for land to feed and house an expanding population. An area of around 75,000 square kilometres – the size of Austria or South Carolina – is destroyed each year (UN, 2005).

But it's not just the environment we're affecting. There's also inequality within our species, exemplified by the historical slave trade, modern production sweatshops, child labour and the sex trade. How far are nations and organizations prepared to go to create wealth?

It's not all bad news. Happily, we've developed 'eco-friendly' bullets, grenades and rockets, and carbon-neutral beer. Even the company Stephen set up in 1999, Corporate Risk Systems Limited, has been carbon free since 2005 (Carbonfund, 2015).

Whenever you read a newspaper, watch the television or listen to a politician, we're urged to 'save the earth'. History shows us that species and civilizations come and go, but the earth has survived. So perhaps it isn't the earth we should be so worried about – perhaps we should be more worried about saving ourselves.

Corporate social responsibility (CSR) is a powerful tool to help our organizations and ourselves to do this. Like our first book on CSR, this new book will help and encourage you to get involved – to take the first steps on your longest journey. It will take you through the theory and practice of CSR; why it's a good idea, how organizations can implement it and how it'll help them to achieve their other goals too. We've also included a chapter on personal social responsibility – or how you can apply the principles of CSR to your personal life, irrespective of what is going on in your organization(s). We recognize too that newer ideas such as these need to be thoroughly tested, so we've also reviewed and summarized the common arguments against CSR.

To bring the theories of CSR to life, we've also included over twenty case studies spread sensibly across our ten chapters. These case studies highlight organizations doing the right thing across the CSR spectrum, use publicly available material and, unless we've said otherwise, are presented here without the knowledge or agreement of the organizations concerned. We've also included a list of 100 CSR actions (see page 249) that will help you start to make a difference.

 Test your thinking

Scattered through the book are 20 'Test Your Thinking' exercises to encourage you to think more about CSR and apply our theories shared in this book to your own organization. For some of these we've

(continued)

(continued)

suggested some answers, but elsewhere we've deliberately left them open-ended. This book doesn't provide all the answers! We hope it'll lead you to read more about CSR and delve further into this fascinating topic. All the 'Test your thinking' exercises can be downloaded from http://www.routledge.com/authors/i8614-stephen-asbury

Throughout the text and in the references we've included a selection of useful web addresses for resources and information we've referred to. Inevitably, links disappear and text on web pages changes over the lifetime of a printed book and you should take this into account when referring to these sites.

> Those who cannot remember the past are condemned to repeat it.
>
> (George Santayana, 1905)

> [The planet] is protesting for the wrong that we are doing to her, because of the irresponsible use and abuse of the goods that God has placed on her. We have grown up thinking that we were her owners and dominators, authorized to loot her. The violence that exists in the human heart, wounded by sin, is also manifest in the symptoms of illness that we see in the Earth, the water, the air and in living things … the attitudes that stand in the way of a solution, even among believers, range from negation of the problem, to indifference, to convenient resignation or blind faith in technical solutions.
>
> (Pope Francis, 2015)

Chapter 1

Business control and risk management

> Good management is the art of making problems so interesting and their solutions so constructive that everyone wants to get to work and deal with them.
>
> –Hawken, 2015

> Effective leadership is putting first things first. Effective management is discipline, carrying it out.
>
> –Covey, 2015

A brief history of business control

We've no idea how the ancient Egyptians (or someone) built the pyramids, despite watching *National Geographic Channel*. Massive structures, huge stone blocks moved from hundreds of miles away, great symmetry and cosmic alignment. Many ideas have been suggested (Asbury, 2013, p.48), but there remains little or no certainty.

As Paul Hawkens and Steven Covey reflect, good management certainly concerns prioritizing; making problems interesting and controls constructive. We also know very little about the absolute origins of management systems, but we suggest that the Chinese military General Sun Tzu was one of the first to understand the benefits of structure in control. Certainly, since its translation into the first European language in 1782, his book *The Art of War* (Tzu, 2009) has been regarded as a masterpiece of strategic thinking. Its significance was quickly recognized; and such towering figures of Western history as Napoleon and General Douglas MacArthur have claimed it as a source of inspiration.

Sun Tzu

The earliest historical record of using a systemic framework for control of an activity and giving some assuredness of consistency of outcome dates back roughly 25 centuries to ancient China. Our suggestion is that the origins of modern management systems go back to the activities and subsequent writing of the military general, strategist and philosopher Tzu. Traditional accounts place him as a military general serving under King Helu of Wu, who lived c. 544–496 BCE. The story of Sun Tzu's life is based on the following legend:

The King of Wu tested Sun Tzu's skills by commanding him to train 180 concubines as soldiers. Sun Tzu divided the girls into two companies, appointing the two concubines most favoured by the King as the company commanders. When Sun Tzu first ordered the concubines to face right, they giggled. Sun Tzu said that the general, in this case himself, was responsible for ensuring that soldiers understood the commands given to them. Then, he reiterated the command, and again the concubines giggled. Sun Tzu ordered the execution of the two company commanders (the King's favoured concubines), even though the King protested. Tzu explained that if the general's soldiers understood their commands but did not obey, it was the fault of the officers. He also said that once a general was appointed, it was their duty to carry out their mission. After both concubines were killed, new officers were selected to replace them. And afterwards, both companies performed their manoeuvres flawlessly. Managers today can learn much from this story.

General Tzu's now famous book *The Art of War* presents a philosophy of war for managing conflicts and winning battles in 385 points set out in thirteen chapters – it is a highly interesting and recommended read. It is accepted as a masterpiece on strategy and is frequently cited and referred to by generals and theorists since its publication, translation and distribution the world over. However, only in recent times (since the mid to late 1950's), has 'strategy' been associated with 'management' per se. For two-and-a-half millennia, 'strategy' was exclusively used as a military term, and defined interestingly as 'The Art of War'.

From Sun Tzu to the twentieth century and since, there has been an evolution of management systems thinkers and thinking, and we have summarised some of the main pillars of this in Figure 1.1.

Bringing this evolution of management systems thinking fast-forwards through 2500 years, we (and many others) feel that another significant initiating moment in the evolution of modern business control was from 14 October 1900 in Sioux City, Iowa, USA.

Deming

Dr William Edwards Deming (14 October 1900–20 December 1993) was an American statistician, professor, author, lecturer and consultant. He trained to be an electrical engineer and worked briefly as an engineer in Chicago before becoming a statistician, working in the US Bureau of Census. His Ph.D. was in mathematical physics, awarded by Yale. He is best known for his work in Japan, where he taught senior management how to improve design, service, product quality, testing and sales through

4th Century BCE	13th Century	15th Century	18th Century	19th Century	20th Century
Sun Tzu	Leonardo Pisano	Luca Pacioli	Adam Smith	Henri Fayol	Konosuke Matsushita
				Frederick W Taylor	William Deming
				Henry Ford	Jehangir Tata
				Toyoda family	Joseph Juran
				Alfred Sloan	Akio Morita
				Tomas Bata	Henry Mintzberg
				Max Weber	Tom Peters
					Rosabeth Moss Kanter
					Kenchi Ohmae
					Michael Porter and others

Figure 1.1 The main pillars of management systems thinking from the 4th to the 20th century.

various methods, including the application of statistical process control and related methods. His continuous quest for understanding processes and deviations from the norm led him to become one of the founding fathers of the quality movement.

Dr. Deming (Figure 1.2) made a significant contribution to Japan's later reputation for innovative high-quality products and its economic power. He is regarded as having had more impact upon Japanese manufacturing and business than any other individual not of Japanese heritage. In the years following World War II, Deming was sent to work in Japan. Working with a fellow American, Joseph Juran, he developed production and management theories that later became known as the 'right first time' philosophy in Japanese industry. These have been exported around the world since the quality revolutions of the 1980s and 1990s.

We say that 'management' is nothing more than motivating other people to deliver what is needed.

> Every business and every product has risks. You can't get around it.
> (Lee Iacocca (2015), former President
> and CEO of Chrysler, 1978–1992)

Academics and industrialists credited Deming and Juran with giving birth to an industrial revolution through the way they developed statistical control of quality levels into a new way of managing business.

Figure 1.2 William Edwards Deming in the 1950s. Photo courtesy of The W. Edwards Deming Institute.

Dr. Deming was the author of *Out of the Crisis* (2000a, originally published in 1982) and *The New Economics for Industry, Government, Education* (2000b, originally published in 1993). The latter includes his 'System of Profound Knowledge' and the '14 Points for Management', which we encourage you to review.

In *Out of the Crisis*, Dr. Deming said:

> The prevailing style of management must undergo transformation. A system cannot understand itself. The transformation requires a view from outside. My aim is to provide an outside view – a lens – that I call a system of profound knowledge. It provides a map of theory by which to understand the organizations that we work in.
>
> The first step is transformation of the individual. This transformation is discontinuous. It comes from understanding of the system of profound knowledge. The individual, transformed, will perceive new meaning to his [sic] life, to events, to numbers, to interactions between people. Once

the individual understands the system of profound knowledge, he will apply its principles in every kind of relationship with other people. He will have a basis for judgment of his own decisions and for transformation of the organizations that he belongs to.

(Deming, 2000a)

Deming said that once transformed, the individual would:

Set an example;

Be a good listener, but will not compromise;

Continually teach other people; and

Help people to pull away from their current practices and beliefs and move into the new philosophy without a feeling of guilt about the past

(Deming, 2000a)

Plan-Do-Check-Act

At the heart of Deming's legacy to the (business) world is the adoption in his teaching of the four steps in the Deming Wheel: Plan-Do-Check-Act (PDCA) also referred to by Deming later in his life as Plan-Do-Study-Act (PDSA).

In his own writing, Dr Deming actually called this cycle of activities the *Shewhart Wheel*, after his friend and mentor Walter Shewhart. Whatever it is called, this wheel (or cycle) can be used in various ways, such as running an experiment:

- PLAN (or design) the experiment;
- DO the experiment by performing the planned steps;
- CHECK the results by testing them;
- ACT on the decisions based on those results.

This cycle, commonly called 'The Deming Wheel', is shown in Figure 1.3. It was proposed as a cyclical process to determine in a never-ending way the next action, with the 'Wheel' illustrating a simple approach to testing information before making a major decision.

The shorthand PDCA mnemonic has borne the test of time despite the efforts of certification bodies, business sector organizations, consultants and academics who have substituted Deming's simplicity with complexity. PDCA lives at the heart of the latest iteration of ISO management systems based on *Annex SL*, which you will read about later in this chapter and which has revolutionized ISO 9001, ISO 14001 and other standards recently. It is also commonly applied as a 'wheel within a wheel' to illustrate the relationship of operational processes to corporate and strategic processes.

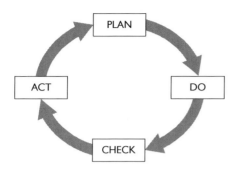

Figure 1.3 The PDCA cycle, commonly known as the Deming Wheel.

Deming saw that the elimination of waste could be achieved by aligning processes coherently and then carrying them out in a manner which was as close to the laid down standards as they could be – the control of variation, so to say. The armaments and munitions industry was one to see the potential of such an approach to manufacturing, since every time ammunitions failed to explode upon impact, all of the resources that were consumed before launching the weapon at its target had zero payback, since the enemy's soldiers and equipment had not been destroyed as intended.

For example, some observers feel that the outcome of the Falklands War (commonly known in Argentina as *Guerra de las Malvinas*) – an effective state of war between Argentina and the UK between 2 April and 14 June 1982 over the long-disputed territories of the Falkland Islands, South Georgia and the South Sandwich Islands – might have had quite a different outcome if more of the bombs launched by the Argentinean air force had actually exploded on impact with their British Royal Navy targets. Would these munitions have exploded as designed if they had been manufactured and assembled by Toyota?

Management truths

In his book *Out of the Crisis,* Deming (2000a) set out his System of Profound Knowledge and his 14 Points of Management some 40 years after his teaching had been listened to, accepted and benefited from by the Japanese.

We think that Deming's ideas remain vibrant signposts for managers today. Deming saw immutable truths in systems of management. For instance, a line manager must understand that all people are different, and understand the interaction of psychology and statistical variation. For example:

• The number of defective items that a quality inspector finds will depend upon the size of the work load presented to him; or

- Another inspector, not wishing to penalize or punish anybody from within his or her own team, may pass an item that is just outside the acceptable manufacturing tolerances.

'Fear' invites improved performance. Bearers of bad news often fare badly in all but the most generative and progressive organisations. And so, to keep their jobs, people present to their boss only good news; a committee appointed by the CEO of a company will report what the CEO wishes to hear. Would they dare report otherwise?

> A eureka moment. It suddenly struck Mintz as so obvious. The executives entrusted with reviewing all of the LJM transactions . . . approached their duties casually, giving everything just the onceover. They seemed to figure that somebody else was doing the tough analysis. But no one was.
> (Eichenwald, on the Enron Corporation, 2005, p.389)

> The company had been engaged in accounting maneuvers since 1997–98, including a flawed internal audit function; Shell had engaged as [group reserves auditor] a retired Shell petroleum engineer – who worked only part time and was provided with limited resources and no staff – to audit its vast worldwide operations.
> (Donovan, 2015)

Other observations made by Deming also remain relevant to today's corporate practices; for example, accounting-based key performance indicators (KPIs) drive managers and employees to achieve targets of sales, revenue and costs by manipulation of processes.

Modern HSEQ management systems and PDCA

Virtually all management systems, frameworks or implementation models that are in use today have elements that can be mapped to the four interconnecting elements of the Deming Wheel. Whether these are owned by the International Standards Organization (ISO), national certification bodies, sector groups or by organizations developing their own approaches, the overall approach used will generally align to PDCA.

Some examples of current management system standards include ISO 9001, ISO 14001, OHSAS 18001/ISO 45001 and ILO-OSH 2001; and we note these have been and/or will be amended through revisions aligned to Annex SL during the life of this book.

ISO 9001

Until 2015, the words used in the international standard for quality management systems were *management responsibility, resource management, product realisation*, and *measurement, analysis and improvement*. These are all aspects of Deming's recognition that senior management is responsible: *plan* what needs to be achieved and provide the resources to do so; ensure an effective realization *do* in accordance with the developed plan; conduct measurement and analysis *check* what has been done; and *act* to initiate improvement where necessary ('better next time').

H&S (OHSAS 18001 and ISO 45001) and Environment (ISO 14001)

Similarly, the words used in these models for health, safety and environment were *policy, planning, implementation and operation, checking* and *review* until 2015–16, but these were all aspects of Deming's recognition that senior management must: *plan* what needs to be achieved in terms of both the significance of OH&S risks/environmental impacts and legal/other requirements; ensure an effective implementation *do* in accordance with the developed plan; conduct verification and measurement *check* what has been done; and *act* to consolidate standards, or alternatively to initiate an improvement where this has been revealed to be necessary (again, 'better next time').

The principle requirements of OHSAS 18001 differed from ISO 14001 in only one clause: 4.2, which is called 'OH&S Policy' in the former, instead of 'Environmental Policy' in the latter. During the life of this book, OHSAS 18001 will be withdrawn and replaced by ISO 45001.

ILO-OSH 2001

Figure 1.4 illustrates the occupational safety and health (OSH) framework developed in 2001 by the International Labour Organization (ILO): a part of the United Nations. ILO aims to create worldwide awareness of the dimensions and consequences of work-related accidents and diseases; to place OSH on national and international agendas; and to provide support to the national efforts for the improvement of national OSH systems and programs in line with relevant international labour standards.

Commenting upon its' own OSH standard, ILO (2001) says:

> At the onset of the twenty-first century, a heavy human and economic toll is still exacted by work-related injuries, ill health, diseases, incidents and deaths. These Guidelines call for coherent policies to protect workers from occupational hazards and risks while improving productivity. They present practical approaches and tools for assisting organizations, competent national institutions, employers, workers and other social partners in establishing, implementing and improving occupational safety and health management systems, with the aim of reducing work-related injuries, ill health, diseases, incidents and deaths. Employers and competent national institutions are accountable for and have a duty to

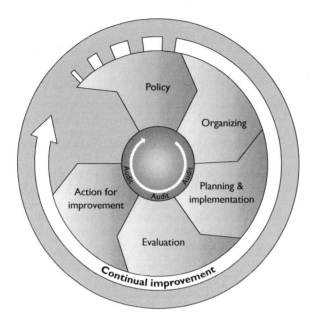

Figure 1.4 ILO-OSH, 2001.

organize measures designed to ensure occupational safety and health. The implementation of these ILO Guidelines is one useful approach to fulfilling this responsibility.

(ILO, 2001)

Annex SL

In April 2012, ISO published *Annex SL* (previously *ISO Guide 83*) of the *Consolidated ISO Supplement of the ISO/IEC Directives* (ISO 2012). This has had – and will continue to have – significant impacts on all ISO management system standards for writers, implementers and auditors.

Over the course of the last ten years or so, many organizations have become interested in, and started to seek to implement and certify combined management system standards (MSS). This has led to a need to allow those organizations to integrate these in an effective and efficient manner. While the main clauses of these MSS map across closely to PDCA, the reality of the detail is that they also have numbering, requirements, terms and definitions that are subtly or substantially different. In the past, this has caused confusion and inconsistent understanding and implementation.

All ISO technical work, including the development of standards, is carried out under the overall management of the Technical Management Board (TMB). ISO/TMB produced *Annex SL* with the objective of delivering consistent and compatible MSS.

Annex SL describes the framework for a generic management system. However, it demands the addition of discipline-specific requirements to make fully functional standards for systems such as quality, environmental, service management, food safety, business continuity, information security and energy management (and so on). *Annex SL* consists of eight clauses and four appendices. Appendix three is in three parts: high-level structure, identical core text and common terms and core definitions.

In the future, all new MSS will have the same overall 'look and feel' because of the adoption of *Annex SL*, and current MSSs will migrate during their next revision. This should be completed within the next few years. The migration of most of the current management system standards will likely not prove arduous; ISO 22301:2012 was developed using a draft version of *Annex SL* and ISO 27001:2013 was developed using the published version. The working groups established to revise ISO 9001 and ISO 14001 published new versions of these standards aligned to Annex SL in September 2015, and at the time of writing, ISO 45001 is in the final stages of development also using Annex SL.

For MSS writers, *Annex SL* will provide the template for their work, and they can thus concentrate their development efforts on the discipline-specific requirements of their MSS, which will be focused on Clause 8: Operation. For management system implementers, this will provide an overall management system framework within which they can pick and choose the discipline-specific standards that they need to include. Very much the intention of the standard is to remove the conflicts and duplication, confusion and misunderstanding from different MSS. In future, it is intended that all MSS owned by ISO should be readily compatible.

The main clause numbers and titles of all ISO management system standards will be identical, such as the introduction, terms and definitions, and operation. The introduction, scope and normative references will have content that is specific to each discipline and each standard is likely to have its own unique bibliography. Overall, there is a reorganization of management system requirements into this structure that may be unfamiliar in the first instance. However, some management system standards have already successfully migrated to this new structure.

Annex SL has 45 'shall' statements (generating 84 requirements). Obviously, each discipline will have its own requirements, so the total for any new standard is likely to have more. Appendix 3, Clause 3 of the Annex lists 22 terms and definitions. These can be in a separate standard, but they must be addressed; they cannot be deleted or changed.

Corporate social responsibility and MSS

Corporate social responsibility (CSR) includes several HSEQ-related themes, as we have discussed and as summarised below. There are several recognized frameworks for managing and implementing a structured approach. These will be described later. We'll start with our original model for CSR MSS, which we introduced in our first book, published in 2009 (Asbury and Ball), and shown in Figure 1.5.

CSR is essentially about organizations moving beyond legal compliance to integrate socially responsible behaviour as core values in recognition of the sound business case, risk mitigation and wider benefits in doing so. We say that CSR is not 'pink and fluffy' nor of 'greenwash', but comprises key elements of the overall corporate responsibility to mitigate risk(s).

Since organizations – and the challenges they face – differ widely, government intervention need to be carefully considered, well designed and targeted

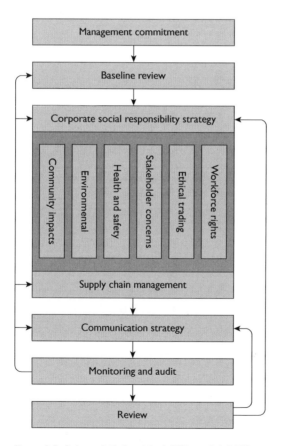

Figure 1.5 Asbury & Ball original CSR model, 2009.

Deming Wheel PDCA	ISO 14001:2004 OHSAS 18001:2007	ILO OSH-2001	ISO 9001:2015 ISO 14001:2015 ISO 45001:2016	Annex SL	Asbury &Ball CSR (2009)
Plan	4.2. Environmental Policy/4.2 OH&S Policy 4.3 Planning	Policy Organizing Planning	4. Context 5. Leadership 6. Planning 7. Support	Context of the organisation Leadership Planning	Management commitment Baseline review CSR strategy
Do	4.4 Implementation and operation	Implementation	8. Operation, including emergency preparedness	Support Operation	Elements of focus Communication strategy
Check	4.5 Checking	Evaluation Audit	9. Performance evaluation, including audit and management review	Performance evaluation	Monitoring and audit
Act	4.6 Management review	Action for improvement	10. Improvement, including NC, CA and continual improvement	Improvement	Review and improvement

Figure 1.6 Mapping of control frameworks to the Deming Wheel/PDCA.

to achieve their objective. The UK Government's approach is to encourage and incentivize the adoption and reporting of CSR through best practice guidance and, where appropriate, intelligent regulation and fiscal incentives.

In our 2009 model, the key themes were:

- workforce rights;
- ethical trading;
- stakeholder concerns;
- health and safety;
- environmental;
- community impacts.

We have developed our model since 2009, having learned a lot from using it and you'll find it on page 44. In Figure 1.6, we have mapped out the correlation between Deming/PDCA, our examples of quality, health and safety, and environmental frameworks discussed here, as well *Annex SL* and the Asbury and Ball CSR model from 2009. At an early opportunity, we encourage you to map out the management system frameworks used in your own organizations so that you completely understand this important relationship.

**Case study 1.1   Hon Hai Precision Industry
Co., Ltd (Foxconn), Taiwan and
Catcher Technologies, Jiangsu,
China**

The DTRT Model © Core Theme Indicator highlights the CSR-related themes addressed by this case study.

Campaign groups are calling on Apple (RoSPA, 2014, p.4) to take action to improve the working conditions faced by staff in its supply chains after a report found health, safety and human rights violations at the Catcher Technologies plant in Suqian, Jiangsu Province, China, which makes iPads and iPhones. It also has contracts with other firms including Dell and Sony. The report found 'extensive violations' of labour laws, company policies and Apple's Supplier Code of Conduct including locked fire exits, use of toxic chemicals without suitable protective equipment, absence of safety training and mandatory overtime of up to 100 hours per month. Workers faced 'harsh and punitive' management and were discouraged from reporting issues. The co-authors of the report, Green America, said: 'We knew that we needed to make this information public to encourage Apple to take immediate steps in addressing toxins and unsafe working conditions.'

Apple said that it is: ' . . . committed to ensuring safe and fair working conditions for everyone in our supply chain', and that it had dispatched a team to the factory to investigate the report.

Meanwhile, another Apple supplier, Hon Hai Precision Industry Co., Ltd. (trading as Foxconn), is a Taiwanese multinational electronics manufacturing company. It is the world's largest maker of electronic components. The most notable amongst its products include the iPad, the iPod and the iPhone. Foxconn has been involved in several controversies over the years; most relating to how it manages employees in China, where it is the largest private-sector employer.

In 2012, Apple hired the Fair Labor Association to conduct an audit of working conditions at Foxconn. Suicides among Foxconn workers have attracted considerable media attention. One was the high profile death of a worker after the loss of a prototype phone. There have been several reports of suicides linked to low pay in 2010. Suicides of Foxconn workers have continued into 2012, with one in June 2012. On Friday 21 September 2012, the iPhone 5 hit the world's shops, selling over 5 million units over its first weekend. On Monday 24 September 2012 Foxconn had to halt production at a plant in northern China after a fight broke out – apparently in a workers' dormitory. Foxconn confirmed that a 'personal dispute' escalated into an incident involving about 2,000 workers, injuring 40 of them. The BBC reported that 5,000 (yes, five thousand) police had attended the scene. Later, comments on a Chinese blogging site suggested the fight broke out after security guards beat a worker.

Reviewing the opportunities presented by CSR, we cannot see sufficient attention at either of these two companies to our six core elements, as shown in the model. It is an important risk mitigation to comply with standards (legal and other), to protect workers' health and safety and to manage labour relations well to achieve good employee relations. Together, these actions will mitigate the opportunity for negative media around key launch events.

Information for management about business control

In teaching people how to understand management systems, it is apparent to us that a critical pre-requisite is commonly missing.

While there is extensive internal control guidance available for auditors, which has been produced over many years by professional auditing bodies, we note there is virtually nothing for the senior management of many organizations. We've set out here to help managers who want to benefit from such professional guidance.

We've noticed that management's bookshelves and e-mail inboxes are overflowing with company policies, governance guides, values and ethics statements, principles of business, vision and mission statements, copies of laws and regulations, approved codes of practice, client and company rulebooks, mandates, organization charts, job descriptions, reporting relationships, accountabilities, roles and responsibilities, competence standards, process maps, training matrices, minutes of meetings, action plans, insurer's reports, plans, standards, strategic and tactical reviews, manuals of authority, audit reports, procedures, risk registers and a whole lot more. But there are very few high-level overview documents written from a management perspective that described how these discrete internal controls should and can be implemented in a coordinated and complementary manner that would tie management's activities in with delivering success for their organizations – the be 'in control'.

In the USA, this lack of guidance for management and boards of directors was eventually recognized and some actions have been taken. For example, the Foreign Corrupt Practices Act of 1977 stimulated a flood of proposals and guidelines from consultants, professional and regulatory bodies focusing on management's responsibility for maintaining a system of internal accounting control.

Following on from their report on Fraudulent Financial Reporting in 1987, the Committee of Sponsoring Organizations of the Treadway Commission (COSO) conducted a review of what written material about internal control was available. This work led on to COSO's well-known project to provide practical, broadly accepted criteria for establishing internal control and evaluating its effectiveness. Management could use it to support their recently emphasised responsibility for establishing, monitoring, evaluating and reporting on internal control. A seminal moment arrived with the publication in September 1992 of COSO's *Integrated Framework of Internal Control* (COSO, 2015a).

Corporate governance

Throughout the 1990s, legislative and regulatory authorities across the world began to demand better standards of corporate governance. This was mainly a reaction to a litany of high-profile corporate failures (anyone remember Enron?) that stimulated outrage from innocent parties who were affected directly, but also vicariously, by the actions of companies operating in their countries, cities and towns. These outraged citizens were voters, and therefore legislators took note that the majority wanted those responsible for running organizations to be held more accountable for their actions than had been the case in the past.

Many professional accountancy bodies across the world have long accepted the need for global standards. The International Federation of Accountants now ensures that all accountants and auditors worldwide subscribe to a global code of ethics. And there has been growing support for international standard setters to develop and promote international standards of accounting and auditing.

The interdependence of individual countrys' economies requires high and globally accepted, applied and enforced management standards, which act as the most effective solution between balancing the needs of regulatory authorities with the needs of commercial and other organizations. It is widely accepted that such standards are what give investors confidence in the companies in which they invest and other stakeholders the confidence to buy from, work for, supply to and live next door to.

They require that organizations and their senior management throughout the world, operating in both private and public sectors, must demonstrate:

- accountability (of senior managers to all of the stakeholders);
- integrity (to attract financial and social support);
- transparency (of their operations and financial positions as reflected in their statutory and other voluntary reports to stakeholders).

Not all organisations achieve these standards, and our case study in Chapter 10 on FIFA and the soccer World Cup provides a recent example of potential problems and/or non-conformity/ies under investigation by authorities in the US and elsewhere at the time this book was being written.

COSO's *framework* became an accepted reference on internal control in the US and around the world. Its implications for corporate governance led other countries to follow with their own expectations: the Cadbury Committee reported in the UK in 1992; in 1995 the Greenbury Committee reported in the UK, the Criteria of Control Board (CoCo) of The Canadian Institute of Chartered Accountants reported in Canada, and Marc Vienot first reported in France, in June 1997 the Peters Commission reported in The Netherlands; the Hampel Committee reported in the UK in January 1998; KonTraG was published in Germany in March 1998; and the Turnbull Committee reported in the UK in September 1999. In the last 10 years, most developed and developing countries have issued guidance regarding the proper governance of major companies that are registered in their jurisdictions. Furthermore, countries are reviewing and updating that guidance in the light of experiences in their own and other countries. Essentially, all of these corporate governance standards have the same message: an organization's senior management (in particular the directors of a public limited liability company) must take responsibility for two things:

1   Really understanding what the risks and opportunities of the company are and what is done to enhance corporate performance on the basis of this knowledge.
2   Informing external parties about what the company has been doing in a transparent and trustworthy manner.

During three of the most turbulent years in the US's corporate history, COSO developed and published in September 2004 their *Enterprise Risk Management – Integrated Framework* (COSO, 2015b), which was intended to meet the needs of these corporate governance expectations by setting out principles and concepts that could become a common language and giving clear direction and guidance on enterprise risk management. The phrase 'wilful blindness' emerged around this time.

Wilful blindness

Wilful blindness is also called ignorance of the law. It is a term used in law to describe a situation where an individual chooses to ignore something they could or should have attended to, and thus seek to avoid a criminal, civil or other liability. Ignorance of the law means intentionally putting themselves in a position where they will be unaware of facts that would otherwise render them liable.

For example, in a number of high-profile cases, persons transporting luggage containing illegal drugs have asserted that they never asked what the contents of the packages were and so lacked the requisite intent ('mens rea') to break the law. Generally speaking, this defense has not succeeded, as courts have been quick to determine that the defendant *should* have known what was inside the luggage, and were willfully blind by failing to determine this.

Internal control reference frameworks and structured means of control

COSO's *Integrated Framework of Internal Control* continues to stand the test of time and is still a broadly accepted standard for satisfying an organization's reporting requirements. Now, in addition, the *Enterprise Risk Management – Integrated Framework* provides management with a more robust and extensive focus on the broader subject of organizational risk management. It was not intended to and has not replaced the internal control framework, since it incorporates the internal control framework within it, but organizations can use it to move toward a fuller risk management process.

The obvious question then is: 'What constitutes a suitable internal control reference framework for achieving corporate governance, or 'structured means of control'?

And in our opinion, the best answer is: 'The structured means of control or reference framework that is currently being used by your own organization'. And if your organization doesn't have a reference framework for corporate governance, now might be the time to select, develop or otherwise acquire one! We'll show you how to do it.

> Present circumstances don't determine where you can go; they only determine where you start.
>
> Stephen Asbury

A problem that does arise for managers in trying to select an appropriate structure for control is the multiplicity of control frameworks they're asked to comply with these days. *Annex SL* should bring some relief here in due course (see pages 12–13). Sometimes events will naturally lead a manger towards a particular reference framework. For example, ISO 9001 is the natural framework to select for quality management assurance, unless there is a more-specific sector standard. It's certainly true these days that ISO 9001 is a 'qualifier' for even an invitation to express interest to tender with some organizations. Likewise, ISO 14001 is the natural choice for those who have pollution concerns, or have been prosecuted and OHSAS 18001 ISO 450017 is for those concerned about matters related to worker safety and health.

But often we find that management has no particular corporate governance framework (or group of frameworks) which they are using because their company does not have a corporate-wide internal control or CSR/risk management framework. Therefore, they are not expecting a structured means of control to give them reasonable assurance that they will meet their business objectives and carry out their activities in such a way that they meet their responsibilities to their particular groups of stakeholders. They just 'do their best' every day, and react to events as they occur. This will not do.

The five principal stakeholder groups interested in the performance of any typical organization are shown in Figure 1.7. We'll discuss the requirements and aspirations of each of these groups in Chapter 5, but it will be immediately apparent that different stakeholder groups have different requirements and aspirations, for example:

- Investors will desire higher sales prices, while customers will prefer lower prices.
- Employees will prefer higher wages, while investors may prefer management to pay lower wages.

Figure 1.7 The five stakeholder groups.

- Business partners may prefer to keep employed numbers low, while society might want more permanent jobs to be available.

Management has to balance off these competing requirements and aspirations at all times, prior deciding what to do.

The DTRT model

In the remainder of this chapter, we will describe a simply structured management systems approach for maximizing the upsides and minimizing the downsides of an approach to meet CSR output requirements, specifically:

- legality (set by government);
- morality;
- ethical practices.

The strength of our DTRT Model as a structured means of controlling and treating CSR-related risks lies in its simplicity. It is readily adaptable for all types of organizations and it reflects all of the features expected of modern risk-based management systems. It provides a robust analysis of the business environment (called 'Context' by *Annex SL*), consideration of the objectives of the organization and an overview of assessing risks. Our framework is, as you might expect, aligned to the Deming Wheel 'PDCA'. When necessary, it will allow managers and auditors alike to map out – and thus understand – any of its own internal controls.

You'll have seen in case study 1.1 (Foxconn and Catcher) our six core elements of CSR. Let's start with a reminder of these; each with examples of their typical coverage.

1 Legal requirements: incorporation, taxation and all other mandated standards, including any requirements in the other five core elements.
2 Health and safety: worker and public protection, product safety.
3 Environmental sustainability: climate change, emissions to air, discharges to land and water, life cycle impacts, biodiversity.
4 Ethical trading (value chain): product quality, product recall, responsible marketing, supply chain.
5 Workforce rights: human rights, equal opportunities, fair pay, working time, zero hours, employee engagement.
6 Community effects: noise and nuisance, community relationships, development and engagement, emergency relief, stakeholder concerns.

All business control frameworks and MSS comprise various categories of control, each of which are rooted in good management practice. Therefore, these categories can be considered both as components of an overall CSR control system and as essential individual criteria for an effective management system; 'wheels within wheels' as Deming may have described these.

These core elements are shaped by three preliminary features unique to each individual organization:

1 The business environment (Context).
2 The organization's objectives.
3 The effects of uncertainty on the organization's objectives, which are called 'Risks' by ISO 31000 (2009), and summarised as 'Managing risk' by risk managers.

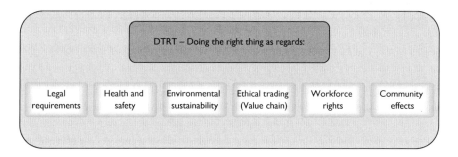

Figure 1.8 The DTRT Model: the six core elements of doing the right thing.

Annex SL: context

Management systems developed using *Annex SL*, Clause 4 require organizations to understand the context (business environment) external and internal to their organizations prior to establishing a structured means of control. Readers should review Figure 1.6 if they wish to be reminded of how the *Annex SL* clauses map to PDCA. In summary, organizations should:

- understand the organization and its context (4.1);
- understand the needs and expectations of interested parties (4.2);
- determine the scope of the management systems (4.3);
- understand the management systems for the specific discipline (4.4), e.g. environment.

The organization and its context/business environment

Figure 1.9 shows the flight deck of the US Space Shuttle with its mass of instrumentation for measuring all of the significant environmental features affecting the mission. Superimposed on the picture are examples of some of the environmental factors applicable to an organization's mission.

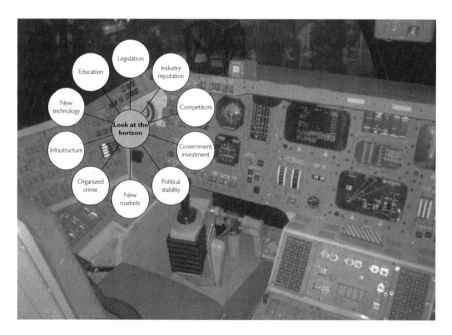

Figure 1.9 Look at the horizon to see factors impacting the mission.

Case study 1.2: Collapse of the Grand Banks Fisheries, Canada

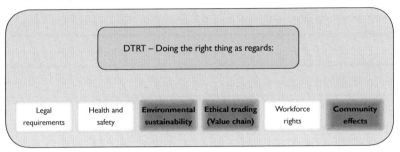

DTRT – Doing the right thing as regards:

| Legal requirements | Health and safety | Environmental sustainability | Ethical trading (Value chain) | Workforce rights | Community effects |

While we can all see the local impact of environmental harm from projects such as building a new road through a forest, or industrial pollution incidents in our rivers and seas, it is harder to see the impacts of wider global concepts, such as climate change, overfishing or loss of biodiversity. Apart from the often quoted Dodo or examples of ancient cultures, such as on Easter Island, what modern examples are there of ecosystems failing in ways that the environmental pressure groups predict? The Earth seems a pretty big place, which has survived for 4.6 billion years: can human activity really affect ecosystems that have adapted for millions or years? Can't we just adapt and use other resources? Are there any examples of sustainability issues having a significant impact on businesses and societies that depend on those natural resources?

The Grand Banks Fisheries off the coast of North Eastern Continental America was once the bread basket of the Atlantic fishing fleets, yet in the 1990's a moratorium of cod fishing stopped all fishing. In this study, we will review the risks of managing a collective resource and the impacts poor management of natural resources can have on the environment.

In 1497, Giovanni Caboto travelled to Newfoundland and remarked that 'the seas were so full of fish that it was possible to catch them by lowering a weighted basket into the water and retrieving it quickly'. The *Canadian Geographic* also reports that seventeenth-century English fishermen commented that the Grand Banks Fisheries had shoals 'so thick by the shore that we hardly have been able to row a boat through them' (Lean, 2011). This abundance of nature's harvest led to an expansion of fishing fleets in the area, with Canadian family fleets using gill and drift nets, long lines and small trawlers to

(continued)

(continued)

maximize the catch. These were small-scale operations keeping close to shore, taking an estimated 100,000 tonnes of fish; within the sustainable limits of the fishing area at that time, as the adult stock would be replenished each year.

However, the conditions that allowed the fish stocks to replenish quickly drew the attention of a broader group, and at the start of the twentieth century the range and capability of the international fleets started to grow. The larger vessels used longer lines and an increased range of vessels to catch more fish. The profitability of the fishing drew in fleets from across the Atlantic from countries as far away as Spain, Portugal, and Scandinavia.

In the post-war era, factory trawlers increased the catch and profits using vast freezers to store the significant hauls. Attempts to control the amount being caught could only be limited to the 12-mile territorial waters off Canadian shores, leaving the international waters open to vessels from as far as the USSR, China and Japan. The range of the fish being caught also expanded from cod to include haddock, hake and all kinds of shellfish. This continued for years, with the peak of the Grand Banks cod catch in 1968, with over 800,000 tons of fish taken in that year alone (British Sea Fishing, 2015).

Newfoundland resident Wilson Hayward spoke to the BBC in 2002 about commercial fishing in the Grand Banks during this time. The 76-year-old described the rush of foreign trawlers that came to the area: 'I remember going out on to the cape in the night, and all you could see were dragger [trawler] lights as far as the eye could see, just like a city in the sea. We all knew it was wrong. They were taking the mother fish which had been out there spawning over the years' (Hirsch, 2002).

In the fifteen years after 1965 the same tonnage of fish was removed from the Grand Banks as in the first 200 years. Unsurprisingly, with hindsight, this level of extraction could not be sustained, so by 1974 the fish harvest had reduced to 300,000 tons. In response to this, in 1976 Canada passed legislation to protect 90 per cent of the Grand banks Fisheries that lay within 200 miles of its coast to create an EEZ (Exclusive Economic Zone). This excluded international fishing in these waters and allowed a more direct control of the fishing rights in the area. While significant action was needed to protect the resource in the long term, it would also have substantial effects on the local fishing industry, which would lead to major job losses and wider societal impacts; so only minor controls were introduced to the quotas.

This inaction led to a spiral of decline in fish stocks, so by 1990 scientific surveys established that cod stock had been significantly overfished and were in terminal decline, (One study estimated that Grand Banks cod levels were 1 per cent of what they were in the 1960s leaving less than 2,000 tons of remaining breeding stock cod (Pringle, 2007). In 1992, the Canadian Government was forced to act and introduced a total ban on fishing less than 500 years from Caboto's original quote.

The fishing moratorium removed around 30,000 fishermen's livelihoods overnight, causing a tidal wave ripple to the Newfoundland economy, as supporting businesses such as shipbuilding were also now no longer needed. The exodus of jobs led around 45,000 people to leave the providence and local commerce in the service and retail sectors was washed away. It was estimated that in the early 1990s the Canadian government paid $1billion in unemployment benefit, housing costs and retraining for people hit by the collapse of the fishing industry, and at least another $1billion was spent in the following years on similar measures.

Since the moratorium the Task Force on Incomes and Adjustment in the Atlantic Fishery (1993) indicated that the following factors had contributed to the collapse:

- Overly high Total Allowable Catch levels, optimistic scientific forecasts, inadequate understanding of stock dynamics and inaccurate data on commercial fishing activity.
- Under-reporting of actual catches, which caused harvesting overruns and misleading data for management and scientific assessments.
- Destructive fishing practices, such as high grading, discarding and dumping of immature fish or non-target species.
- Foreign overfishing of straddling stocks on the Nose and Tail of the Grand Banks.
- Failure to control expansion of fishing effort and failure to minimize the possible adverse impact of fishing gear technologies.
- Unforeseen and possible long-term ecological changes, which adversely affected the growth, abundance and distribution of various species.

In 1992, when the ban was introduced, it was thought that the moratorium would last until 2000, however as stocks have not yet returned to viable levels it remains in place. Dr. George Rose, a fisheries scientist at St. John's Memorial University of Newfoundland, commented:

(continued)

(continued)

> I am not optimistic that we will ever let it come back to what it was. If we get [higher cod stocks] there will be unbelievable pressure to fish it . . . We found 15,000 cod in the South Bay, and everyone said the cod are back. Hold on! Ten years ago, the biomass of the population, was 1.2 million.
>
> (Rose, 1997)

After over 20 years of severe limitations on commercial cod fishing in the Grand Banks, cod stocks are still only at approximately 10 per cent of 1960s levels (British Sea Fishing, 2015)

The Grand Banks fisheries example is not unique: every continent has its own story of overfishing, from Peruvian coastal anchovy fisheries to the North Sea in Europe and the Indian Ocean. So where a common resource exists, so many nations will plunder it, for short-term gain and fear to take the short-term pain to reserve the resource for the future. Modern rates of consumption outstrip the centuries that have gone before; each organization needs to review its supply chain and consider the impacts of resource depletion on the price and demand for the commodity it supplies if it wishes to survive over the longer term.

Senior management's interpretation of their own business context

Senior management's role is to take account of the business environment considered by them to be relevant to their sphere of operation, and to reflect this output of their analysis in the decisions that they make, based on their most realistic interpretation of the opportunities and/or threats faced. The most usual place for this to be written down will be within the business plan, with specific objectives and KPIs contained within it.

Management will often express its analysis of the business environment, and any subsequent developments expected, in a series of corporate documents. The first of these is often a statement of the 'Vision' of how the organization will be in the future. A 'Mission' statement, which provides the purpose of the organization and a series of business objectives for the plan year and beyond will be established. These documents are commonly used as a means to cascading the essential activities (as seen by the top management) in a consistent language throughout their organization. Figure 1.10 shows how this 'cascade' might look.

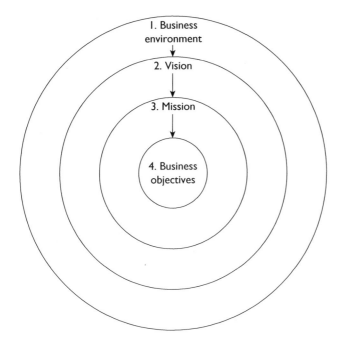

Figure 1.10 Business environment – vision – mission – business objectives cascade.

Shareholders generally have some means to replace the board if they don't like the direction the organization is heading. In a public limited company, directors commonly retire in rotation and may offer themselves to an AGM for re-election. In recent years, there have been some very vocal representations of stakeholder anger inside and outside AGM venues and we expect this to continue in the future.

The organization's objectives

Every organization and its stakeholders need a vision of what and where it wants to be – a picture of itself in the future. With such a vision in mind, management can create strategies and specify business objectives that take full account of the opportunities and constraints inherent in a range of possible business environments, the resources that should be deployed and the enterprise's existing competitive position.

Figures 1.11–1.13 show samples of published 'Vision' statements from three leading global organisations:

At JCB we design and manufacture construction, agricultural and material handling equipment, for use in both established and emerging markets. As such we embrace the challenge of helping to deliver a future based upon environmental, social and economic sustainability.

Our aim is to develop products and services that delight the customer and exceed their expectations. In doing this, we recognize the potential impact we have on:
The welfare of the communities in which we operate
The health and safety of our employees
The environmental footprint we generate
We do everything that is reasonable and practicable to optimise the benefits and minimise the negative effects of these.

Our future prosperity depends not only in providing quality products and services, but understanding that quality means:
Ensuring that our employees and the communities in which we operate are better off because of us
Tackling workplace and product safety responsibly
Taking the need to operate within environmental limits seriously
We are therefore, committed to continuous improvement in how we design and manufacture our products and services to ensure that our contribution to a sustainable future is realised.
From: http://www.jcb.com/csr/Vision.aspx (April 2015)

Figure 1.11 JCB's vision statement.

As a global energy company, we set high standards of performance and ethical behaviours. We are judged by how we act – our reputation is upheld by how we live up to our core values honesty, integrity and respect for people. The Shell General Business Principles, Code of Conduct and Code of Ethics help everyone at Shell act in line with these values and comply with all relevant legislation and regulations.

From: http://www.shell.com/global/aboutshell/who-we-are/our-values.html (April 2015)

Figure 1.12 Shell's vision statement.

Heinz Vision:

To be the best food company, growing a better world

Heinz Values:

Quality
Integrity
Consumer first
Ownership/meritocracy
Innovation

From: http://www.heinz.com/our-company/about-heinz/vision-and-values.aspx (April 2015)

Figure 1.13 H.J. Heinz's vision statement.

1   JCB;
2   Shell;
3   H.J. Heinz.

As you'll see, some are detailed, some are descriptive and some provide (just) the principal themes. We encourage you to remind yourself of your own organization's vision.

Even though they are a means of realising an organization's vision, business objectives are not themselves controls, but rather the necessary start and end points for an integrated control framework.

Business objectives should:

- be lawful;
- accord with published codes of conduct or ethics;
- guide the business processes of the organization;
- apply to each level of management;
- give timeframes for the achievement of required results;
- have wide-participation in their development;
- be communicated to and understood by all employees and others whose performance can affect them;
- pass the 'red face' test (will managers have a red face any time in the future?);
- form a coherent whole and be internally consistent – as illustrated by Figure 1.14.

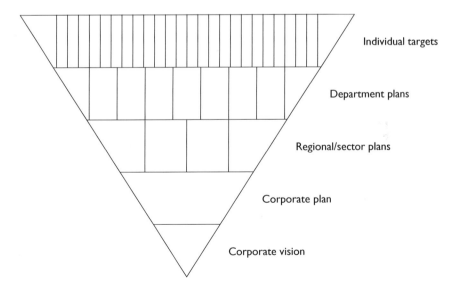

Figure 1.14 Achieving success by aligning objectives.

Risk

The effect of uncertainty on objectives.

(ISO, 2009)

Risk, according to ISO 31000, is the effect of uncertainty on objectives; or anything that may impact upon the achievement of the organization's objectives.

An organization needs to know what is in its risk universe – some inventory of all the things that can harm its potential to be successful so that the significant matters may be managed (managing risks). Figure 1.15 shows some examples of risks in an organisation's 'risk universe'.

Risk assessment is a vital management activity these days, and in some countries and disciplines, it is a legal requirement. This does not de facto imply that all risks can, or indeed should be avoided. The inability or failure to identify and seize business opportunities may itself be a significant risk. Managers should ensure that an organized risk assessment process is embedded in their organization's strategy and the implementation of that strategy.

An effective risk assessment process would require:

- Management to have a detailed knowledge of the political/legal, economic/financial, social/demographic and technical/infrastructure (PEST) features of the market environment in which their organization operates.
- Creation of strategic and operational objectives, which are well known and clearly understood throughout the organization.
- Addressing methodically risks (impacts) in all of their major business activities.

People	Environment
Loss of key personnel	Emissions (air)
Loss of clients	Discharges (land, water)
Health and safety	Nuisance, complaints
Human rights, right to work	Sustainability
Fair pay, discrimination	Biodiversity
Empowerment, morale	
Strikes and disputes	
Assets	**Reputation/Legal**
Natural disasters	Prosecution, litigation
Security	Paying taxes
Fire	Complaints
Life cycle – design, commission, operate,	Media portrayal (local/global)
maintain, decommission	Fair trade
Management of change (MOC)	Sweat shops, forced/child labour

Figure 1.15 Examples of risks in an organisation's 'risk universe'.

- A structured description of the factors that are critical to the organization's success and the opportunities and threats that may help or hinder achievement of the set objectives.
- Estimation of the organization's exposure to these factors, opportunities and threats in quantitative or qualitative terms of i) probability of occurrence and ii) the consequences of their possible impact.
- Collating these exposures in the format of a risk profile or risk matrix (see example in Figure 1.18), which enables management to prioritise the areas for risk responses.

If we were to ask a reasonably-well-informed manager today 'What is risk?', more likely than not you'll be told that it is an estimation of the *probability* and *consequence* of some physical harm occurring. Health and safety managers have been busy in many organizations and 'risk assessment' is a common requirement in Europe, organized companies and developed territories.

In this understanding of risk, managers will commonly use words such as *frequency* or *likelihood*, and some will use words such as *impact* or *severity*. Either way, most will know that risk concerns a reasoned view of the future that can be estimated and planned for. The greater the risk, the greater the resulting need for control. Sometimes, the level of fear drives the level of risk.

Gardner (2009) says fear amongst the people can be a constructive emotion. When we worry about risk, we pay more attention to it and take action where warranted. Occasionally, fears burst into full-bore panics – untreatable diseases, paedophiles lurking in parks and internet chat-rooms are recent fears; in the 1990s it was road rage. A decade earlier, it was herpes. Satanic cults, legionella, mad cow disease, school shootings and crack cocaine have all raced to the top of the public's list of concerns often driven by events.

Organizations have to think about risks too:

> No director can ignore the risk to the reputation of his (sic) company and its brand that health and safety and environmental expectations present.
> Sir Nigel Rudd, one of *The Times* Power 100, and holder of four FTSE directorships (in Eves and Gummer, 2005)

> There is a need for a sensible and proportionate approach to risk management, in short, a balanced approach – this means ensuring that paperwork is proportionate, does not get in the way of doing the job, and it certainly does not mean risk elimination at all costs.
> Judith Hackitt, HSE Chair (Health and Safety Executive, 2013, p.14)

Risk then should be defined as the scale of any type or source of impact on objectives, whether this is reputational, financial, legal, HSEQ and so on.

The opposite face of risk is 'opportunity', achieved by addressing an opportunity to reap the resulting reward.

A good way to think about and refer to these two opposing outcomes is:

1 Value protection (where the harm is the potential for impact upon the achievement of the organization's objectives); and
2 Value creation (the reward for addressing effectively a suitable and acceptable opportunity).

A sample of other definitions of 'risk' are presented below:

> The combination of the severity of harm with the likelihood of its occurrence . . . ; the nature and level of the risks faced by your organisation.
> (Health and Safety Executive, 1997a)

> A combination of the hazard and the loss and, in any given set of circumstances, risk takes into account the relevant aspects of both.
> (Boyle, 2002)

> The chance of a particular situation or event, which will have an impact upon an individual's, organization's or society's objectives, occurring within a stated period of time.
> (Fuller and Vassie, 2004)

> Combination of the likelihood and consequence(s) of a specified hazardous event occurring.
> (OHSAS 18001, BSi, 2007)

> Risk is potential of losing something of value. Values (such as physical health, social status, emotional well being or financial wealth) can be gained or lost when taking risk resulting from a given action, activity and/or inaction, foreseen or unforeseen. Risk can also be defined as the intentional interaction with uncertainty. Uncertainty is a potential, unpredictable, unmeasurable and uncontrollable outcome; risk is a consequence of action taken in spite of uncertainty. Risk perception is the subjective judgment people make about the severity and/or probability of a risk, and may vary person to person. Any human endeavour carries some risk, but some are much riskier than others.
> (Wikipedia, 2015a)

Risk can be considered, expressed and measured in two main ways:

1 Inherent;
2 Residual.

Inherent or unmitigated risk

Inherent risk implies the risk exposure before the effect of the selected controls is accounted for. Some call this the 'unmitigated' risk.

Residual or mitigated risk

The residual risk is the remaining risk exposure after the mitigating and compensating factors of the controls are accounted for. Some call this residual risk the 'mitigated risk'.

Some intentionally selected controls tend to reduce probability (e.g. preventative controls, such as a well-trained workforce or fixed guards on machines), and some controls tend to reduce the consequences (e.g. early detection, containment, mitigation and restoration controls). Other controls can reduce both probability and consequences (e.g. elimination and substitution controls, such as replacement of the hazardous with the less-hazardous).

A brief history of risk

'Risk' has a fascinating history, which is beautifully narrated by Peter Bernstein in his book *Against the Gods* (1998). You would not have to go back in time many years for modern clarity of approach and measurement to be lost. A well-educated individual a thousand years ago would not recognise the number '0', and would probably not pass a basic maths test. Five hundred years later, few would do very much better. Without some form of measurement, some numbers, risk was a matter of gut feel or superstition.

The 'power of numbers' arrived in West in the early thirteenth century, when a book entitled *Liber Abaci* appeared in Italy – a wholly hand-written work of fifteen volumes written by Leonardo Pisano (but commonly known as Fibonacci).

Fibonacci is best known for a series of numbers, which provided the answer to the problem of how many rabbits will be born during the course of one year from one pair, while assuming that every month, each pair produces another pair, and that rabbits start breeding aged two months – the answer is 233; and the dozen month-end totals for the year would be 1, 2, 3, 5, 8, 13, 21, 34, 55, 89, 144, 233. Each successive number is the sum of the two preceding numbers, and if one number is divided by the next, the answer is approximately 1.6. This ratio features in nature (e.g. in shell spirals, leaves and flowers) and in architecture (e.g. the General Assembly Building of the United Nations in New York). Playing cards are similarly proportioned. Fibonacci identified the powerful nature of numbers in the West for the first time (Asbury, 2013), but using them to assess risk remained many years distant.

Bernstein (1998) commented on the development of humans' understanding of risk over the last millennia:

What is it that distinguishes the thousand years of history from what we think of as modern times? The answer goes way beyond the progress of science, technology, capitalism and democracy . . . The revolutionary idea that defines the boundary between modern times and the past is the mastery of risk: the notion that the future is more than a whim of the gods and that men and women are not passive before nature. Until human beings discovered a way across that boundary, the future was a mirror of the past or the murky domain of oracles and soothsayers.

(Bernstein, 1998)

He gives an interesting account of this history, suggesting that:

The ability to define what may happen in the future and to choose amongst alternatives lies as the heart of contemporary societies.

(Bernstein, 1998)

Hazard and risk

A modern definition of hazard is 'the potential for harm'. The word hazard is said to derive from the Arabic word for dice – *al zahr.*

We have seen a representative sample of definitions of risk on page 34, though there are many others. The word risk is said to derive from the early Italian *risicare*, which means 'to dare'. To dare implies the freedom to choose and as a result, possibly to fail.

Dice is a game of luck – of pure chance – of potential for harm, of hazard. Whilst lots of things have potential for harm ('*al zahr*'), managers can choose – to dare or not – how and when to respond to hazards. This choice influences the probability of the harm occurring and the consequences should the harm be realized.

This 'daring' to participate actively in the business environment includes managers making choices. The first choice, the first option for managers is to *Terminate* the activity, or not start it in the first place if the risk is beyond the appetite of the organization, or in absolute terms, is too great.

If the risk cannot or should not be terminated, it could be *Treated* or mitigated with selected controls to a lower residual level. Use of our DTRT Model as described in this book is a risk treatment.

Other choices for managers include to *Transfer* the risk to someone else (e.g. to insure it financial, or to participate in a joint venture).

After the choice or choices have been made, the residual risk is *Tolerated*. Tolerating a risk in this context means 'not happy with the situation' or 'living with the risk'. Managers need to be vigilant and review how well their risk control measures continue to be effective. Tolerating risk is ultimately fatalistic and defeatist, as it implies 'passive acceptance'.

We call these four choices the '4Ts', illustrated in Figure 1.16.

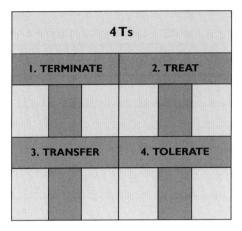

Figure 1.16 The 4Ts.

Black swans

Experience influences choice, and the example here shows how the most experienced sea captain of his day was so influenced:

> When anyone asks me how I can best describe my experience of nearly forty years at sea, I merely say uneventful. Of course there have been winter gales and storms and fog and the like, but in all my experience, I have never been in an accident of any sort worth speaking about. I have seen but one vessel in distress in all my years at sea ... I never saw a wreck and have never been wrecked, nor was I ever in any predicament that threatened to end in disaster of any sort.
>
> (From a paper presented by
> E.J. Smith in 1907; Toone, 2004)

On 14 April 1912, RMS Titanic sank with the loss of 1500 lives. The captain went down with the ship. His name – E. J. Smith.

The absence of previous loss is no guarantor that future loss is impossible. We call these types of risks – of low probability, but very high consequence – 'Black Swans', as they do not come along very often.

The practicalities of understanding risk

In the simplest terms, business concerns the conversion of inputs (land, labour, capital and materials) to outputs (the product or service and the associated wastes).

Figure 1.17 shows the reality of this for any business; the essence of enterprise. On the left-hand side are shown the aspirations of the entrepreneurs, seeking funding for the enterprise, and investment in the necessary resources. We call this the Mission – the reason an organization exists.

On the right-hand side is the Vision of achievement and success stated in whatever terms those entrepreneurs have decided. Connecting the two sides is identifying and responding (the 4Ts) to risks. Or 'risk management' as risk managers call it.

Treatment is applied by the effective implementation of assured management system controls.

Of course, not all organizations are equally successful. Almost every day brings news of organizations that dared and subsequently failed. How (and whether) any organization identifies and responds to the risks in its own context / environment will be a significant feature of *its* success (or failure).

Figure 1.18 shows a simple risk-ranking matrix. Organizations and sectors have taken this basic model and developed it with greater numbers of boxes, and ever-more technical and (sometimes) fanciful ways to determine probability and consequence. But whatever they do, the principle remains the same. Higher risks require greater attention; it is the principle, and the relative positions of the identified risks rather than any absolute 'scoring' that matters.

The greater the inherent risk, the greater the (implied) urgency for response and treatment of the risk. These days, some organizations are rightly interested in activities with significant consequence potential, regardless of the probability (or Black Swan risks). High impact losses can (and have) ended careers and organizations. We remind readers to consider this combination too.

> We're sorry for the massive disruption it's caused their lives. There's no one who wants this over more than I do. I would like my life back.
> BP CEO Tony Hayward, commenting on BP's 'impossible' oil spill disaster in the Gulf of Mexico, which claimed 11 lives, killed thousands of animals and spewed millions of gallons of oil in May 2010. Mr Hayward was replaced in October 2010 (CNN, 2010)

Just *how* low a residual risk should be depends upon the 'appetite' for risk in the management of the organization. Some readers will be familiar with terms such as 'ALARP' (As Low As Reasonably Practicable) and/or 'so far as reasonably practicable', but lengthy discussions of these concepts are beyond the scope of this book. We summarise the basics here.

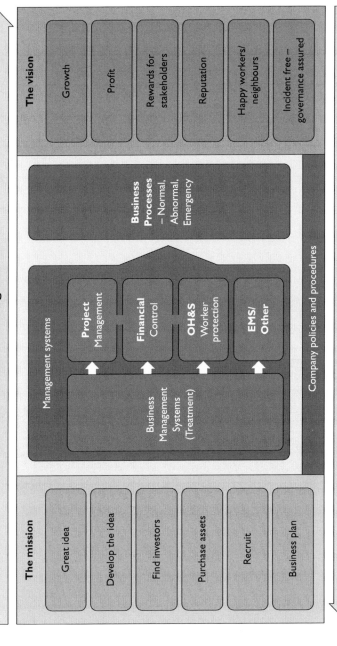

Figure 1.17 The essence of enterprise.

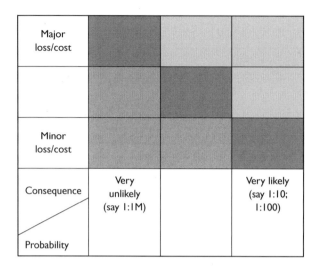

Figure 1.18 A simple risk-ranking matrix.

ALARP

Controls should be applied to business operations in an effective and efficient manner – not too few, and not too many. This finely tuned balance is commonly known as 'ALARP' (As Low As Reasonably Practicable). This means that the controls selected are ALARP if the cost of additional control is grossly disproportionate to the level of residual risk. The final test of what is reasonable and what is not is sometimes carried out by court judges and in some territories, juries. The bottom line is that each risk must be managed well enough to prevent significant impacts on objectives.

The '4Ts' illustrated in figure 1.16 assist any manager to maintain or exclude activities, processes or services. Where 'Treat' is the selected strategy, there is an established hierarchy of control, commonly referred to as 'ERIC', as follows:

- Eliminate: terminate exposure to the hazard;
- Reduce: less time or intensity of exposure, to fewer people;
- Isolate: contain the hazard or energy by physical or other means;
- Control: mitigation by other means, including rules, procedures, training and (last of all) PPE

Tip: Remember 'famous Eric', when a significant risk is identified. Many readers may have a 'famous Eric' – whether a parent, relative, friend or work colleague. In our training, to encourage participants to remember 'ERIC', we encourage referral to Eric Cantona (famous footballer), Eric Morcambe (famous comedian) or Eric Clapton (famous musician) as aide memoires.

The human factor

How people behave in an organization is critical to the success of any control framework.

Critical success factors are:

- The tone at the top set by the highest management level regarding the ethical values, standards and actions of everyone associated with an organization.
- The quality of all levels of staff and their understanding, support and compliance with the business controls in their area.
- Adequacy of time and competent resources for proper operation, maintenance and review of business controls.
- Good communication between individuals and between groups of people.
- Reliable, timely and useful information to enable staff to discharge their responsibilities efficiently, and to measure their achievement of specified objectives.

The impact of culture and human factors were illustrated powerfully in the late Carolyn W. Merritt's (then Chairman and CEO of CSB; the US Chemical Safety and Hazard Investigation Board) statement to the BP Independent Safety Review Panel in Houston, Texas on November 10, 2005:

> One of my aspirations is that all industrial managers treat safety and major accident prevention with the same degree of seriousness and rigor that is brought to financial transactions. Few people would operate a major corporation today without a strict system of financial controls and auditing, where everyone within the corporation recognizes the severe consequences for non-compliance.

> That same standard of diligence is not always applied to risk management and safety. If you get away with a flawed safety decision one day or repeatedly, far from facing a penalty you may actually end up rewarded, perhaps for boosting production. You may come to believe that what was thought to be unsafe is actually safe, based on your experience. It is a phenomenon that is sometimes called 'normalization of abnormalities.
>
> (Merritt, 2005)

Management and risk

An essential first step is to consider risks in the context of the environment in which the organization is operating. It is unlikely that any two business environments could be exactly the same, even if they are in the same county or country.

As we have discussed, the process for estimating risks is by using a risk assessment matrix to assess qualitatively the significance of each identified potential impact using the independent variables of probability and consequence.

Three prompting questions first proposed in 2005 (Asbury) invariably assist managers to decide the significance of the risks they have identified:

1   How often will this happen (the likelihood, frequency, probability)?
2   How big could the impact be (the severity, impact, consequence)?
3   Who might be affected by any occurrence (which stakeholders)?

NB By 'stakeholders', we mean five specific groups – Investors, Employees, Supply chain partners, Customers and Society as discussed on pages 21–2.

Readers may wish to research some of the many quantitative risk evaluation / estimation methodologies and software toolkits available in organizations and commercially. Our view however remains this: Too much focus on precise risk scoring can easily become counter-productive. This is supported by our experience of over 1000 implementations of business and risk management systems over a (combined) 50 years in over 70 countries on six continents. We say it is wise to avoid the 'numbers game' (Asbury, 2005).

Earlier in this chapter, we have described the evolution, development and rise of business control frameworks, aka management system standards, as a reliable approach to making a successful transition from business vision to business reality. This, of course, includes compliance with legal and other mandatory requirements. So you may wonder where do business laws fit in to all of this?

This is not a law book. Nor is it aimed at a particular country or continent. It goes without saying that organizations have to look at (research) the legal requirements of their territory and other requirements of their insurers, trade associations or head offices. What is certainly true is that some of the business control frameworks we have discussed specifically require organizations to identify the relevant legal and other requirements as a mandatory element of conformity.

CSR is the expectation on organizations for transparency of operations and the consequent impacts. This means meeting legal requirements before and in addition to any use of enhanced risk mitigations. The business response to CSR has provided both effective programs with meaningful improvement, as well as lots of 'greenwash' (such as pictures of waterfalls, trees and smiling children). Our DTRT Model supports the former and addresses meaningfully the latter.

DTRT Model

We introduced you to the core elements of the DTRT Model in the Preface and in Case Studies 1.1 and 1.2, earlier in this chapter. It is re-presented here for your convenience in Figure 1.19.

Now that you appreciate the importance of understanding organizational contexts, organizations' objectives and organizations' risks, we have developed

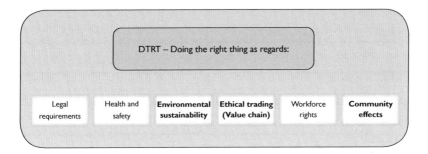

| Legal requirements | Health and safety | **Environmental sustainability** | **Ethical trading (Value chain)** | Workforce rights | **Community effects** |

Figure 1.19 The DTRT Model: the six core elements of doing the right thing.

our model (Figure 1.20) to make it practical and useful to you. Our model links the preliminary understanding of Context to the Organization's objectives and how Risks are identified and prioritized for attention using a significance test. Identification of corporate responsibilities – both corporate legal responsibilities and corporate social responsibilities – allows you to develop a CSR strategy based across the six core themes and likely to lead to business success. The Model shows the interconnectivity of Verification, Communication and Improvement. This is our advice to organizations on how to identify, treat and respond to CSR-related risks. We'll refer to and use this model throughout the rest of the book to illustrate to you our major points.

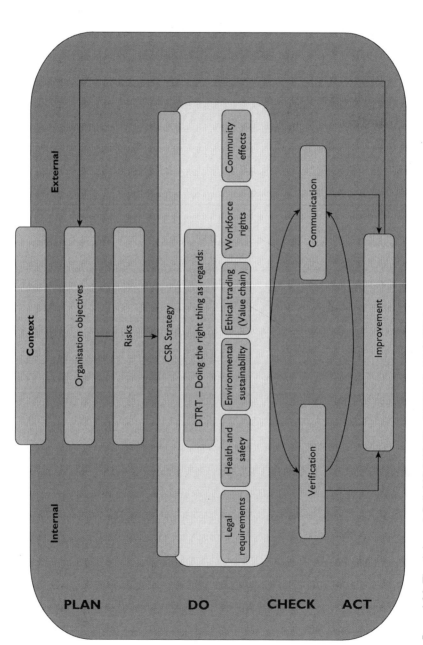

Figure 1.20 The Asbury & Ball CSR MSS, The DTRT Model ©, 2016.

Chapter 2

The evolution of CSR

Symbiotic relationships mean creative partnerships. The Earth is to be seen neither as an ecosystem to be preserved unchanged, nor as a quarry to be exploited for selfish and short-range economic reasons, but as a garden to be cultivated for the development of its own potentialities of the human adventure. The goal of this relationship is not the maintenance of the status quo, but the emergence of new phenomena and new values.

–René Dubos (1901–1982), Bacteriologist at Rockefeller University and Pulitzer Prize recipient

The history of corporate social responsibility

An organization[1] is inevitably intertwined with the society[2] in which it operates and interacts willingly or otherwise with it. It will usually make some positive contributions to society. Organizations of all types may create employment and social environments, they may provide goods, services and information needed by their customers or service users and they generally invest in communities by paying salaries to employees and taxes to governments. But they can also have negative impacts. The downsides might include environmental damage by polluting land, the air and water, poor workforce conditions resulting in injuries, disability or illness to workers, or unreasonable exploitation of people – for example very long hours, or employing children. As Dubos highlights the role of CSR is to set values in how organizations should operate.

CSR involves acknowledging these negative impacts and promoting ways of eliminating or mitigating them as much as possible. In this chapter we'll start by looking at the origins of CSR and consider whether it's here to stay or just the latest fashion. Is CSR a new concept? If not, where did it come from?

Depending on your definition of CSR its origins vary, but probably date from about 4,000 years ago. What is the history of protecting and defending the rights of communities? And what records of this survive today? Another important question is what should be included in any commitment to social responsibility:

- Workers' rights?
- Health and safety?

- Personal health and fitness?
- Ethical trading?
- Environmental impact?
- Bribery and corrupt practices?

The earliest quoted community framework was the Hammurabi Codex, dating to 1780 BCE (King, 2004). This code of law was carved on a black stone monument 2.4 metres high for public view in ancient Babylon in Mesopotamia; an example of which stands in the Louvre in Paris. It included these laws:

> If a builder build a house for someone, and does not construct it properly, and the house which he built fall in and kill its owner, then that builder shall be put to death.
>
> (Law 229)

> If it kill the son of the owner the son of that builder shall be put to death.
>
> (Law 230)

> If it kill a slave of the owner, then he shall pay for a slave to the owner of the house.
>
> (Law 231)

> If it ruin goods, he shall make compensation for all that has been ruined, and inasmuch as he did not construct properly this house which he built and it fell, he shall re-erect the house from his own means.
>
> (Law 232)

Was this the beginning of CSR, building regulations and health and safety?

It's hard to establish for certain where CSR started. It has evolved from many disconnected disciplines. From ancient times, mankind has battled with the dilemma of making gain through the exploitation of others. Where a society has imposed some rule or regulation to encourage 'fairness', its rules have been dependent on the society's definition of equality. The Code of Hammurabi aims to protect society but also explicitly refers to slavery! Similarly, in our modern world, the approach to protecting UK workers may be different from the approach to workers overseas. And what about animals? Should we consider their suffering too?

We don't have to look as far back as ancient Mesopotamia to see the value of CSR. In the context of the British Empire, the Slave Trade Act, which outlawed trading of slaves, received Royal Assent in 1807, some five years after the earliest recognized health and safety legislation, the Health and Morals of Apprentices Act 1802. But slavery was still legal in the British overseas territories until the Slavery Abolition Act received assent in 1833. In the same year, the Factory Act established a regular working day in the textile industry, and wider protection for workers. The main provisions were that:

- children under nine could not be employed in textile factories:
- children aged nine to 13 could work a maximum of nine hours per day and 48 hours per week;
- young people aged 13 to 18 could work a maximum of 12 hours per day and 69 hours per week;
- night work for children and young people was not permitted;
- children were to attend school.

The 1833 Act also appointed four independent factory inspectors to cover the whole of the country, with the power to investigate accidents and to prosecute factory and mill owners. These principles, over 175 years old in the UK, still form part of CSR standards today, such as the Ethical Base Code for sourcing suppliers in developing nations, which, among others, includes the principles that:

- employment should be freely chosen;
- working conditions should be safe and hygienic;
- child labour mustn't be used;
- working hours should not be excessive;
- no harsh or inhumane treatment is allowed.

During the Victorian period in Britain, the development of CSR continued. Increasing industrialization led to more pollution and a degradation of living conditions for many, affecting the health and productivity of workers. In nineteenth-century Britain, there were no fewer than 10 Factories Acts that sought to reform working conditions. Some Victorian philanthropists realized that social reform, including relocating workers from slums to out-of-town developments, benefited not only the workers but businesses as well. These philanthropists' legacy lives on today in the form of businesses formed then which still survive, such as Lloyds Bank, Rowntree and Cadbury.

Case Study 2.1: Cadbury pioneers CSR, UK

The common perception is that CSR is something new, developed as part of the environmental movement as a post-modern juxtaposition to the capitalism and industrialism of the later twentieth century. The paradigm that space exploration and the 'Earthrise' photograph by Apollo 8 (our first manned rocket to the Moon) gave a new perceptive on our fragile green planet we call Earth? However, on a closer review, business and work welfare extends much further back. In the later part of the nineteenth century a similar movement was in place in the United Kingdom, which focused on the links between a better environment

(continued)

(continued)

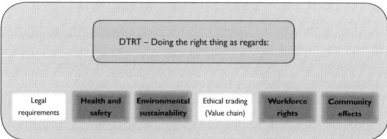

with worker living conditions, occupational standards and increased productivity. The wealthiest in society recognized the benefits to themselves of tackling the urban pollution and their moral duty to act upon it. How much can be learnt from the Victorian philanthropic movement in today's modern context?

From the start of the development of the industrial revolution workers health was a concern for society to some degree; the Abolition of Slavery, Morals and Apprentices Acts and the setting up of the Factories inspectorate in the first part of the nineteenth century was in response to the working conditions in the fast growing cities in the UK. With cities such as Liverpool expanding in population from 4,240 in 1701 to 222,954 in 1841 (Philanthrocapitalism, 2015) the services within the cities where continually pushed to breaking point creating a range of social and public health issues, causing these areas to become a haven for disease. This is illustrated by the fact that in 1842 the average age at death of a labourer in Bethnal Green, East London was just 16 years, for tradesmen it was 26 years, whilst the average gentlemen lived to 45 (Philanthrocapitalism, 2015).

In response to these facts, many rich industrialists responded in a number of ways, these included the foundation of a number of charity organizations that are still in existence to this day. Examples of this are the National Society for the Prevention of Cruelty to Children (NSPCC), which gained its royal charter from Queen Victoria in 1895 and the Royal Society for the Prevention of Cruelty to Animals (RSPCA), which was formed in 1824; both where financed by public donations from wealthy individuals. A study of 466 wills published in *The Daily Telegraph* in the 1890s showed that on average, men left 11% and women left 25%, of their estates to charity. Another response was for organization's, lead by their charismatic owners, to participate in what would now be known as CSR activities, whilst not the first, one of the most well known of these was the Quaker movement, which included the Cadbury and Rowntree confectionary brands.

After taking over from his father, George Cadbury expanded the chocolate production to a scale that the existing factory could not support, so he started to look to develop a new factory away from the industrial pollution, smog and squalid conditions of the inner city. However in an age when commuting was by foot, the new factory workers would also need housing in close proximity. Guided by his Quaker Principles, he was quoted as saying:

> No man ought to be condemned to live in a place where a rose cannot grow.
>
> (Cadbury, 2015)

A new factory site was selected, and a new community built, called 'Bourneville', of which the conditions are described in more detail on the Cadbury website. These mostly semi-detached houses were well built and spaced out with ample gardens. Production began at the Cadbury Brothers' 'Bourneville factory in a garden' in September 1879. When the workers arrived, they found facilities that were simply unknown in Victorian times. There was a field next to the factory where men were encouraged to play cricket and football; a garden and playground for the girls; a kitchen where workers could heat up their meals; and properly heated dressing rooms where they could get changed. As George said, 'If the country is a good place to live in, why not to work in?' (Cadbury, 2015). Keen sportsmen, Richard and George, encouraged sports and recreations, often playing cricket

(continued)

(continued)

themselves. Sports facilities grew to include football, hockey and cricket pitches, tennis and squash racquet courts and a bowling green. Gradually women's and men's swimming pools were built and every young boy and girl joining the company was encouraged to become a good swimmer. Work outings to the country were organized, together with summer camps for the young boys. Morning prayers and daily bible readings first started in 1866, helping preserve the family atmosphere. These continued for another 50 years, until the workforce grew too large for such an assembly.

However the area also had no public houses in line with the Quaker origins of abstinence.

In 1899 the death of George Cadbury's brother Richard from diphtheria greatly affected him, and led him to establish a trust deed of 330 acres of land and over 300 houses; thus creating a long term CSR legacy for people not only for the workers at the chocolate factory but also from a wide range of backgrounds. Today the Bourneville Estate covers over 1,000 acres, 10 per cent of which has been set aside as parkland and open space. There are almost 8,000 houses of mixed tenure on the Estate, which is now home to about 25,000 people.

Which brings us to Cadbury's of the twenty-first century. In 2007, the brand launched its 'Purple Goes Green' strategy, drawing on its distinctive purple branding and setting targets to reduce its impact on the global environment. The Cadbury 'Purple Goes Green' website says:

> The Cadbury 'Purple Goes Green' initiative sets a vision for our company to tackle climate change. We intend to shrink our global environmental footprint by cutting our energy use, reducing excess packaging and managing our water use.
>
> (Cadbury, 2015)

The company aimed to achieve this through a set of specific aims, i.e.:

- reducing carbon emissions 50 per cent by 2020;
- reducing standard packaging by 10 per cent and seasonal packaging by 25 per cent;
- implementing water reduction programs in all 'water-scarce' sites;
- advocating green business practices with colleagues, suppliers, customers, peers and consumers.

These goals were then incorporated in to broader goals when Cadbury became part of the Mondelēz International group. Their aims were to tackle social and environmental goals, which the whole of Mondelēz organization materially affects, and they have stated the following areas for improvement:

Environmental

1 environmental footprint of agriculture;
2 supply security of key agricultural commodities;
3 environmental footprint of our operations.

Social

1 mindful snacking – to promote better health of consumers;
2 promoting well-being through community partnerships;
3 safety of our people and products.

It would appear the that philanthropic principles continue, as in 2013 Cadbury's owner Mondelēz International reported that it achieved the 'Roundtable for Sustainable Palm Oil' (RSPO) standard for 100 per cent of the palm oil it bought in 2013 – two years ahead of schedule.

'Achieving 100 per cent RSPO is an important milestone toward our long-term commitment to only buy palm oil that's produced on legally held land, doesn't lead to deforestation or loss of peat land, respects human rights, including land rights, and doesn't use forced or child labour,' said Dave Brown, VP of Global Commodities and Strategic Sourcing (Mondelez International, 2014). 'We recognize the need to go further, so we've also challenged our palm oil suppliers to provide transparency on the levels of traceability in their palm oil supply chains. Knowing the sources of palm oil supplies is an essential first step to enable scrutiny and promote improvements in practice on the ground.'

Looking to the future, Mondelēz International is working on an action plan for suppliers to give priority to supplies that meet its sustainability principles and eliminate supplies that do not meet their standards by 2020 (Ethical Performance, 2015), continuing a heritage of CSR of over 150 years.

However, not everyone had access to such positive opportunities. The Victorian age saw the development of a range of piecemeal and industry-specific legislation, such as the Shop Hours Regulation Act, 1886 and the Metalliferous Mines Regulation Act, 1872. These were later consolidated into the Factory and Workshop Act, 1901. This Act gave the power to the Secretary of State to make regulations for particular industries, separating Parliament from the day-to-day setting of regulations, a process that remains in place today.

This period also saw the beginnings of ecology in the era of classification and exploration of the natural world. Darwin's book *On the Origin of Species*, first published in 1859, led to an awakening in the scientific understanding of the natural world. This interest prompted the quest to identify and classify

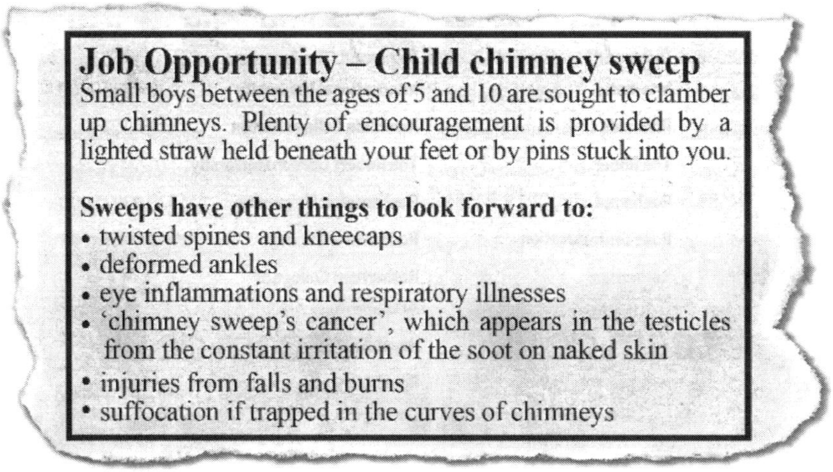

Job Opportunity – Child chimney sweep
Small boys between the ages of 5 and 10 are sought to clamber up chimneys. Plenty of encouragement is provided by a lighted straw held beneath your feet or by pins stuck into you.

Sweeps have other things to look forward to:
- twisted spines and kneecaps
- deformed ankles
- eye inflammations and respiratory illnesses
- 'chimney sweep's cancer', which appears in the testicles from the constant irritation of the soot on naked skin
- injuries from falls and burns
- suffocation if trapped in the curves of chimneys

Figure 2.1 Spoof job advertisement for nineteenth-century chimney sweeps.

species, resulting in macabre but colourful collections of butterflies, beetles and birds; pinned, stuffed or bottled in formaldehyde. The Victorian period also saw the expansion of a Philanthropist movement: in 1845, Benjamin Disraeli, a British Prime minster, described the difference between rich and poor in England as 'two nations between whom there is no contact and no sympathy; we are as ignorant of each other's feelings as if we were dwellers in different zones or different planets' (Disraeli, 1998). The Quaker movement shaped the principles of organizations such as Cadbury, Lever Brothers and Rowntree to bridge this gap, through the provision of garden villages for workers, however these came with conditions to abide by specific behaviours. Lord Leverhulme, one of the founders of Unilever was reported as saying:

> A good workman may have a wife of objectionable habits, or may have objectionable habits himself, which make it undesirable for us to have him in the village.
>
> (History, 2015)

The early twentieth century saw a new power in CSR – the tort of negligence and the principle of 'neighbour'. While the concept of 'negligence' had existed in common law for many centuries, it tended to apply only in the narrow context of a contractual 'master and servant' relationship. The famous case in 1932 of the snail in the ginger beer extended this duty to take 'reasonable care to avoid acts or omissions which you can reasonably foresee would be likely to injure your neighbour' (Baihlii, 1932). This established what is known as the 'neighbour principle'.

The possibility for legal claims for compensation became a new battleground for CSR, and this continues to allow individuals, groups and communities to mount legal challenges against large organizations, with financial implications large enough to compel them to consider their actions in a wider context. CSR is an extension of this principle. Case law has developed to extend the neighbour principle to trespassers who you could reasonably foresee may enter your site, to contractors under your supervision and to users of your products or services. In a globalized market place, who will be your 'neighbour' tomorrow? Could the Inuit living inside the Arctic Circle sue developed nations for the loss of the Greenland ice shelf, and thus their homes, as a result of climate change?

The increasing democracy of wealth, production and growth, which followed the end of World War II, took a while to gain momentum. But this also brought its problems. Thick 'pea soup' smog in London in the 1950s brought the capital to a standstill for five days, and led to the reported death of around 4,000 people from respiratory and other diseases. In response, the first Clean Air Act was introduced in 1956; it was updated in 1968 and 1993. A few years later, the publication of *Silent Spring* by Rachel Carson in 1962 questioned the impact of pesticides on the wider environment, and made society question the impact of organizations on society and the environment. This laid the foundations for the public appetite for the modern environmental movement, and for CSR.

In 1974, the UK Health and Safety at Work etc. Act received Royal Assent. This new law provided 'umbrella' legislation for the protection of virtually all workers in Great Britain, and has been extended to cover offshore installations within British territorial waters. The Act has many elements that are important for the CSR practitioner.

The general duty for every employer to 'ensure so far as is reasonably practicable the health, safety and welfare at work of all his employees' (Health and Safety At Work, etc. Act, 1974) brings a standardized statutory framework across industrial sectors, although there are some exclusions, such as a domestic servant in a private household. This duty implies the common approach of balancing the size of a risk against the cost of its solution; a philosophy that can be extended to CSR. The Act also sets out duties to protect 'those not in his [the employer's] employment' and places duties on designers, manufacturers, importers and suppliers which, together with consumer protection legislation (such as the Sale of Goods Act 1979), codify every organization's legal duties to consider society, the wider public and users in its operations and interactions.

The Health and Safety at Work etc. Act also requires organizations with five or more employees to have a written statement of health and safety policy. Could – and should – this be extended to include a statement of CSR and environmental protection policy for all organizations in years to come? What if every organization had a legal duty to use the earth's resources as efficiently as is reasonably practicable?

In 1975, the CITES (Convention on International Trade in Endangered Species of Wild Fauna and Flora) list came into force. This outlawed trade in any species listed as endangered by signatory countries. While this is a voluntary code, it signaled the ability of governments to agree international protocols on environmental grounds. Today, the following are on the CITES (2015) endangered lists:

- Mammals – 886 species;
- Birds –1471 species;
- Reptiles – 798 species;
- Amphibians –146 species;
- Fish –103 species;
- Invertebrates –2,254 species;
- Plants –29,817 species.

The Ethiopian famines of the 1980s brought the inequality of where people live to every television set in the world. Scenes of wide-eyed babies, with skeletal limbs and flies around their mouths, held in the arms of a rocking mother

Figure 2.2 An audience of 72,000 attended the Live Aid concert at Wembley Stadium in 1985. A further 90,000 filled the JFK Stadium in Philadelphia, while a global audience of 1.5 billion in 100 countries watched the concerts on television.

became burned into our minds. These were famines of biblical proportions, and with millions dead from starvation and thirst, it forced millions of people in the developed world to question their own lifestyles and ask how they could help.

'Compassion fatigue' may have taken hold in later years, but the Live Aid images from 1985 opened another generation's minds to the principles of CSR and personal social responsibility (PSR), with charitable fundraising moving from the individual to the national government agenda.

While environmental and social issues had been discussed in academia for some time, they now began to reach a wider public awareness. In 1987, the Brundtland Report *Our Common Future* highlighted the importance of including environmental and social elements in the economic framework, and provided a widely quoted definition of sustainable development:

> Development that meets the needs of the present, without compromising the ability of future generations to meet their own needs.
>
> (World Commission on
> Environment and Development, 1987, p. 27)

One year on, the Intergovernmental Panel on Climate Change (IPCC) was formed. This panel of experts and politicians was drawn from a wide range of backgrounds, including climatology and oceanography. The IPCC has played a critical role in building a consensus on climate change processes, effects and adaptation strategies. It was clear that only through international agreement would any single state consider it worthwhile to introduce environmental protection at a scale that would have a reasonable effect.

Several such agreements have since been signed, including the Montreal Protocol on Ozone Depleting Substances (1989) and a series of Earth Summits (most notably at Rio de Janeiro in 1992 and Kyoto in 1997, RIO20+ 2012) which led to 'Agenda 21' and a treaty to stabilize greenhouse gas concentrations in the atmosphere at a level that would prevent dangerous man-made influences on the climate.

Johnson, Bush and Gore, highlighted the perspective of a growing concern for what was at stake stating:

> Once our natural splendour is destroyed, it can never be recaptured.
>
> Lyndon B Johnson, US President,
> 1963–1969 (in Sreenivasan, 2009)

> Let us remember as we chase our dreams into the stars that our first responsibility is to our Earth, to our children and to ourselves.
>
> George H W Bush, US President,
> 1989–1993 (in Environmental Law Reporter, 1988)

> We could really lose it . . . what we take for granted might not be here
> for our children
>
> Al Gore, former US Vice-President and
> international environmental campaigner
> (in *An Inconvenient Truth*, 2006)

The signatories to the Kyoto Protocol agreed to limit greenhouse gas emissions. While some countries have reduction targets, developing countries must control their increases. The European Union agreed to an eight per cent reduction in carbon dioxide equivalent emissions based on 1990 emission levels, by 2012.

The Kyoto agreement set in motion the legal framework that has resulted in an EU-wide carbon emissions trading scheme and the UK Climate Change regulatory framework, which created:

> [A] new approach to managing and responding to climate change in
> the UK through setting ambitious targets, taking powers to help achieve
> them, strengthening the institutional framework, enhancing the UK's
> ability to adapt to the impact of climate change and establishing clear
> and regular accountability to the UK Parliament.
>
> (Institute of Environmental
> Management & Assessment, 2007)

This new target-setting approach has led to increasing pressure on UK organizations to report and minimize their greenhouse gas emissions. Performance so far in a selection of countries against their agreed obligations is shown below.

Prospects for success in the world's struggle to combat global warming were transformed in November 2008 when the US President-elect, Barack Obama, made it clear that America would play its full part in renewing the Kyoto Protocol treaty on climate change. His words brought to an end eight years of objections to Kyoto by George W Bush's administration, which withdrew the US from the treaty in 2001.

President Bush had justified withdrawal from Kyoto by casting doubt on whether climate change was happening and whether it was caused by human activities. The scientific consensus on both points has become so great that the US administration had to accept that they were true.

President Obama's words injected a new mood of optimism among negotiators preparing for the conference at which the Kyoto agreement was due to be renewed and extended.

> Once I take office, you can be sure that the United States will once again
> engage vigorously in these negotiations, and help lead the world toward
> a new era of global co-operation on climate change.
>
> Barack Obama, US President,
> 2009–(in Change.Gov, 2009)

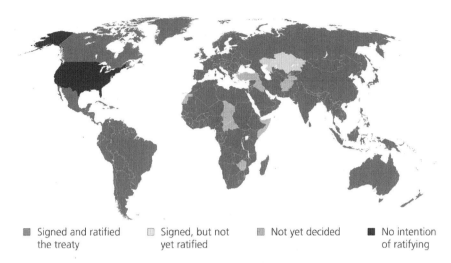

Signed and ratified the treaty   Signed, but not yet ratified   Not yet decided   No intention of ratifying

Figure 2.3 Map showing the 178 states (at April 2008) which have ratified the Kyoto Protocol to the United Nations Framework Convention on Climate Change.

This change of heart signaled that the US was at last coming in from the cold – an essential prerequisite for success at the Copenhagen Conference in 2009. The conference could be described as being of limited success at the very best. The Copenhagen Accord was a declaration that the signatories recognized climate change as a significant problem and that they will try to map out a way for the world to hold global temperature rises to two degrees Celsius above the pre-industrial level. This is regarded as the maximum short-term increase the earth and its human communities can safely sustain. The main groups of UNFCCC signatory nations involved in the formal negotiations were:

- the African Group; see African Group and climate change negotiations for further details on their role in the post Kyoto negotiations;
- the Alliance of Small Island States; see Alliance of Small Island States and climate change negotiations for further details on their role in the post Kyoto negotiations;
- the Coalition of Rainforest Nations;
- the Environmental Integrity Group;
- the European Union;
- G-77/China;
- the Least Developed Countries; and
- the Umbrella Group, including Australia, Canada, New Zealand, Iceland, Japan, Norway, the Russian Federation, Ukraine and the United States.

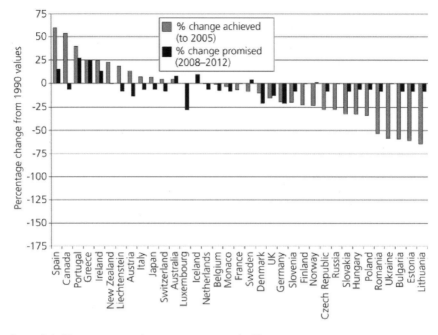

Figure 2.4 Changes in greenhouse gas emissions by Kyoto signatory countries since 1990.

The lack of an agreed process has led to a broad spectrum of countries making pledges to reduce carbon emission nationally, impacting on organizations and encouraging other countries to follow. The EU has set a range of targets in relation to carbon management setting three key objectives for 2020:

- a 20 per cent reduction in EU greenhouse gas emissions from 1990 levels;
- raising the share of EU energy consumption produced from renewable resources to 20%;
- a 20 per cent improvement in the EU's energy efficiency.

And beyond – Key EU targets for 2030:

- at least 40 per cent cut in greenhouse gas emissions compared with 1990;
- At least 27 per cent of total energy consumption from renewable energy;
- At least 27 per cent increase in energy efficiency.

With the following long-term goals:

- By 2050, the EU aims to cut its emissions substantially – by 80–95 per cent compared to 1990 levels, as part of the efforts required by developed countries as a group.
- Turning Europe into a highly energy efficient and low-carbon economy will also boost the economy, create jobs and strengthen Europe's competitiveness (EU, 2015).

In 2014, China and the US pledged to cap carbon emission, speaking at a joint press conference at the Great Hall of the People, in China President Obama said:

> As the world's largest economies and greatest emitters of greenhouse gases we have special responsibility to lead the global effort against climate change. I am proud we can announce a historic agreement. I commend President Xi, his team and the Chinese government for their making to slow, peak and then reverse China's carbon emissions.
>
> (Guardian, 2014)

This statement recognized that governments and organizations have a duty to act on climate change, and shows there is sufficient pressures on world superpowers to make a commitment. Whether that agreement was sufficient or will be followed through will be a matter for history.

CSR's dramatic evolution over the last generation has not been limited to the environmental risk area. Other risk areas, such as bribery and corruption, fair trade and ethical sourcing, are all now central to the core principles of what CSR is or should be. In January 1999, the UN Secretary-General Kofi Annan challenged world business leaders to embrace and enact the United Nations Global Compact. This agreement seeks support for nine principles of human rights, labour and environmental sustainability as they apply to business practices and public policy.

Social Media and the digital age now add another dimension to CSR. Anyone can publish statements about an organization, making any story a potential viral internet hit. This has driven a requirement for clear verification and reporting systems so that stakeholders and investors have some assurance that risks are consider, evaluated and managed effectively. To support this, a broad range of globally recognized reporting standards have been developed, these include the Global Report Initiative a set of globally recognized standards to which many organizations develop their CSR report, ISO 26000:2010 the International Standards Organization's guidance framework on social responsibility, together with a revision to ISO 14001 Environmental Management Systems Standard that includes elements on considering strategic business risk and opportunities in relation to the environment, closer working with value chains (a broader scope than supply chain, as it also looks at any who might receive value from the organization such as recycling), and a life cycle approach. The development over past decade of recognized auditable standards allow third parties to distinguish between the truth and the hype of organization's CSR claims and social media commentaries. These standards are summarized in Chapter 6.

These standards include the principles of international human rights norms as described in International Labour Organization conventions, the United Nations Convention on the Rights of the Child and the Universal Declaration of Human Rights. The last focuses on:

- child labour;
- forced labour;
- health and safety;
- free association;
- collective bargaining;
- discrimination;
- disciplinary practices;
- working hours;
- compensation.

Ethics vs. the need to compete in the global economy

As we've already discussed, organizations inevitably interact with the societies and macro-environments within which they operate. In this book, you'll learn the key points in relation to CSR (and, in Chapter 9, PSR) and how some organizations are working to tackle these issues.

We'll look at the benefits for organizations and society which can be gained from broad adoption of CSR principles and also the potential difficulties of trying to balance ethical practice against the need to compete in a global economy.

We've already shown that organizations can have both positive and negative impacts on society. Without organizations, we'd have no goods or services, no employment and reduced tax revenues to fund the public sector in areas such as health, education, defense and welfare support. But with the increasing commercialization and globalization of business, there are potential negative impacts too.

Fundamentally, businesses operate to make profits and to grow year on year. Other organizations will have other objectives, for example to provide information or charity. Businesses are often seen as the 'bad guys'. Their need to expand and make profits for their owners or shareholders can sometimes be to the detriment of society and the environment. This presents businesses and society with a dilemma: how to balance the needs of society against the benefits of a dynamic and developing economy.

Test your thinking 1

To bring these dilemmas into sharp focus, consider the following scenarios:

1   If a manufacturing company chooses to move its production plant from a developed nation to a under developed nation to reduce costs, what impact will this have on the local economy and local suppliers? If it does not move, it might be undercut by a competitor and close.

2   What are the effects if a furniture supplier has a sustainable purchasing policy? Its decision not to sell tropical hardwoods from rainforests may mean it has to increase the price to its customers of the goods it sells.

3   How much money should an oil company invest in leak detection systems in pipelines when it extracts oil in sensitive tundra or marine environments, such as Alaska?

4   If a company invests significant resources to extract minerals in an underdeveloped country, how should subsequent profits be divided between the local community, the country's government and the investors who funded the work?

All of these examples represent real issues to businesses and governments across the world. Companies, governments and people have to engage with each other to make sure that the net benefit of business is to society, and not just to a few individuals.

Case Study 2.2: The evolution of CSR at Unilever, International

Through its 400 international brands, such as PG Tips tea, Lynx deodorants, Domestos and Cif cleaning products, as well as food ranges such as Walls ice cream and Flora spreads, Unilever is in every sense a household name. With over 165,000 employees operating in 180 markets, and two billion people using its products every day, inevitably it can identify a broad range of social, environmental and economic impacts.

(continued)

(continued)

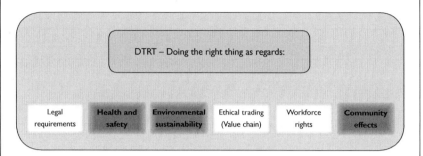

From its origins, Unilever recognized CSR as an important part of its long term operating strategy. Its founder Lord Leverhulme developed a village for its workers between 1888 and 1914 called Port Sunlight, from the name of the company's key product, Sunlight Soap. Port Sunlight was a garden village for the workers of the factories and included two replicas of Shakespearian Houses as well as a school to educate 500 children; later came a concert hall, a library, a gymnasium and an open-air swimming pool. The Port Sunlight project was a huge success producing 5,000 tonnes of soap a week with the addition of products such as 'Lifebuoy', 'Lux' and 'Vim' and subsidiaries are set up in the United States, Switzerland, Canada, Australia and Germany. However these benefits came with a balance, adherence to the Quaker principles of strict ethical codes. Breaking these standards could mean losing your job, and as the cottages are tied to your employment, losing your job meant losing the roof over your head.

Today, Unilever continues to recognize the importance of CSR in its corporate strategy. It has developed a 'Sustainable Living Plan' that aims to meet environmental and social objectives whilst doubling the size of its business. The plan's purpose is 'to make sustainable living common place' (Unilever, 2015) and sets out a range of goals for the organization' The plan aims to set itself out from the competition, through its range of coverage in terms of products, countries, issues and value chain. (Unilever quotes that the plan covers the entire portfolio of brands, all markets in which products are sold, social and economic dimensions – from the sourcing of raw materials to factories and the way consumers use their products). But with such as broad scope and scale, in an organization the size of Unilever, how was the plan developed and how did they select which issues to focus on?

When the initial plan was developed in 2009–2010, Unilever completed an in-depth materiality assessment to determine the issues to include, set targets for and report on. The organization used four factors to defining the issues that were material to the business. These were:

- the degree to which an issue is aligned with the vision and purpose, brand portfolio and geography;
- the potential impact on operations, or on sourcing and consumers;
- the extent of Unilever's influence on the issue;
- the importance of an issue to key stakeholders (Unilever, 2015).

After a review in 2014 this was refined into two key factors:

1   The potential for an issue to help us grow our sales or increase profitability, in line with our business model.
2   The level of stakeholder interest and then studying the potential for Unilever to drive transformational change for that issue (Unilever, 2015).

The result of the exercise identified the following top 15 material issues:

- deforestation;
- sustainable agriculture and smallholder farmers;
- safe drinking water, sanitation and hygiene;
- brands and innovation;
- enhancing women's lives;
- inclusive business models;
- trust and transparency;
- domestic water solutions;
- waste;
- food fortification;
- fairness in the workplace;
- obesity and non-communicable diseases;
- non-renewables;
- climate change advocacy;
- chemicals (Unilever, 2015).

The plan itself highlights the importance of integrating sustainability into the business to drive growth, not to mitigating the sustainability impacts of growth. Unilever recognize that CSR can create new opportunities as consumers select brands they associate with and can trust. This supports each consumer to do the right thing, such as selecting products that use less energy and resources. Unilever also want to work

(continued)

(continued)

more directly with small-scale suppliers to improve benefits through-out the value chain improving farming practices and livelihoods. On its website it recognizes that this will need a transformational change stating:

> We are at a turning point in history, a point when change is needed for the sake of all life on the planet. The world needs a new business model with sustainability at its heart. Only the businesses that grasp this will survive. Only those who grow sus-tainably will thrive. There has never been a better time to create a brighter future.
>
> (Unilever, 2015)

These are not the words of not an eco-warrior or CSR professional but an organization where pre-tax profits for 2014 rose 7 per cent to €7.6bn (£5.7bn). The chief executive, Paul Polman has a different approach to business to many:

'People assume that if you do something good, it must cost money. I don't know where they get that idea from', he has reported as saying, adding that business leaders 'don't need to compromise'.

> If you make closed loop systems [manufacturing operations that pro-duce no waste], you de-risk your model and it's good for the planet.
>
> (Burn-Callander, 2015)

According to Mr Polman, the consumer goods giant has been invest-ing in creating a greener business model, using sustainably sourced materials in its packaging, acting against deforestation and ensuring all factories are 'zero waste'.

Across the organization, Unilever has set 2020 as a key target date and aims to make the following changes:

- Improving Health and Well-being – By 2020 we will help more than a billion people take action to improve their health and well-being.
- Reducing Environmental Impact – By 2020 our goal is to halve the environmental footprint of the making and use of our products as we grow our business.
- Enhancing Livelihoods – By 2020 we will enhance the livelihoods of millions of people as we grow our business.

In order to deliver these goals it has developed a broad range of spe-cific projects and initiatives, such as climate action, new leaders, and 'Project Sunlight'. Project Sunlight aims to:

> Motivate millions of people to help create a brighter future for children everywhere through a new global initiative . . . it is all about making sustainable living desirable and achievable by inspiring people, and in particular parents, to help build a world where everyone lives well and within the natural limits of the planet.
>
> (Unilever, 2015)

Another project is 'Brands with Purpose' which recognizes:

> Our brands play a major part in helping us achieve our sustainable living aims of helping more than a billion people improve their health and well-being; halving the environmental footprint of our products and sourcing 100% of our agricultural raw materials sustainably.
>
> (Unilever, 2015)

Through these cross-brand campaigns Unilever is taking a multi stranded approach to achieve its 2020 goals. The Plan appears to be delivering results as Unilever (2015) state:

- Since 2008, we have reduced CO_2 from energy by 32% per tonne of production. Compared to 1995, this represents a reduction of 62% in absolute terms.
- We've rolled out eco packs, which use up to 70% less plastic and give reductions of 50-85% in greenhouse gases per use.
- By 2020, 100% of all our agricultural raw materials will be sustainably sourced, including our palm oil, 100% of which will be from certified sustainable and traceable sources by 2020.
- Over 90% of our 13 most used vegetables in Knorr products are now sustainably sourced.
- Across all of our 240 factories in 67 countries, we are now sending zero non-hazardous waste to landfill.

This is backed up with external verification for 14 out of the last 15 years; Unilever has led the Food, Beverage and Tobacco industry group of the Dow Jones Sustainability Index (DJSI). In the FTSE4Good Index, it has achieved the highest environmental score of five. It led the list of Global Corporate Sustainability Leaders in the 2014 GlobeScan/ SustainAbility annual survey for the fourth year running, and in 2015 was ranked the most sustainable food and beverage company in Oxfam's Behind the Brands Scorecard.

Unilever was one of the 186 companies globally awarded an 'A' for climate performance in 'The A List: The CDP Climate Performance Leadership Index Report 2014,' produced by international NGO CDP (formally the Carbon Disclosure Project) and it is one of just 15 companies to have been a member of the DJSI World Index since it began in 1999.

Test your thinking 2

Let's take the UK supermarket sector as an example. Since the 1980s, there has been a significant increase in the number of big supermarkets in the UK. These supermarkets are generally controlled by four big chains: Tesco, Asda/Walmart, Sainsbury's and Morrison's. As these chains have expanded, smaller retailers have struggled to compete as the market leaders have significant advantages in terms of buying power and stock availability.

The large supermarkets provide quick access to a wide choice of goods at low prices, but this can come at a cost, causing damage to local communities, local economies and the environment. The big supermarket chains can now wield a huge influence over our lives – economically, socially, environmentally and culturally. Suppose a new supermarket is being built in your area. What positive and negative impacts would the new facility bring? The extract below outlines some of the positive impacts claimed for a new supermarket.

> Independent planning consultants looked at our new store in Beverley . . . . Far from damaging Beverley and its economy, the study found that Tesco acted as a magnet . . . . Two-thirds of our customers visit other stores in the town centre, and local business leaders say that it has boosted Beverley's reputation as a place where people want to go to shop. So I would argue that strong supermarkets can also benefit local economies and local people.
>
> Sir Terry Leahy, (former) chief executive officer of Tesco, at the IGD Conference (in Corporate Watch, 2005)

The quotation below outlines some of the negative impacts of a new supermarket.

> East Riding Council says we must have a Tesco . . . because footfall will bring trade into the town centre. But Tesco has caused a loss of distinctiveness, a change in the texture of the town. Take a look at what is on offer in Tesco compared to the home-baked pies and cakes in the deli. I can't imagine the discerning visitors we say we want to attract will keep on coming when they realize what is happening. Beverley's charm is declining and its prosperity has very little to do with multinationals, pound shops and mobile phone outlets.
>
> Retired lecturer and Beverley resident, Richard Wilson (in Corporate Watch, 2005)

The following questions should help you to explore the CSR-related impacts in this scenario fully.

1   Make a list of some other positive impacts of the new supermarket.
2   Make a list of some other negative impacts of the new supermarket.

Here are some suggested answers to help you develop your understanding.
   The positive impacts could include:

- employment;
- local investment;
- additional facilities;
- better accessibility;
- redevelopment of disused land or buildings;
- re-investment;
- local supply chain development;
- increased choice for consumers;
- lower prices;
- increased local business;
- improved infrastructure and roads;
- relocated public services.

The negative impacts could include:

- impact on local businesses, e.g. loss of trade;
- habitat destruction;
- increased traffic;
- less accessibility if an out-of-town development;
- loss of community;
- use of resources;
- litter;
- noise;
- waste;
- 'ghost town' effect;
- loss of distinctiveness;
- the 'clone town' effect (all towns the same);
- loss of essential services such as post offices, car parks and access to public transport;
- loss of public and community space.

Depending on the location of the supermarket and the surrounding conditions, the balance of the negative and positive impacts could

(continued)

(continued)

result in a net benefit or net loss to the community. If organizations don't consider and consult communities, planning permission may not be granted for the new development or customers could boycott their stores or products. In this information and media age, pressure groups can be formed and information easily distributed to highlight the impacts that organizations have.

CSR – what does it mean?

We've seen that the decisions that companies make can have a dramatic effect on society, economics and the environment. CSR really is all about organizations acknowledging their interactions with the environment and society, and considering and responding to the implications of the decisions they make.

Different organizations have different definitions of CSR, although there's considerable common ground between them. Consider the following definitions:

'The responsibility of enterprises for their impacts on society'. Respect for applicable legislation, and for collective agreements between social partners, is a prerequisite for meeting that responsibility. To fully meet their corporate social responsibility, enterprises should have in place a process to integrate social, environmental, ethical and human rights and consumer concerns into their business operations and core strategy in close collaboration with their stakeholders, with the aim of:

- maximizing the creation of shared value for their owners/shareholders and for their other stakeholders and society at large;
- Identifying, preventing and mitigating their possible adverse impacts (European Commission (2011).

ISO 26000:2010 defines CSR as the:

Responsibility of an organization for the impacts of its decisions and activities on society and the environment, through transparent and ethical behaviour that:

- contributes to sustainable development, including health and the welfare of society;
- takes into account the expectations of stakeholders;
- is in compliance with applicable law and consistent with international norms of behaviour; and
- is integrated throughout the organization and practiced in its relationships.

(International Organization for Standardization, 2010)

Or there's this slimmed-down version from the Philippines:

> CSR is about business giving back to society.
>
> (Holmes and Watts, 2000)

The World Bank agreed with us that:

> CSR is no longer seen as corporate social assistance or philanthropy, but as essential to a good business strategy, helping reduce investment risks and enhancing business profits by improving transparency and accountability. It is about working together – with government, with civil society, and with the community – to improve the lives of millions of people by making growth more inclusive.
>
> (World Bank, 2013)

The Global Reporting Initiative G4 guidance on reporting standards states:

> An ever-increasing number of companies and other organizations want to make their operations sustainable. Moreover, expectations that long-term profitability should go hand-in-hand with social justice and protecting the environment are gaining ground. These expectations are only set to increase and intensify as the need to move to a truly sustainable economy is understood by companies' and organizations' financiers, customers and other stakeholders.
>
> (Global Reporting Initiative, 2013)

Test your thinking 3

Considering these examples, how would you define CSR in your own words?

Notes

1 By 'organization' we mean any sort of established or informal entity, including legally founded companies and charities, public sector organizations, partnerships and sole traders, clubs and societies, and similar groups.
2 By 'society' we mean all organizations, governments, regulators, neighbours, individuals and media with interests in the community.

Chapter 3

The appetite for CSR and the triple bottom line

> There are three bottom lines: the traditional measure of corporate profit is the first bottom line of the profit and loss account; the second bottom line is of a company's 'people account' – a measure of how socially responsible an organization has been; and the third is the bottom line of the company's 'planet' account – a measure of how environmentally responsible it has been.
>
> –Adapted from *The Economist*, 2009

> Puma [sportswear] has pioneered the concept of environmental profit and loss reporting which has made a huge impact on how businesses see their impact, it is much more environmentally dominated than socially, but it is a real step change forward.
>
> –Authors' comment, 2015

Triple bottom line

As *The Economist* suggests, triple bottom line (aka TBL or 3BL) is an accounting framework and the nexus between the societal, environmental and financial performance of an organization. These three divisions are sometimes called the three Ps: People, Planet and Profit, or the 'three pillars of sustainability'. And some organizations are really getting there, such as Puma.

John Elkington, co-founder of consulting group, SustainAbility, first used the TBL phrase in 1994 (Elkington, 1997), and the 3Ps language was first used by oil giant, Shell, in the title of its first sustainability report in 1997 (Shell Global, 2007).

TBL accounting expands upon the traditional reporting framework to take into account social and environmental performance in addition to the common measures of financial performance. The currencies of the calculations are different and challenging, but some (like Puma) are trying. How you calculate and report this measurement is (of course) up to you; whether this is financially based or benefits-based. The Global Reporting

Initiative G4 Sustainability Reporting Guidelines (2013) provide a range of indicators for all CSR related matters – we recommend that you review these. For practitioners requiring a very simple approach, you could commence with a qualitative assessment against each of our DTRT core elements as follows:

- **Red** = foundational expectations not met, and no progress planned;
- **Amber** = requirements understood, but implementation of current plan is incomplete;
- **Green** = advanced implementation, with progress on target.

Elements may also be not applicable, such as when a service sector organization has no or limited product liabilities.

In summary, TBL demands that a company's responsibility lies with all of the stakeholders rather than just the shareholders. We discussed 'stakeholders' in Chapter 1, and we encourage you to review page 22 to remind you of these five groups if necessary.

TBL and the DTRT model

Our DTRT Model focuses organizations on the first and second elements of TBL and the 3Ps, and its use assist selection of those approaches that impact positively and most significantly upon the third element – profit.

According to this broader responsibility commended by TBL and our DTRT Model, organizations become a vehicle for coordinating the interests of all of the stakeholders, instead of maximizing shareholder (owner/investor) profits. Only a company that produces a TBL (which might be akin to a balanced scorecard approach) is taking account of the full cost involved in doing business.

Example: when an organization reports a money profit, but their asbestos mine causes thousands of deaths from asbestos-related diseases, and their bauxite mine pollutes a river, a government can end up spending taxes on healthcare for its citizens and clean up of the environment. TBL adds these two more "bottom lines" of social and environmental (ecological) concerns, and allows a full societal cost-benefit analysis.

A growing number of institutions incorporate a triple bottom line approach in their work, including multinationals FedEx, Nike and Tesco. An organization's intent towards CSR is a powerful reason to bring the 3Ps to your own organization's business plan. However, it's not the only reason. A recent report by MIT (2012) is only one of many that show how the approach can be profitable too. The results are less tangible, yes; but benefits related to competitive advantage, brand reputation and the creation of opportunities for improved innovation should not be ignored.

The MIT study also advised that companies must set concrete goals and prepare targeted plans to reap the benefits of sustainability; in other words, sustainability needs to be treated seriously to really pay off. Our DTRT Model provides precisely this impetus.

For reporting their progress towards CSR and TBL, organizations may demonstrate their commitment through the use of some or all of the following:

- Top-level involvement (CEO, Board of Directors);
- Policies;
- Specific implementation programmes;
- Engagement with voluntary standards such as SA8000, AA1000, ISO 14001, BS OHSAS 18001, ISO 45001, ISO 26000 (aka ISO SR), ETI base code of labour practice, and others;
- Core principles of CSR (UN Global Compact);
- Reporting (Global Reporting Initiative).

We review and discuss these voluntary standards and core principles in greater detail in Chapter 6.

As with other new(er) concepts, there are also variants which summarized here for completeness: DBL and QBL.

Double bottom line

Double bottom line (aka DBL or 2BL) is a concept to extend the conventional bottom line (profit or loss) by adding a second bottom line to measure performance in terms of positive social impact. This idea that for-profit organizations have an obligation to support social causes beyond their interest in short-term profits dates back to the 1960s (DeGeorge, 2010).

Example: founded in 2000, Khushhali Bank Limited (2015) is a part of the Government of Islamic Republic of Pakistan's Poverty Reduction Strategy and its Microfinance Sector Development Program (MSDP). MSDP was developed with the facilitation of Asian Development Bank (ADB). With its headquarters based in Islamabad, Khushhali operates under the supervision of the State Bank of Pakistan (SBP) and many central (commercial) banks are its shareholders. Its mandate remains to retail microfinance services and to act as a catalyst in stabilizing the country's newly formed microfinance sector. While the bank wants to generate profits so that it can grow, it has a second bottom line of reducing local poverty. Its annual report provides 'audited financial statements and indicators of financial performance such as the bank's credit rating, portfolio at risk and efficiency ratio', but also notes that the bank was 'established to mobilize funds for providing microfinance services to poor persons, particularly poor women for mitigating poverty and promoting social welfare and economic justice'. Its website

(Krushhali Bank Limited, 2015) highlights ten current DBL programs, which we believe readers will find to be of interest.

Quadruple bottom line

We'll summarize too the so-called quadruple bottom line (QBL). This additional fourth pillar of sustainability proposes future-oriented thinking, including impacts upon future generations and equity between the generations; long-tail impacts so-to-say. QBL adds a long-term outlook that sets sustainable development and sustainability concerns apart from historic social, environmental and economic considerations.

The appetite for CSR

Since our first book on CSR in 2009, we have noticed considerable growth in interest in this fascinating subject. This time, we found no difficulty whatsoever in identifying the case studies we have presented in this book from organizations as small as a UK regional insurance broker with 400 employees (see Case Study 3.1), to a global blue chip educational organization with over 60,000 workers in 96 countries (see Case Study 3.2), through to the world's most valuable company (case study 7.1).

To make this engagement clearer still, we'll defer to the Association of British Insurers (ABI), which says that 80 per cent of the UK's top 100 listed companies now report to some extent on their CSR performance. Growing awareness and engagement indeed . . . .

> There is growing awareness among large companies of the importance of managing corporate responsibility risks. The evidence suggests that companies that do this well are more competitive and provide a better return for shareholders.
>
> Mary Francis, Director
> General of the ABI (in Mallenbaker, 2015)

Case Study 3.1   Donate-a-Day at Henderson Insurance Brokers, UK

Henderson Insurance Brokers Limited (HIBL), based in Leeds, is one of the UK's top six leading independent insurance brokers, operating from twelve offices across the UK and employing about 400 people.

HIBL is committed to supporting charities on both a local and national level. Founded in 1986, it has raised hundreds of thousands of pounds for good causes including Macmillan Cancer Support and

(continued)

(continued)

| Legal requirements | Health and safety | Environmental sustainability | Ethical trading (Value chain) | Workforce rights | Community effects |

DTRT – Doing the right thing as regards:

BBC's Children in Need. In addition, it has pledged more than £20,000 to aid the ongoing development of St Andrew's Hospice in Grimsby, which is located close to its Kirmington branch. The hospice looks after more than 1,000 adults and children with life-limiting illnesses.

For the whole of 2015, HIBL has launched a new community engagement programme, which encourages all staff to donate a day of their time to a charity or worthy cause of their choice and to really make a difference to peoples' lives. In return, HIBL rewards it staff with a day off in lieu.

Figure 3.1 *Michael Wright* (Director – Executive Board), Danielle Roe (Marketing Manager), Megan Turner (Events Coordinator), Lily Proctor (HR/ Training Apprentice) and Tanya Parker (Receptionist) spent a day helping staff at the facility to paint fences, tend to the hospice garden, bake with some of the patients and help sort through clothing at the Shop and Drop Donation Centre.

And some staff have already got their hands dirty in the name of charity. Five employees from across the group kicked off the campaign by volunteering at St Andrew's Hospice.

> We're proud to have raised so much for charities across the UK over the years, but I feel that we can help support such worthy causes in so many more ways. By taking the time to volunteer, we have the potential to make a real difference to other people's lives – I'll be encouraging everyone in the group to participate in the Donate A Day initiative this year.
>
> Joe Henderson, HIBL Chief Executive
> (in *Grimsby Telegraph*, 2015)

In organizations, the department or function responsible for communicating on CSR publishes information related to the environmental and social performance to its stakeholders. This information is intended for use by the wide variety of stakeholders, including shareholders and potential investors, who are interested in understanding the context of non-financial performance in driving corporate profitability in the future.

While our own research in preparation for writing this book supports that at a societal level, shareholders are increasingly using this information to inform their investment decisions, firms are currently struggling with understanding the appetite of investors for communication at the company level.

Our continued research will aim to capture the expectations for this information, and a broader characterization of the current interests and appetites of socially responsible, retail and institutional investors, and we will report this in our blogs and future editions of this book. In the meantime, now might be the time to review your own stakeholders' expectations – Chapter 4 explains how you might go about this.

Case Study 3.2   Pearson plc. wins global health and safety award, International

About Pearson plc.

Pearson plc. is the world's leading learning company. With head offices in London and New York, it employs 52,688 people (over 40,000 direct employees and over 12,000 temporary employees) at over 1000 locations in 96 countries. Around 93 per cent of employees are located in eleven countries – 63 per cent in the US and UK, and a further

(continued)

(continued)

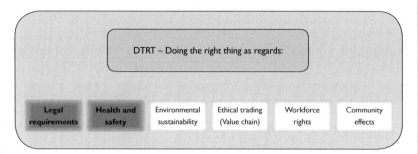

30 per cent in nine other countries: China, India, South Africa, Brazil, Australia, Canada, Germany, Hong Kong and Mexico.

This is a summary of Pearson's main activities:

- Direct delivery: it owns and operates learning institutions/schools (physical, virtual and/or blended), providing teaching direct to the learner.
- Learning services: individual learning materials that are increasingly digital in nature and operating as part of an integrated learning ecosystem.
- Inside services: it provides integrated learning services to institutions (public and private) that have an institution-wide impact on improving learning outcomes.
- Assessment: Pearson provides services that enable an institution or system to measure and validate learner progress towards relevant standards or to certify competency. For example, in the UK, it runs the DVLA driving theory and construction skills/CSCS tests.
- Pearson is the publisher of the *Financial Times* newspaper, and it owns 47 per cent of Penguin Random House books – adult and children's fiction and non-fiction. Its publishing lists include more than 70 Nobel Prize laureates and hundreds of the world's most widely read authors, including Dan Brown and John Grisham.
- It is a member of the FTSE100, with turnover (2014) of £5.2 billion.

Adoption of a global health and safety policy

Pearson plc. launched its global health and safety policy in December 2013, and won a RoSPA Occupational Health and Safety Award in June 2015 at the first attempt. This is how they did it.

The board of Pearson plc. decided that a global health and safety program should succeed a plethora of national programs of varying intent and quality in spring 2012. The VP, Insurance, Risk and Health and Safety was appointed to lead the program and became the line manager of the country and regional Health and Safety Managers.

The new global health and safety team drafted proposals – subsequently accepted – to add health and safety responsibilities into the job descriptions of top management.

In summer 2012, the Head of Group Insurance and Risk interviewed several health and safety practitioners from several consulting firms, and selected Stephen Asbury of Corporate Risk Systems Limited as the provider of external support to her and the Group.

In October 2012, the Head of Group Insurance and Risk assembled a team of around 30 interested managers from Group businesses across the world to collaborate in the development of a Group health and safety policy, and series of standards. Regular telephone conferences were carried out, where it was agreed that the policy and standards should be aligned to BS OHSAS 18001:2007, ANSI Z10-2012 and AS/NZS 4801:2001. Pearson in the UK is externally certified to BS OHSAS 18001, and much of the global health and safety policy and standards were shaped from these experiences, with additional input from its US Injury and Illness Prevention Program (I2P2). The statement of health and safety policy was signed by the Group Chief Executive.

Meanwhile, in spring 2013, the Board's Audit Committee requested a 'special project' governance review of health and safety management in the Group. This project was conducted in parallel with the policy and standards development between April and June 2013. Interviews were conducted with 39 individuals from 32 Group businesses, collectively employing 52,155 staff (then 89 per cent of Group total staff) as well as managing the interfaces with third party contractors,

(continued)

(continued)

students and others, including the public. The report contained seven high-level recommendations, and was published and accepted by the Audit Committee.

During the development of the Group health and safety policy and standards, great care was taken to work with regional representatives from as many businesses/territories/companies as possible.

During this development, this group also identified the benefits of a (proposed) best practices guidance document, and some work was done to develop this. There were many contributions from around the world. The development of the guide however was paused, while implementation of the standards progressed as a matter of greater urgency. Pearson anticipates that the best practices guide will be further developed and published in the future.

Incident rates

The global health and safety team has pressed hard for better, more-accurate reporting of incidents, and have produced posters and other promotional materials to promote this. It collects data from all its facilities in the world on a six-monthly basis and calculates total employee injury rates (all employees reporting any injury) per 100,000 employees for each six-month period:

- 1/11/2012–30/4/2013 = 743/100,000
- 1/5/2013–31/10/2013 = 564/100,000
- 1/11/2013–30/4/2014 = 720/100,000
- 1/5/2014–31/10/2014 = 683/100,000

These (low) rates are considered to be world class.

Pearson safety news

Pearson commenced a journal of safety best practices in its new 'Pearson Safety News' publication in early 2014. This is published quarterly, circulated globally in ten languages and is used to provide information to employees across the world on hazards, risks and preventive measures. Every edition includes an introduction by a member of the Board or a Senior Vice President.

Below is a summary of the areas covered:

- May 2014 – road safety, stress, violence and aggression;
- August 2014 – fire safety, incident reporting, results of incident data collection: 1/2013–4/2014;

- November 2014 – risk assessment, setting SMART health and safety objectives, health and safety inspections;
- February 2015 – DSE and VDU safety, safeguarding (of children and vulnerable adults), results of incident data collection: 5/2014–10/2014.

Conclusions

Pearson has set formal health and safety standards for all its businesses all over the world. These are owned, coordinated and promoted by the global health and safety team managed by the VP, Insurance, Risk and Health and Safety. Effective senior commitment and top-down leadership has been proven to work across geographical, language and cultural differences.

The UK certification to OHSAS 18001, along with high performance and management standards in the USA and some other territories (e.g. Australia, Canada) assisted as benchmarks where other territories did not have the same high standards.

Pearson has shown that setting, measuring and enforcing high-standards from the centre of its business has triggered strides forward in its overall health and safety performance. It collected a RoSPA Bronze Award for it occupational health and safety performance in 2014 in London on 16 June 2015.

> We want to do all we can to protect our 52,688 employees, as well as our contractors, and quite literally millions of students in our classroom and virtual learning environments. Using our expertise from our 'best' territories, we can leverage improvements in our 'developing' territories. We look forward to developing and demonstrating our progress through many future years. Pearson is committed to high standards of occupational health and safety.
>
> Pearson RoSPA award
> entry of January 2015, unpublished

Branding, advertising and CSR

The first patented logo in the world was Bass Ale – the familiar red diamond – in 1876. Other logos in common use today date back as far as 1366 (Stella Artois). USA Today (2015) identifies the ten oldest corporate logos still in use today. In order to be considered, the logo had to currently have an international presence, and could not have been meaningfully changed. In addition to the two above, the other oldest company logos in the world are:

- Peugeot (1850)
- Heinz (1869)
- Levi Strauss & Co (1886)
- Twinings Tea (1887)
- Johnson & Johnson (1887)
- Prudential Insurance (1896)
- Shell (1904)
- Sherwin-Williams Paint (1905)

Current business norms continue to show a persistent and growing use of branding and logos in advertising as part of concerted communication and marketing campaigns. As consumers become increasingly aware of their own social preferences and purchasing responsibilities, organizations seek to meet their needs by providing real or perceived 'green' and 'friendly' products.

A major criticism of CSR has been that organizations may care more about their brand than the people it might affect – that it's more about media, marketing and presentation than actually making a real difference. You can read some of the arguments against CSR in Chapter 7.

> Not whitewash, but greenwash!
>
> Authors

For many organizations, their brands are likely to be some of their core assets – some organizations go as far as to put a monetary value on their brands in their accounts. This is as true of some large multinational companies as of the pressure groups that seek to influence their behaviors.

 Test your thinking 4

Think of some big own organizations known to you and their well-known brands. Aim to identify the most prominent, strongest brands that you've heard of.

Below are the names of some example organizations that are well known to us. What does their brand make you think of? Add those you thought of to our examples, and complete the exercise.

- Body Shop
- World Wide Fund for Nature (WWF)
- McDonald's

- Greenpeace
- Adidas

We've prepared some possible responses, based on common views of these organizations. Compare them with your own.

1   Body Shop – an ethically based chain established by the late Anita Roddick, which was bought by a large pharmaceutical company (L'Oreal). It sells a range of plant-based cosmetics, body scrubs and lotions. It avoids animal testing.
2   WWF – an environmental charity that campaigns to save species at risk of extinction, such as pandas, tigers and polar bears. Its logo is a panda.
3   McDonald's – Big golden arches/capital 'M' in every town. A place to get cheap fast food, such as Big Mac, Chicken McNuggets, shakes and fries. 'Happy Meals' include collectible toys for children. Starting to add salads to its menus.
4   Greenpeace – an environmental pressure group that believes in direct action to get media publicity. Some members occupied the Brent Spar oil platform in the North Sea a few years ago. Their ship, called *Rainbow Warrior*, was sunk in New Zealand.
5   Adidas – a leading sportswear brand worn by top teams such as the All Blacks and Real Madrid, and top athletes such as Lionel Messi and Justin Rose. In a design partnership with Stella McCartney. Three stripes. German. Often faked.

Organizations spend large quantities of money to create brand imagery and protect it. As we become more aware of CSR, we may start to think that organizations could and should include some of the CSR-related issues within their branding. Whether the brand is based on ethical trading, such as the Body Shop, or whether it's a fast food retailer or even a tobacco company, a strong 'image' is critical if it's to remain visible, profitable and viable in the longer term.

Naomi Klein (2000) provides a fascinating review of branding in her book *No Logo*, which became one of the most influential texts about the anti-globalization movement, and an international bestseller. Throughout the book's four parts – No Space, No Choice, No Jobs and No Logo – the author comments on issues such as sweatshops, culture-jamming and corporate censorship. She pays special attention to the deeds and misdeeds of some of the organizations and brands we prompted you to consider earlier.

In this media age, the internet allows anyone to publish virtually anything without any sort of proof or validation. It can be difficult to establish what to believe and what not to believe. The exercise below allows you to consider two sides of the same coin.

 Test your thinking 5

Here are two articles about the Body Shop: one from a pressure group and one from the organization itself.

Fuelling consumption at the Earth's expense

Body Shop has over 1,500 stores in 47 countries and aggressive expansion plans. Their main purpose (like many multinationals) is to make lots of money for their rich shareholders. In other words, they are driven by power and greed. But the Body Shop try to conceal this reality by continually pushing the message that by shopping at their stores, rather than elsewhere, people will help solve some of the world's problems. The truth is that nobody can make the world a better place by shopping.

Natural products?

Body Shop gives the impression that their products are made from mostly natural ingredients. In fact, like all big cosmetic companies, they make wide use of non-renewable petrochemicals, synthetic colors, fragrances and preservatives, and in many of their products they use only tiny amounts of botanical-based ingredients.

Body Shop claims to be helping some third world workers and indigenous peoples through so-called 'Trade Not Aid' or 'Community Trade' projects. In fact, these are largely a marketing ploy, as less than one per cent of sales go to 'Community Trade' producers.

(www.mcspotlight.org, 2015)

1   Does this article make you reconsider your image of the Body Shop? If so, how?
2   How far do you think a company such as this that sells consumer products should go in marketing a green image?

Now, let's read the other side of the story:

Statement from the Body Shop

We take our commitment to ethical trade seriously and our approach is one of constructive engagement and capacity building. We believe that we should source from suppliers who share our values and support them in providing ethical employment standards. But what do we do when a supplier just won't co-operate?

In 2004, we conducted 62 on-site factory audits and worked successfully with suppliers around the world to improve the working conditions of their employees. However, in the course of the year, Body Shop also had to disengage from five suppliers – located in China, the Philippines and Taiwan – as a result of their failure to meet our ethical standards. The decision to disengage from each of these suppliers was based on their lack of commitment to improving working standards.

For example, in the case of a factory in China, an audit identified that the supplier was not paying medical insurance for workers. We offered to contribute towards the cost of medical insurance, but the supplier refused to participate on the basis that the Body Shop business made up only a small part of their total sales. Due to this non-compliance we withdrew our orders from this supplier.

(The Body Shop, 2005)

1   How far do you think a company should go in managing the behaviors and the impacts in its supply chain?
2   Which do you believe more: the first (from the pressure group) or the second (from Body Shop)? Why do you say this?
3   Does Body Shop's own statement enhance their credibility?
4   What are the dangers of only reading one source of information about an organization's (CSR) performance?

As we've seen, it's important to look and read very carefully, to look beyond the 'greenwash' and to do your homework, if we're truly to completely fulfill your appetite for CSR.

The only way of finding the limits of the possible is by going beyond them into the impossible.

(Clarke, 1962)

Nature never did betray the heart that loved her.

(Wordsworth, 1798)

Chapter 4

Stakeholder expectations

> A Corporation [is] an ingenious device for obtaining individual profit without individual responsibility.
>
> –Ambrose Bierce, 1842–1914

Society

A society is a diverse but connected population of humans interacting in an economic, social and industrial infrastructure. What impact is your organization having on society?

A central principle of CSR focuses on how an organization relates to all of its stakeholders. The CSR concept is that we should look at the impacts of our organization 'beyond the factory gates'. As we saw in Chapter 2, throughout the evolution of CSR the standards to which an organization should operate have varied according to its location in both time and place. The society in which the organization operates will have a range of expectations, but in the global village – full of conflicting agendas and pressures – how can any organization hope to measure up to the expectations of everyone else?

In this chapter, we'll look at some of the pressures stakeholders can bring to bear on organizations, and the approaches that can be used to manage these expectations in an increasingly media-led age.

Stakeholders

Society is increasingly interested in the impact of organizations' activities. As Ambrose Bierce highlights, society has questions over the motivation of business. Society, and its media and special interest groups, looks at what organizations have done – good or bad – in terms of their products and services, their impact on the environment and local communities and how they treat and develop their workforces. In an age of social media, an organization's action can be broadcast to the world through a viral spread of images and comments without censorship, or the balance of libel or slander, as enforcement in social media is so difficult to action.

While the precise definition may vary, the groups of people interested or affected by the organization's activities are called 'stakeholders'. ISO 26000:2010 defines a stakeholder as individual or group that has an interest in any decision or activity of an organization (International Organization for Standardization, 2010). A broader definition of 'stakeholders' is provided by the International Finance Corporation, part of the World Bank:

> Stakeholders are persons or groups who are directly or indirectly affected by a project, as well as those who may have interests in a project and/or the ability to influence its outcome, either positively or negatively. Stakeholders may include locally affected communities or individuals and their formal and informal representatives, national or local government authorities, politicians, religious leaders, civil society organizations and groups with special interests, the academic community, or other businesses.
>
> (International Finance Corporation, 2008)

The stakeholders of an organization may include (see pages 21–2):

- shareholders (who provided the money for the enterprise and expect to be rewarded);
- employees (on our payroll);
- suppliers and contractors (the people we do business with);
- customers (consumers of our products or services);
- society (everyone else, including government, regulators, media and the public).

We want you to understand who the specific stakeholders may be in a particular organization. One way to do this is to develop a 'mind map'. Mind mapping is a useful tool to help you think about complex ideas and issues, and find connectivity between themes. To make notes on a subject using a mind map, make a sketch in the following way:

1   Write the title of the subject in the centre of the page, and draw a circle around it.
2   For the major subject subheadings, draw lines out from this circle; label these lines with the subheadings.
3   If you have another tier of information belonging to the subheadings, draw these and link them to the subheading lines.
4   For individual facts or ideas, draw lines out from the appropriate heading line and label them.
5   As you come across new information, link it in to the mind map appropriately.

For more information on the mind mapping approach, visit: https://www.mindtools.com/pages/article/newISS_01.htm.

Test your thinking 6

Choose a major sports equipment manufacturer and develop a mind map to identify as many of its stakeholders as possible.

Start with the main five discussed above, but also consider subsets such as media, pressure groups and governments – what will their key objectives be and what kind of pressure could they apply?

The typical stakeholders of a sports equipment manufacturer could include:

- customers (e.g. retail outlets);
- consumers – end users;
- suppliers;
- retail traders;
- sports governing bodies;
- athletes and sporting participants;
- endorsing personalities;
- endorsing teams;
- employees;
- neighbours;
- governments;
- non-governmental organizations;
- health advisers;
- media companies (including those that sell advertising space);
- pressure groups;
- investors or shareholders;
- insurance companies.

Each stakeholder will doubtless have their own opinions, motivations and interests, which can quite easily come into conflict with each other. Crucially, each stakeholder will exert different types and levels of pressure.

Case Study 4.1   Prohibition and American college football, USA

American college football may seem an unlikely case study to illustrate an application of CSR. The boyhood dream of playing quarterback for the Texas Longhorns, and to become a draft pick for the NFL is not a natural link to stakeholder engagement plans and business risk

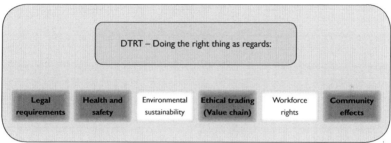

management. However US college football teams are facing a dilemma similar to many organizations; how to balance finances, brand image and stakeholder requirements. How far should business opportunities and capitalism push an organization from its core values and goals? Is short-term gain the only way to survive, or should long-term growth be the answer? Furthermore in this case study we will look at the importance of stakeholder analysis to establish the correct approach for your organization, as often it is not the case that one size fits all.

The scale of US College Athletics departments and their associated football teams is comparable to any sporting league in the world. The 2015 College Football Playoff National Championship attracted some 85,689 attendees (ESPN, 2015), while average attendances and overall attendances rank amongst the highest of world-wide attendances for any league-wide sport. Despite these high attendances the financial challenge is as tough as any, with only around 10 per cent of the 120 National Collegiate Athletic Association (NCAA) Division

(continued)

(continued)

One Football Bowl Subdivision (FBS) schools reporting a profitable programme (Wolken, 2014). With a limited number of revenue streams, Athletics Departments are considering all options, and with a limited number of major events funding a range of minor sports and activities the focus has been on maximizing the income from these high attendances.

One way to maximize game day revenue is through the sale of food and beverages and more specifically alcohol, but this has been controversial. One of the Governing bodies, the South Eastern Conference (SEC), has specific regulations controlling alcohol sales stating:

> No alcoholic beverages shall be sold or dispensed for public consumption anywhere in the facility and the possession and/ or consumption of alcoholic beverages in the public areas of the facility shall be prohibited. These prohibitions shall not apply to private, leased areas in the facility or other areas designated by the SEC. There shall be no advertising displays mentioning or promoting alcoholic beverages in the facility.
>
> Saturday Down South, 2014

This ban on alcohol sales mimics the 18th amendment of the US Constitution, which introduced prohibition in 1920 but was later repealed. However this does not exclude the sale of alcohol in corporate areas, and has led to the arrangement of other practices including fans 'chugging' alcohol prior to games outside of the venues and a range of 'tailgate' parties where fans hold BBQs and drink alcohol in the parking lots of stadium from the rear of their pickups. Other conferences leave it to each institution to make their own decision.

If alcohol is already being consumed at events then should it be done in car parks and through pre-match binging, or within the stadium where there are controls in place, where age identification checks can be made and where security and medical support is on hand?

> 'Sometimes if you wanted to go to a game and were used to drinking beer, people chose to go to a bar instead of the venue,' said Trespalacios, a 22-year-old graduate student. 'It's good to bring everyone together and enjoy the same environment.'
>
> ESPN, 2014

In 2014, *USA Today* reported 32 teams current have taken the decision to sell alcohol at their stadiums:

Campus stadiums:

- Akron
- Bowling Green
- Cincinnati
- Colorado State
- Houston
- Kent State
- Louisiana-Lafayette
- Louisiana-Monroe
- Louisville
- Minnesota
- Nevada
- North Texas
- SMU
- Syracuse
- Toledo
- Troy
- Tulane
- UNLV
- UTEP
- Western Kentucky
- West Virginia

Off-campus stadiums

- Connecticut
- Georgia State
- Hawaii
- Massachusetts (Three games at Gillette Stadium)
- Memphis
- Miami
- San Diego State
- South Alabama
- South Florida
- Temple
- Texas-San Antonio

Despite this, the majority of high-profile programs in the Football Bowl Subdivision have currently chosen not to go in that direction. This is for reasons that range from philosophical and religious interests, to concerns about crowd control and unease about the appearance of profiting off alcohol, but as financial pressures grow, few have ruled out the idea, looking to their stakeholders for further guidance.

(continued)

(continued)

Jan Withers, president of Mothers Against Drunk Driving, high-lights: 'Kids are watching adults all the time. If they see the only way to have fun is to drink a lot, then they're going to model after that. That's not the message we want to be sending to them' (Ferguson, 2015). She comments that 'in a college environment most undergraduates are under the legal drinking age in the US.'

This is supported by the findings of a research paper into the topic by Huang and Dixon (2013) 'Examining the Financial Impact of Alcohol Sales on Football Game Days: A Case Study of a Major Football Program in the Journal of Sport Management' which concludes:

> At the collegiate level, the inundation of alcoholic beverage names, pictures, and product sends mixed messages to students. Research shows an individual's choices with regards to alcohol consumption depend on the drinking patterns of his or her peers. Thus, underage students surrounded by individuals consuming alcohol causes unnecessary peer pressure. Additionally, further research has shown a positive relationship between the availability of alcohol in the campus environment and its consumption, particularly binge drinking. With the documented problems surrounding high-risk drinking among college students, condoning alcohol consumption through alcohol sales and advertisements on game days to the general public only worsens the perilous situation.
>
> Huang and Dixon, 2013

While this approach tackles the root cause and promotion of alcohol consumption in areas where it currently has a limited social impact, should the same approach be used in areas where consumption of beer and spirits is already a problem; or would in-stadium purchases reduce underage sales, excessive consumption in pre-game tail gate events? *USA Today* reporter Dan Wolken captures the balance in his report on Virginia Tech athletics director Whit Babcock:

> But it's a cultural issue at a place of higher education where there's a tradition (of not selling it). I don't know that it will be one of the top things on my agenda. But as more people do it . . . I'll definitely be watching.

At Cincinnati, his previous job, beer was sold at practically every on-campus sporting event — including green beer on St. Patrick's Day to help attract fans to a baseball game. . . . Availability of beer wasn't just non-controversial at Cincinnati, it was viewed as a given in a more competitive, pro-oriented market.

"In my 2½ years there, we didn't have any alcohol-related incidents, so it worked," Babcock said. "It opened my eyes that it could be done in a responsible way."

(Wolken, 2014)

 Test your thinking 7

Below is a list of the sports equipment manufacturer's five main stake-holder groups. Think about what each group's key objectives are and how they could apply pressure to the company to get what they want.

- Shareholders;
- Employees;
- Suppliers;
- Customers;
- Society (e.g. the media, NGOs/pressure groups, the government).

The following table gives some examples of what the stakeholders may want and how they could achieve it:

Stakeholders' objectives and how they could achieve them

Group	Objectives	Means of applying pressure
Shareholders	Return on their investment through share dividends, profits and capital growth in the shares.	Direct shareholder pressure on management or by investing in alternative businesses.
Employees	Good pay and conditions, safe working environment, long-term secure employment.	Internal requests, strikes, contact with media.
Suppliers	To make a profit on the goods or services they are providing you.	Raise price of good or services, choose if to supply you or not, contact with the media.
Customers	Good quality, stylish products at a reasonable price.	Buying other products if they are better.

(continued)

(continued)

Group	Objectives	Means of applying pressure
Society, e.g. media	To increase their revenue through greater circulation and more advertising.	Interesting (negative?) news stories of interest to the wider public.
Society, e.g. NGOs, pressure groups	To further the cause of the group.	Direct action, bad publicity, alternative reports. Providing information to other groups such as shareholders or consumers.
Society, e.g. government	Protect society, maintain votes.	Information, policy, tax incentives and regulation.

The figure on the opposite page illustrates some of the competitive forces found in the business environment.

Now consider your own organization. Who are its stakeholders? How could they apply pressure? How could you manage these relationships?

Stakeholder engagement

The function of managing the relationships and expectations of the people and groups your organization is likely to affect is called 'stakeholder engagement'. The aim of stakeholder engagement is not to gain unanimous consensus, for this would probably be impossible. It includes consulting pro-actively with key stakeholders in order to decide how best to manage your organization's CSR-related impacts – in other words, in a way that mitigates negative impacts and maximizes the contribution of positive impacts. The key principles of effective engagement include:

- providing meaningful information in a format and language that is readily understandable and tailored to meet the needs of the target stakeholder group;
- providing information in advance of consultation activities and decision-making;
- sharing information in ways and locations that make it easy for stakeholders to access it;
- respect for local traditions, languages, timeframes and decision-making processes;
- two-way dialogue that gives both sides the opportunity to exchange views and information, to listen and to have their issues heard and addressed (such as open meetings);

- making sure that the views of traditionally disadvantaged groups are heard equally;
- processes that are free of intimidation or coercion;
- clear mechanisms for responding to people's concerns, suggestions and grievances;
- incorporating feedback into the proposed project or programme design and reporting back to stakeholders.

The depth, style, nature and frequency of this engagement with key stakeholders depends on a range of factors, including:

- the nature and scale of the activity – the more impact the organization is likely to have on society and the environment, the greater the level of engagement needed;
- the stage of the project – new installations or shutdowns are likely to alter the status of the organization or affect its stakeholders. Change is likely to raise more concern than continuing with the status quo;
- statutory requirements – depending on the type, scale and impact on the environment or working conditions, the law may require the organization to engage its stakeholders;

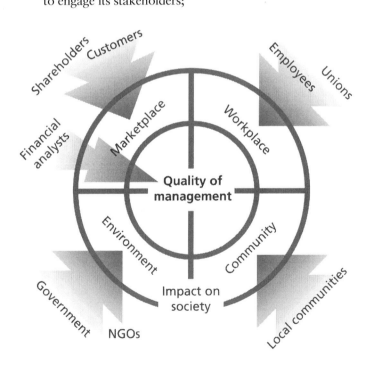

Figure 4.1 The business in society (Mallenbaker, 2015).

- the target group – its characteristics and how easy it is to engage with;
- resource availability – how much time, labour and money the organization has available to invest in an engagement programme;
- economic sector – public sector initiatives are likely to require more in-depth engagement than private sector projects;
- location – the local environment may be especially sensitive (e.g. if it's close to a Site of Special Scientific Interest), or the project may be close to a school, hospital, place of worship or residential area;
- organizational policy – what the organization's long-term approach is for engaging with its key stakeholders.

The different levels of stakeholder engagement can vary from simple information provision as part of a drive to be more transparent through to in-depth negotiations, where the extended involvement leads to participants materially contributing to the formulation of proposals and the organization's operations.

Stakeholder engagement can be broken down into eight key areas, as defined by the International Finance Corporate Report (2008):

1   Stakeholder identification and analysis: invest time in identifying and prioritizing stakeholders and assessing their interests and concerns.
2   Information disclosure: communicate information to stakeholders early in the decision-making process, in ways that are meaningful and accessible, and continue this communication throughout the project.
3   Stakeholder consultation: plan out each consultation process, consult inclusively, document the process and communicate subsequent decisions.
4   Negotiation and partnerships: for controversial and complex issues, negotiate in good faith in a way that satisfies the interests of all parties. Add value to the project's benefits and your plans to mitigate impacts by forming strategic partnerships.
5   Grievance management: establish accessible and responsive means for stakeholders to raise concerns and grievances about the project throughout its life.
6   Stakeholder involvement in project monitoring: involve stakeholders in monitoring project impacts, mitigation and benefits, and involve external monitors where they can improve transparency and credibility.
7   Reporting to stakeholders: report back to stakeholders on environmental, social and economic performance. Include stakeholders that you've consulted directly and those with more general interests in the project and parent company.
8   Management functions: build and maintain sufficient capacity within the organization to manage processes of stakeholder engagement, track commitments, and report on progress.

Figure 4.2 on the following page outlines the key elements of these core areas.

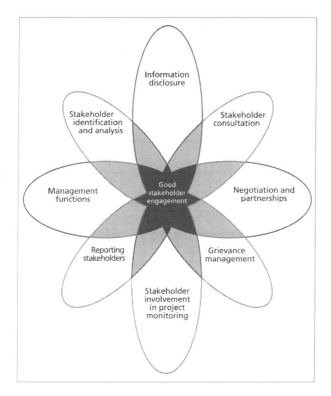

Figure 4.2 Good stakeholder engagement (International Finance Corporate
          Report, 2008).

The core principles can be developed into a detailed stakeholder engagement plan, which sets out a clear standard for your organization's approach
to working with its key stakeholders.

Stakeholder engagement plan

A good stakeholder engagement plan should:

- describe requirements for consultation and disclosure imposed by regulators, lenders, the organization itself and others;
- identify the key stakeholder groups and prioritize work with them;
- provide a strategy and timetable for sharing information and consulting
  with each of these groups;
- describe resources and responsibilities for implementing stakeholder
  engagement activities;
- explain how stakeholder engagement activities will be incorporated into
  the organization's management system.

The scope and level of detail of the plan should be scaled to fit the needs of the project or operation. This example, based on guidelines from the World Bank Group in *Stakeholder Engagement* (International Finance Corporation, 2008) follows the process through in ten logical sections.

1. Introduction

A brief description of the project (or the organization's operations), including design elements and potential social and environmental issues. Where relevant, include maps of the project site and surrounding area.

2. Regulations and requirements

Summarize the legal, regulatory, lender or organizational requirements for stakeholder engagement that are relevant to the project or the organization's operations. This may involve a requirement for public consultation and disclosure during the social and environmental assessment process.

3. Summary of any previous stakeholder engagement activities

If your organization has already carried out any activities, including information disclosure and consultation, add the following details:

- the type of information disclosed and in what forms (e.g. presentations, brochure, reports, posters, radio);
- the locations and dates of any meetings held so far;
- individuals, groups and organizations that have been consulted;
- key issues that have been discussed and key concerns raised;
- agreements that have been reached;
- the organization's response to issues raised, including any commitments or follow-up actions;
- the process chosen for documenting these activities and reporting back to stakeholders.

4. Project or organizational stakeholders

List the key stakeholder groups you'll need to tell and consult about the project or operations. These should include people or groups that:

- are directly or indirectly affected by the project (or the organization's operations);
- have commercial or financial interests in the project or organization;

- have the potential to influence project outcomes or operations, such as affected communities, neighbour organizations, NGOs and government authorities. Stakeholders can also include individual politicians, other organizations, trade unions, academics, religious groups, national social and environmental public sector agencies and the media.

5. Stakeholder engagement programme

Summarize the purpose and goals of the programme (either project-specific or corporate), and describe what information will be disclosed and in what formats, and the types of method that will be used to communicate this information to each of the stakeholder groups identified. The methods you use may vary according to the target audience, for example:

- newspapers, posters, radio, television and the internet;
- information centres and exhibitions or other visual displays;
- brochures, leaflets, non-technical summary documents and reports;
- interviews with stakeholder representatives;
- surveys, polls and questionnaires;
- public meetings, workshops and focus groups;
- participatory methods – encouraging people to become lay members of working groups and management teams;
- other traditional mechanisms for consultation and decision-making, such as involving local councils.

6. Timetable

Draw up a schedule that outlines the dates and locations of stakeholder engagement activities.

7. Resources and responsibilities

List the staff and resources that will be allocated to managing and implementing the organization's stakeholder engagement programme. Add details of:

- who within the organization will be responsible for carrying out these activities;
- what budget has been allocated toward these activities.

For projects or complex operations with significant or diverse impacts and multiple stakeholder groups, it's good practice to recruit a qualified community liaison officer to arrange and facilitate these activities. Integration of the community liaison function with other core business functions is also important, as is management involvement and oversight.

8. Grievance mechanism

Describe the process by which people affected by the project or operations can bring their grievances to the organization for consideration and redress. Describe how responses will be fed back to the correspondent.

9. Monitoring and reporting

Describe plans to involve the key stakeholders in monitoring the impacts of the project and ways of controlling them. Say how and when the results of stakeholder engagement activities will be reported back to affected stakeholders, as well as broader stakeholder groups. Tools that can be used for this include:

- social and environmental assessment reports;
- organization newsletters;
- annual monitoring reports;
- company annual reports;
- corporate sustainability reports.

10. Management functions

This section shows how stakeholder engagement activities will be integrated into the organization's core business functions. It may include:

- the name of the management representative responsible for overseeing the programme;
- the plans for hiring, training and deploying staff to undertake stakeholder engagement work;
- the reporting lines between community liaison staff and senior management;
- internal communication of the stakeholder engagement strategy;
- the management tools that will be used to document, track and manage the process, e.g. a stakeholder database or commitments register (a formal record of the agreements made with stakeholders);
- details of the interaction between appointed contractors, stakeholders and the organization.

Case study 4.2   200 thousand hotels and 17.5 million hotel rooms, International

Internet hotel reservations agent Booking.com is apparently growing quickly (van Poll, 2012). It is adding 852 new hotels to its offering every week. At the time of writing, it offers 202,842 hotels to its clients across the world.

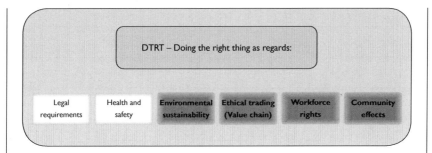

According to travel industry website Tnooz (2014), there are about 187,000 hotels in the world, offering 17.5 million guest rooms. It says that this rises to perhaps 500,000 hotels when B&Bs and hostels are added

From the world's largest hotel since 2008 – the Venetian Las Vegas, with 7117 rooms on 53 floors – down to the smallest – with just a room or two – hotels provide 13,443,014 hotel rooms as of February 2012, according to the DestinAsian (2015) census database. That's 2,315,000 more rooms than in their last census in 2000. The global hotel inventory compound annual growth (CAGR) increased by 1.6 percent over the 12 year period, led by the Asia-Pacific and the Middle East/Africa regions, which grew respectively by 2.7 per cent and 2.5 per cent CAGR through February 2012.

As of February 2012, almost two thirds of hotels are in North America and the Asia/Pacific regions:

- North America: 41.4 per cent.
- Asia Pacific: 21.4 per cent

In all regions, rooms from branded hotels increased compared to those from independent hotels in the 12 year period to February 2012.

Estimating use of resources in the world's hotels is not easy, but we'll hazard a guestimate. If there are around 15 million hotel rooms averaging (say) 50 per cent occupancy, there may be 1.5 billion hotel-night stays. That is a lot of hotel guests, with their meals, bed linen, bathroom towels and air conditioning.

As we've all seen on our travels, some hotels have started to address some of their impacts, and Figures 4.3 and 4.4 show examples of initiatives many of us will have seen.

Marriott

Marriott International, Inc. is a major hospitality company with more than 3,800 properties, 19 hotel brands and associates at more than

(continued)

(continued)

BigHotelCo

Dear Guest

We love our planet. Can you help us?

Millions of sheets are washed daily in hotels around the world using valuable water, energy and detergents.

We're trying to reduce our water consumption and our carbon footprint and need your help to do this. That's why we only change bed linen every three days, or after each departing guest of course.

Naturally, the choice is yours – if you'd like your bed changed daily, just pop this card on your pillow.

Think planet, and thank you for your help!

The Management

Figure 4.3 Reducing water consumption and carbon footprint.

BigHotelCo

Dear Guest

Here at BigHotelCo, we are trying to be as environmentally friendly as possible. To help us with this, please place your recyclables listed below into the bag attached to this tag.

- Plastic and glass bottles
- Cans
- Newspapers and paper

Thank you for your help!

The Management

Figure 4.4 Promoting hotel-room recycling.

3,800 managed and franchised properties around the world (Marriott, 2015). Founded by J. Willard and Alice Marriott and guided by Marriott family leadership for more than 80 years, the company is headquartered in Bethesda, Maryland, USA, and reported revenues of nearly $12 billion in fiscal year 2012.

The U.S. Green Building Council (USGBC) for Leadership in Energy and Environmental Design (LEED®) empowers hotel development companies to build 'green' hotels. In 2005, Marriott was the first major hotel company to design and develop a LEED®-certified hotel. At the time of writing, Marriott has 106 LEED®-registered hotels, and 31 LEED®-certified hotels.

Marriott partners with the World Tourism Organization, the United Nations Office on Drugs and Crime and the United Nations Educational, Scientific and Cultural Organization in a global campaign aimed at raising awareness and providing guidance on how tourists can help fight the trafficking of persons, wildlife, cultural artifacts, illicit drugs and counterfeit goods.

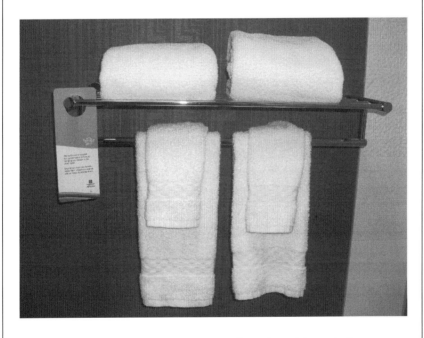

Figure 4.5 Encouraging us to replace our towels on the rail, instead of on the floor.

(continued)

(continued)

The 'Spirit To SERVE Our Communities®' social responsibility and community engagement initiatives focus on five areas of giving: shelter and food, environment, ready for jobs, vitality of children and empowering diversity.

Marriott says that it has contributed more than $2 million to the Amazonas Sustainable Foundation (FAS) and raised nearly $300,000 through its supply-chain partners, guests and associates to protect 1.4 million acres of rainforest in Brazil. In addition, it has set the following five environmental goals (Marriott, 2015):

- Further reduce energy and water consumption by 20 per cent by 2020 (Energy 20 per cent per kWh/conditioned m^2; Water 20 per cent per occupied room (POR). Baseline: 2007);
- Empower our hotel development partners to build green hotels;
- Green our multi-billion dollar supply chain;
- Educate and inspire associates and guests to conserve and preserve;
- Address environmental challenges through innovative conservation initiatives including rainforest protection and water conservation.

Marriott says that responsible management of natural resources in its hotel operations has been part of its business since the first hotel was opened in 1957. Since 2015, it has planted a tree for each of its hotels participating in Earth Hour (Saturday 28th March 2015), and it has designated April as its environmental awareness month, aiming to engage guests and its employees (known as associates) in initiating and celebrating achievements.

An example of this awareness building is the 'origami towel sculpture' initiative. In-room promotional materials show guests how to fold a towel into a swan, and are then encouraged to post a photograph of it on social media. Marriott plants one more tree for every post up to 50,000 trees.

More may be found on Marriott's corporate responsibility policies, approaches, and reports under four main themes/headings – responsible business, environment, society and performance – at http://www.marriott.com/corporate-social-responsibility/corporate-responsibility.mi.

Materiality

Stakeholder Engagement is not merely a process of managing external bodies and interest groups, but also a significant part of the internal process of selecting materially important risks for the organization, not only to manage as risk but also to report upon. In 2013, the Global Reporting Initiative released its G4 reporting standards; its predecessors have become the corporate standard of choice for agreeing a frame working of reporting standards. The Standards set out the elements that should be included in CSR reports, with specific indicators, and set out six essential elements to include in your G4 Report:

- Choose the 'in accordance' option that is right for your organization, and meet the requirements. This can be the core option, which sets out a requirement to report at least one aspect in each Material issue, or the comprehensive option, which adds broad management strategy reporting.
- Explain how you have defined the organization's material Aspects, based on impacts and the expectations of stakeholders.
- Indicate clearly where impacts occur (Boundaries).
- Describe the organization's approach to managing each of its Material Aspects (DMA).
- Report Indicators for each material Aspect according to the chosen 'in accordance' option.
- Help your stakeholders find relevant content by providing a GRI Content Index.

The GRI G4 standard makes specific reference to Stakeholders highlighting that:

> Key stakeholders – such as investors, market regulators, civil society, suppliers, employees or customers – have a vital role to play in informing an organization's materiality assessment. Taking stakeholders' views into account is central to developing a robust understanding of a company's economic, environmental, and social impacts, and of how these relate to business value and resilience.
>
> (Global Reporting Initiative, 2013)

Furthermore, of the four key principals of 'defining the report content' the standard raises stakeholder inclusiveness as its first, with sustainability context, materiality and completeness as the others. More specifically it states:

Stakeholder Inclusiveness Principle:

The organization should identify its stakeholders, and explain how it has responded to their reasonable expectations and interests.

Stakeholders can include those who are invested in the organization as well as those who have other relationships to the organization. The reasonable

> expectations and interests of stakeholders are a key reference point for many decisions in the preparation of the report.
>
> (Global Reporting Initiative, 2013)

Stakeholder views are also included into the Materiality Principal. Materiality is a key concept in CSR; it is the equivalent of significance in environmental management systems. In risk evaluation there will always be a broad range of possible risks: some that are important, those that can be realized and will have an impact and those that are insignificant. The challenge for any risk analysis process is to devise a methodology for filtering out the trivial and impossible without ignoring the highly unlikely but major impact risks.

For example, in Time Management the variables to determine what should be prioritized are importance of the task and imminence of the deadline; tasks that are neither of these should be completed after those that are both. Another example is in health and safety, where the variables of risk assessment are severity and likelihood. In CSR, the risk analysis filter is known as 'Materiality'; the variables are the organization's significant economic, environmental and social impacts; and issues that substantively influence the assessments and decisions of stakeholders. The organization can use a range of tools to define what is material or not, from rating systems and scatterplots, but stakeholder engagement in the selection is a critical part of the validity of the process and should be recorded and reported.

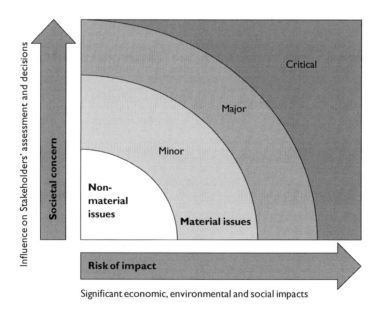

Figure 4.6 Materiality scatter matrix.

CSR tries to manage the impact of the organization on others and the environment. Stakeholders are the individuals and groups with which your organization interacts – with their consent or otherwise. It's clear that you won't please every group or every individual all of the time. But through transparent disclosure of information, active engagement at relevant stages, and timely and accurate consultation, problems can be managed at the earliest stages to prevent, minimise and mitigate the possible social, economic and environmental effects not only of your organization on your stakeholders, but also of stakeholders on your organization.

Chapter 5

Opportunities for organizations

There is a general mood across the corporate world and society that people have to return something, so there is a huge pressure . . . and once they [companies] start to accept that they can do something, then the chances of influencing them increases.

–Tyler-Rubenstein, 2015

Companies are likely to have activities scattered across the map, but that's not where they have to stay—nor is it how the benefits of CSR are maximized. Many companies start with pet projects, philanthropy, or propaganda because these activities are quick and easy to decide on and implement. The question is how to move toward CSR strategies that focus on truly co-creating value for the business and society.

–Keys, T., Malnight, T.W. and van der Graaf, K., 2009

The need and the opportunity

For an organization that has already seen CSR as an opportunity to strengthen its business proposition, the next challenge is implementation. As Tyler-Rubenstein suggests, there is huge pressure to do something. Finding an appropriate balance of benefit between business and society can cause even a well-intended participant to stumble, as Keys et al. have identified, present activities may not be coordinated. But the need and the opportunity is gigantic – we (the passengers of spaceship Earth) need to find the new products, services and business models for a world that needs to be able support nine billion sustainable lifestyles by the year 2050.

It is easy for an organization's CSR activities to become 'pet projects' – deeds, donations and decisions that reflect the personal interests of the directors or owners. These programs are often presented with great noise and gusto, but may offer very little benefit to either business or society.

Another family of actions might include partnerships and ventures that can make both sides feel good, but that generate only limited or very one-sided benefits. Organizations select a charity and make a donation to it, for example. In this instance, most of the benefit swings towards society, though there will be those that argue for the potential (but often questionable) reputational benefits to the business. Frankly, this may be no more than paying for advertising by a different means – working only to build a reputation as some cynics have suggested.

Our first two questions for any leader are:
Where have you focused CSR activities in the past?

And, more importantly: Where should you focus them for the future?

All organizations will have to balance their invariably limited resources and efforts against the forecast rewards, so the challenge is how best to deploy to maximize the benefits to your business (and your shareholders and stakeholders), as well as to society.

Something different is thus needed, and it should be focused to meet the needs of stakeholders, rather than only the partisan wishes of the executives.

Each member of the stakeholder groups (shareholders, employees, suppliers, customers, society) can – and does – apply a range of pressures for their interests to be heard. These pressures can be regarded as an opportunity and lead to a more meaningful implementation. By consulting wisely, organizations can plan in detail how they're going to meet some or all of these needs and simultaneously address any concerns of these people and groups. Doing this for all groups at the same time can be a challenge, as different people often want different things. For example, suppliers may want to deliver more frequently to reduce their warehouse stocks, while society may prefer to see fewer vehicles on the roads.

By including CSR in high-level business planning, organizations can reap benefits, including:

- a more motivated and loyal workforce;
- greater productivity;
- reduced overheads and greater efficiency;
- increased sales;
- improved access to capital;
- increased customer loyalty;
- improved reputation;
- a reduced risk of prosecution;
- access to investment and larger market shares.

Good for society, good for business

Companies that take CSR seriously not only achieve benefits to society; they can also enhance their own reputations; concurrently improving competitiveness and strengthening their risk management. Here are some introductory facts and figures about CSR (Ipsos MORI, 2000):

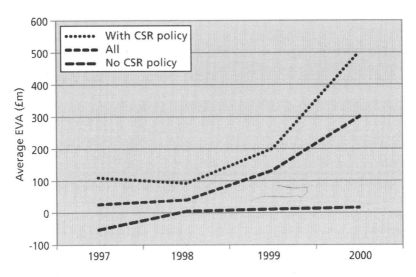

Figure 5.1 Added value from CSR.

- 81 per cent of customers agree that when price and quality are equal, they are more likely to buy products associated with a good cause;
- 73 per cent of workers agreed that they would be more loyal to an employer that supports the local community;
- 17 per cent of consumers were likely to be influenced by ethical considerations when making purchasing decisions.

An increasing number of companies of all sizes are finding that there are real business benefits from being socially responsible. Figure 5.1 shows the extra value added (EVA) by organizations with CSR policies.

CSR has thus become a core issue to be managed for many large businesses. As we identified earlier, more than 80 per cent of UK FTSE-100 companies now provide information about their environmental performance, social impact or both. And these trends are not confined to big businesses; a recent MORI (2015) survey of small and medium-sized enterprises found that 61 per cent were involved 'a great deal' or a 'fair amount' in the local community.

 Test your thinking 8

Consider each of the following five stakeholder groups for your own organization. Identify the potential benefits to each of a meaningful CSR policy and approach:

- Shareholders (aka investors);
- Employees;
- Suppliers;
- Customers;
- Society.

The scope of CSR

If an organization is to harness some or all of these benefits, it needs to consider a wide range of factors. Our DTRT Model identifies the six core elements of doing the right thing, and the Business in the Community Toolkit (BITC, 2015) is superbly aligned with these, saying that the scope should include community, environment, ethics, human rights, responsibility in the market (market responsibility and ethical trading) and its workplace/workforce. Each of these factors is summarized, before we analyze each more thoroughly.

Community

An organization should consider its impacts on the local and wider community. Investment into the community may take the form of jobs and salaries, charitable donations, staff time and skills, and donations in kind. Transport is an important factor – for example, employees commuting to and from work will affect the local roads.

Environment

An organization should identify the impact its goods and services have on the environment. As part of its planning, it should seek to maximize positive impacts by reducing its waste arising, and minimizing negative impacts, for example by investing in habitat creation schemes.

Ethics

An organization will inevitably be judged on how it makes its decisions, and how these decisions are implemented. For example, would it be ethical to explore for fossil fuels in Antarctica, even if it were allowed?

Ethical principles reflect the values of the organization, which are seen in the context of the values of its stakeholders and the society in which it operates.

Human rights

A civilized society recognizes the right of every individual to liberty, freedom of association, free speech and personal safety. These form the basis for codes of human rights found at the core of national and international laws, such as the UN Declaration of Human Rights.

Responsibility in the market (ethical trading)

Organizations can have a real impact on society through their marketing activities. For example, should cigarettes or sugary drinks be advertised during screenings of films for children? Responsibility in the marketplace can strengthen organizations' competitive edge – or damage it.

The key issues include ethical advertising, relationships with suppliers, relationships with customers, distribution, packaging and the process of creating the product or service itself.

Workplace/workforce

Recognizing organizations' impact in their workplaces means understanding the business benefits and the wider social impact of good employment policies. This not only covers the traditional areas of recruitment, remuneration, training and health and safety, but also the growing concerns – and opportunities – of issues such as diversity and equal opportunities.

We will now consider each of these elements in greater detail.

Community

No organization operates in a social vacuum. They employ people, use suppliers and have relationships with customers. Organizations' decisions on their operating location(s) affect the local community/ies, as do the employment and procurement decisions they make.

In Chapter 2, we considered the community impacts of the location of a supermarket, but communities can be equally affected by opening a new major manufacturing plant or closing down a mine, using (or not) local suppliers or investing in deprived areas.

By aligning the organization's goals with the community's needs, both can benefit. A technique that's gaining increasing interest, particularly in connection with new projects, is the ESIA, or environmental and social impact assessment.

The five steps in an ESIA are:

1   Baseline study;
2   Impact assessment;
3   Management planning;
4   Monitoring;
5   Community consultation.

Baseline study

Field studies are carried out to assess the local demographics (including social groups), flora, fauna, water, soil and pollution levels.

Impact assessment

All of the social and environmental impacts associated with a project are identified and evaluated.

Management planning

Agreed measures aimed at avoiding, minimizing and correcting the negative impacts are detailed in a management plan. There is hierarchy of mitigation measures included s. This will look familiar to health and safety specialists, as it is rather reflective of the hierarchy in the Health and Safety at Work Act and the Management of Health and Safety at Work Regulations:

- Prevent;
- Minimize;
- Restore;
- Compensate or offset.

Consultation and local development actions should take place throughout the process.

Monitoring

A programme of monitoring is developed and implemented to make sure that all management measures are being correctly and effectively applied.

Community consultation

Through all of the steps in this process, contact is maintained with interested parties. The most popular community initiatives tend to be links with local councils, education and charities, but joint projects are also becoming more common with local regeneration and arts organizations. By investing in local education, such as offering work experience placements, organizations can help to develop a future workforce that will meet their future needs. Organizations can also consider the impact on the community of the decisions they make. They can improve 'social capital' through donations to charities or supporting voluntary organizations. In this way, organizations are perceived to be profiting with the community rather than from it. The challenge remains to balance the benefits between the organization and society in a way that is meaningful to both.

Environment

All that comprises 'the environment' has now become a critical consideration for most (all?) types of organization, whether this is through the money it spends on dealing with its waste, its use of energy, or how and from where it buys its raw materials. Each of these factors directly affects the impact the organization has on the environment. If an organization can plan to use less material and energy and create less waste, not only will it help the environment, but it will save the company money, which, if safeguarded, goes straight to the bottom line, aka profit.

Early examples of projects that proved this included the Aire and Calder Project and Project Catalyst. Space here does not allow other than a summary of these projects, but interested readers may find these interesting further reading. In summary, these projects were both based on 'waste clubs', where members would meet regularly to discuss savings and how they had made them. These types of project have since been repeated by many organizations; in some cases facilitated by local authorities under the Agenda 21 banner established by the Intergovernmental Conference on Climate Change in Rio de Janeiro in 1992.

A range of Acts and regulations have been developed seeking to prevent organizations from damaging the environment. In the UK, the Water Resources Act 1991 makes it an offence to knowingly allow 'noxious or polluting matter' into rivers and other controlled waters, whilst the Environmental Protection Act 1990 places a duty of care on producers of waste to make sure it is stored securely, described accurately when transferred to a licensed waste carrier (or one with an exemption from the need to hold a license), and disposed of at an approved site.

Some wider issues, such as transport infrastructure, are also considered as part of planning application processes, particularly on larger scale projects, such as out-of-town developments and airport expansions. Environmental protection can play a pivotal role in the application and approval process, and therefore has a direct effect on the overall viability of the project or operation.

Case Study 5.1   Heathrow Airport Terminal 5, London, UK

British Airports Authority (BAA) planned and built the new Terminal 5 at London's Heathrow Airport, which opened in March 2008. The main building is the largest freestanding structure in the UK, costing £4 billion, and taking almost 20 years from conception to completion, including the longest public enquiry in British history, sitting for 525 days.

BAA was aware of the significant impact the construction of a new major terminal would have. The project cost included a range of mitigating measures to minimize the impact of the construction work on the environment. The planning approval process took over four years. A construction team environmental plan was developed to tackle

planning, legal and design elements, community concerns and contingency and mitigation measures, including:

- guidance, checklists and control plans;
- supplier awareness initiatives;
- audits and reviews;
- environmental performance indicator monitoring.

The plan tackled material use, including minimizing the use of non-sustainable and toxic materials. Over 85 per cent of the waste material from the site was recovered and recycled. Around 100,000 tonnes of carbon dioxide emissions were saved during design and construction. Around 70 per cent of the water used was from non-potable sources, and two rivers were diverted (BAA, 2002).

Figure 5.2 Construction of Terminal 5 at Heathrow Airport, London.

So, when considering the environment and their impacts upon it, organizations need to look at all of their functions in a structured way to identify:

- the inputs to the organization;
- the processes;
- the outputs.

At each stage, environmental improvement opportunities can often be identified.

Inputs

Consideration of where employees live in recruitment decisions. Careful analysis of purchasing records, including the utilities, and contracted works will allow an organization to focus efforts to only buy what its needs, from sustainably managed resources. Avoid having to throw material away by not buying too many short-shelf-life products.

Example: An organization found 80 cans of aerosol paint in its waste stream. Each had passed its end-of-shelf-life-date. An investigation found that the purchasing department had been offered an opportunity to reduce its per-can price in return for a larger order, and had accepted the opportunity placing an order for 100. The usage of the product was 20 cans. The balance over the 20 required went past the expiry date and were discarded as waste. The disposal fee was higher than the original purchase price.

Processes

Concerns making the most out of what you have purchased – some call this efficiency. Use energy efficiently; turn lights and machinery off when they're not being used. Have things serviced and drive belts correctly tensioned. Turn off computers, printers and photocopiers overnight, and don't leave electrical equipment in a standby mode.

Outputs

Only dispose of what you really have to. Consider and apply the waste hierarchy – reduce, re-use and recycle before resorting to disposal. If you incorporate meaningful environmental objectives into the organization, you'll see benefits through better use of resources, a reduction in waste, and the chance to make environmental sustainability one of your unique selling points.

This whole approach minimizes your current and future environmental liabilities and reduces your corporate risk, while enhancing your business reputation.

Ethics

Every organization relies on human relationships; they're at the heart of the interactions between the organization and its workers, its consumers and its suppliers. By establishing clear values and principles for the organization, each decision made throughout the enterprise can be aligned with its strategic purpose.

For any organization to grow and develop, it can choose to put long-term relationships before short-term profit. It should demonstrate its ethical principles in every way it can – for example, in the way it recruits and employs staff, in the products it offers the customer, and in the contracts it offers to its suppliers.

An ethical approach to business can be critical to the organization's long-term success.

Human rights

If organizations are to be socially responsible, they need to take on board one of the most basic elements of a CSR strategy – a respect for human rights. The three most important internationally recognized human rights instruments are:

- the UN Universal Declaration of Human Rights;
- the International Covenant of Civil and Political Rights;
- the International Covenant on Economic, Social and Cultural Rights.

Together, these protocols form the International Bill of Human Rights and include a set of freedoms for every human being, regardless of race, religion or sex. These are enforced by national governments, the UN Human Rights Council and the UN Security Council, although the latter has been criticized several times for not acting quickly enough – for example, in Rwanda, Bosnia and Darfur.

 Test your thinking 9

What do you consider to be your own basic human rights?

To guide and assist your response, it's worth looking at the International Bill of Human Rights, which includes the following:

- everyone has the right to life, liberty and personal security;
- no-one may be held in slavery or servitude; slavery and the slave trade are prohibited in all their forms;
- no-one may be subjected to torture or to cruel, inhuman or degrading treatment or punishment;
- no-one may be subjected to arbitrary arrest, detention or exile;
- everyone charged with a criminal offence has the right to be presumed innocent until proven guilty;
- no-one's privacy may be arbitrarily interfered with;
- everyone has the right to leave any country, including their own, and to return to that country;
- men and women of full age, without any limitation due to race, nationality or religion, have the right to marry and to found a family;

(continued)

(continued)

- everyone has the right to own property alone as well as in association with others;
- everyone has the right to freedom of thought, conscience and religion;
- everyone has the right to freedom of opinion and expression;
- everyone has the right to freedom of peaceful assembly and association;
- everyone has the right to take part in the government of their country, directly or through freely chosen representatives;
- everyone has the right to work, to free choice of employment, to just and favorable conditions of work and to protection against unemployment;
- everyone, without any discrimination, has the right to equal pay for equal work;
- everyone has the right to a standard of living adequate for the health and wellbeing of themselves and their family;
- everyone has the right to education.

We recommend you look at the full UN Declaration of Human Rights, presented in 30 articles, available at http://www.un.org/en/documents/udhr/.

As significant players in society-at-large, organizations should check carefully as a foundational expectation that they comply with these basic human rights. Beyond these, they should consider the impact of purchasing from or investing in countries that don't have the same respect for human rights as their own.

Market responsibility

An organization's impact on society in the marketplace is made up of the effect of what it produces, and how it buys and sells its wares. How much value or harm do its products and services generate? Is its approach to marketing, advertising and procurement fair and honest, as well as effective?

While price, quality and service all play an important role in consumers' purchasing decisions, they're increasingly influenced by our CSR factors, as we discussed earlier. Some consumers are now willing to pay a higher price for fair trade, ethically produced, organic or environmentally friendly products. So what is 'fair trade'?

> With Fairtrade you have the power to change the world every day. With one simple choice you can get farmers a better deal. And that means they can make their own decisions, control their futures and lead the dignified life everyone deserves.
>
> (Fairtrade Organization, 2015)

Test your thinking 10

1   We want you to think about your own purchasing decisions. How have you taken into account the societal impacts of what you buy in the past?
2   Have you decided against purchasing a company's goods because of a particular issue?
3   Do you choose goods because the products are organic, not tested on animals, or include the fair trade logo? Do you avoid products from companies that have received negative publicity in the media?
4   What CSR factors will influence your purchasing decisions in the future?

Organizations are aware of their customers' answers to (some of) these questions and have responded in a range of ways. Some market their products and services specifically on CSR factors – remember the Body Shop example you considered earlier, and how it emphasizes the responsible manufacture and testing of its products.

It is important to recognize the major opportunities for and threats to any organization, and to observe standards of behaviour in such matters as advertising, selling and purchasing. This still raises a number of issues for organizations.

Consider the following three examples. Is it socially responsible to:

- Market food and drinks with a high fat or sugar content specifically at children by offering a series of free toys?
- Reduce the social impact of selling tobacco products by having an award-winning CSR policy?
- Produce 'environmental friendly' weapons? (In 2006, the British arms manufacturer BAe Systems was first reported as designing 'environmentally friendly' weapons, including 'reduced lead' bullets, 'reduced smoke' grenades and rockets with fewer toxins).

Organizations' social responsibilities should always be set against the business context in which they operate. The examples above show that it's easy to focus only on the negative practices and ignore the positive policies of organizations in different markets. Arms suppliers and tobacco manufacturers will still have a significant impact, but how can these be minimized?

Workplace/workforce

Recognizing organizations' impact in the workplace means understanding the business benefits and the wider social impact of good employment policies. By providing a safer and more equitable place to work, organizations can improve their employees' prosperity and standards of living. A workforce that is safe, healthy and well motivated is generally thought to be the most productive. Workers should go home from work in the same condition they arrived – with all of their fingers and with their health intact. Not only is it unethical for organizations to provide an unsafe working environment; it is also uneconomic and, in most countries, illegal.

If organizations fail to invest in suitable training and safe systems of work, accident rates will tend to be higher. The financial impacts of this can include:

- loss of skilled workers
- increased downtime or overtime
- reduced productivity
- increased property damage
- increased liabilities
- higher risk of criminal prosecution
- fines and/or imprisonment
- bad publicity
- reduced morale
- increased retraining costs
- increased recruitment costs
- reduced investor confidence
- increased overheads
- reduced profits.

> Prevention is not only better, but cheaper than cure . . . There is no necessary conflict between humanitarianism and commercial considerations. Profits and safety are not in competition. On the contrary, safety is good business.
>
> (Prof. Peter McKie, DuPont Corporation,
> Health and Safety Executive, 1997a)

Although you can transfer some of the financial risks (costs) to an insurer, we know that the proportion of insured costs resulting from accidents and ill health at work compared to the uninsured costs is very small. An old, but we think still-relevant, study by the Health and Safety Executive in the UK (Health and Safety Executive, 1997b) reported that the ratio of insured costs to uninsured costs may be between 1:8 and 1:36.

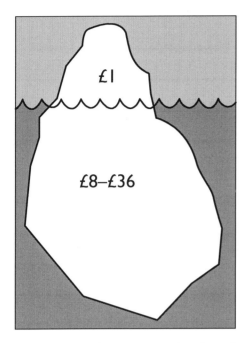

£1

£8–£36

Figure 5.3 The tip of the iceberg: the relationship between insured and uninsured costs.

Similar benefits can be realized through having equality-based recruitment and non-discriminatory employment policies. Workforce diversity can help organizations to bridge gaps between their workplace and their marketplace, and to help them to understand and open up new markets. Organizations that mirror their customer base can enhance their image and send a positive signal to stakeholders and potential investors.

Protection by minimum standards

In order to make sure that basic minimum standards are in place for CSR, some key issues are already being enforced around the world through legislation with a range of legal requirements to establish basic minimum standards for a variety of common hazards.

Our research suggests that legislation works, as following implementation of primary worker protection laws in the USA (1970) and the UK (in 1974), fatal accident rates were reduced. This is true for all the territories we have analyzed, and we encourage readers to review their own statistics where these are available.

Worker safety and health

In the UK, the Health and Safety at Work Act and the Management of Health and Safety at Work Regulations, along with their supporting regulations, protect workers' health and safety and ensure basic welfare standards are met in workplaces. Equivalents are provided in Europe as required by Directive 89/391/EEC, and in many other countries there are laws providing worker protections, as broadly described by the UN/ILO conventions.

Employment rights

In the UK, the National Minimum Wage Act 1998 provided the first instrument for employees' rights to be paid at least a national minimum wage and to receive paid annual leave. Rates of pay are reviewed each year by the Low Pay Commission, which makes recommendations for change to Government.

The Working Time Regulations 1998 stipulate maximum hours and minimum rest periods that employers can impose on employees.

Employment laws also give rights to employees not to be discriminated against on recruitment and promotion, and also set out minimum requirements for redundancy pay.

So, let's start to consolidate Chapters 1–5 with a case study, which will enable you to use your learning so far to review and understand the CSR impacts of one of the world's best-known organizations – Coca-Cola.

Case study 5.2   Two views of Coca-Cola, International

Consider Coca-Cola, the leading carbonated soft drink manufacturer. Coca-Cola is a global market leader with over 500 globally recognized brands, including Coke, Fanta, Sprite and Powerade.

The following text is taken from Coca-Cola's *2013/2014 Sustainability Report* (Coca Cola, 2015):

> Sustainability is at the heart of our business. And as a business, we know that sustainability efforts are themselves only sustainable when they help our enterprise grow and prosper. Indeed, we believe this work must be integral to our mission of refreshing the world, inspiring moments of optimism and happiness, creating value and making a difference.

> As a result, we've chosen to focus our leadership on three areas of fundamental importance to our business—areas where we believe

we have the best opportunity to make a lasting positive difference. We call them the "Three Ws": Women, Water and Well-Being. We also continue to implement sustainability programs across other areas of our operations.

We know that we don't have all the answers, all the access or all the know-how. On the contrary, we believe that, in a world of great challenges and even greater opportunities, we must work side by side with our bottling and industry partners, non-governmental organizations, universities, government agencies and others.

Working together, we can unlock the collaborative power of the "Golden Triangle" of business, government and civil society organizations, making a much greater collective impact than any one organization or even sector could hope to achieve alone.

As for our overarching goals, we're striving to enable the economic empowerment of 5 million Women entrepreneurs within our global value chain by 2020. Since launching this initiative, which we call 5by20™, in 2010, we've made a difference in the lives of more than 550,000 women and their families as we pilot, scale and replicate the best ideas.

In Water, we're working to balance the water we use by 2020, returning to communities and nature an amount of water equal to that used in our beverages and their production. We're currently on track to achieve this water goal, replenishing an estimated 68 percent of the volume of our finished beverages in 2013 and returning a calculated 108.5 billion liters to communities and nature.

As for Well-Being, we're committed to, among other things, helping our consumers make informed choices by providing an ever-expanding selection of reduced-, low-, and no-calorie beverages along with front-of-package nutritional labeling. And we're working toward our goal to support physical activity programs in each of the more than 200 markets we serve. To date, we've supported more than 290 programs in nearly 125 countries and territories.

(Coca-Cola, 2015)

An alternative view of the Coca-Cola Company is presented by War on Want (2015), which comments as follows:

This is [an] alternative company report . . . to compare and contrast the rhetoric of corporate social responsibility (CSR) with the reality of companies' actual practices. The reports form part of War

(continued)

(continued)

on Want's ongoing campaign for a global framework of corporate regulation, and each recommends action that ordinary people can take to rein in the power of multinational corporations across the world. This report looks at the international beverage company Coca-Cola, one of the most recognized brands in the world. Coca-Cola has built a global empire and now sells close to 400 brands in almost 200 countries. The company claims to adhere to the "highest ethical standards" and to be "an outstanding corporate citizen in every community we serve". Yet Coca-Cola's activities around the world tell a different story. Coca-Cola has been accused of dehydrating local communities in its pursuit of water resources to feed its own plants, drying up farmers' wells and destroying local agriculture. The company's own workers have also suffered: workers in Coca-Cola and supplier plants have seen their rights violated in countries such as Colombia, Turkey, Guatemala and Russia. Only through its multi-million dollar marketing campaigns can Coca-Cola sustain the clean image it craves.

(War on Want, 2015)

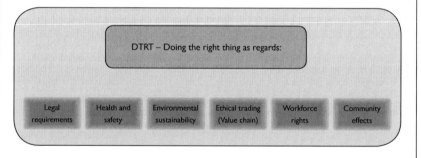

DTRT – Doing the right thing as regards:

| Legal requirements | Health and safety | Environmental sustainability | Ethical trading (Value chain) | Workforce rights | Community effects |

Test your thinking 11

Considering both of these reports, complete a review of the reported performance at Coca-Cola against our DTRT Model, including the areas we've discussed above. You'll need to look at both of these reports in full to do this successfully.

For each area, list examples of good practice, poor practice and impacts that you feel haven't been addressed satisfactorily. For example, under 'Community' impacts, you might identify the initiatives to empower women or promote children's sport and physical activity as examples of good practice, and the use of water or marketing of high-sugar drinks directly to children as examples of bad practice.

The six core elements of our DTRT Model:

- legal requirements;
- health and safety;
- environmental sustainability;
- ethical trading (value chain);
- workforce rights;
- community effects.

Getting started

Now that you have proven to yourself that you can use the learning so far to review and understand the CSR impacts of Coca-Cola, we think you can now start to think about your own organization.

Throughout this book you have gained ideas and concepts that will help you to identify and tackle your own CSR issues. While every organization is obviously different, we set out below our possible approach to implementing a CSR strategy.

Action plan

- Get senior management commitment – remember to 'sell' the benefits to your organization. See Chapter 9 for our advice on how to become an 'agent for change'.
- Set up a core working group. We recommend that you include a cross-section of workforce representatives. Decide whether you want to work to a verified standard, to seek accreditation, or perhaps just to use good practices.
- Carry out a baseline review of the key issues and establish the materiality – the relevance or significance – of each issue in terms of its potential impact on your stakeholders and on your business. Our DTRT Model will help you to cover the key areas.
- Develop a CSR plan to tackle your key areas and define targets, policies, roles, responsibilities, training and action plans to make sure the strategy is effectively implemented.
- Establish a communication strategy to respond effectively and promptly to stakeholder issues in a transparent and sensitive way, and make sure action is taken to tackle the important issues. The strategy should also cover regular reporting to stakeholders on progress and market the CSR strategy to internal and external stakeholders.

- Review the supply chain. If your organization is at a stage to consider an external CSR strategy, it's less likely that the key issues will be internal, as you'll probably have many good practices already in place – but your supply chain might be a different matter. You'll need to develop a program to assess suppliers' current status, develop a support and development program and confirm their status through auditing.
- Develop key performance indicators, and regularly monitor and continually review their effectiveness and impact on your organization.

If you want to see a high-level illustration of the framework we've described here, it is shown in Figure 1.19.

Opportunities for organizations – conclusion

To be successful, organizations must focus on specific choices, and to conclude Chapter 5, we present our three guiding principles for doing the right thing:

DTRT Principle 1: concentrate your CSR efforts

Management time and resources are invariably limited, so the greatest opportunities will come from areas where the business significantly interacts with –and thus can have the greatest impact on – society. Use of our DTRT Model will help you to identify these. It will likely reveal areas where your operation cannot only develop a deeper understanding of its mutual dependencies upon society, but also where the greatest potential for mutual benefit exists.

DTRT Principle 2: build a deep understanding of the mutual benefits

Even after selecting your chosen areas of opportunity, finding the potential for mutual value creation is not always straightforward. The key is finding symmetry between the two sides of organization and society, and understanding the context (business environment) well enough to understand the issues from both perspectives. Develop a means of measuring and reporting upon these in a currency (at least red, amber, green) that will resonate within the organization and with stakeholders.

DTRT Principle 3: be in this for the journey, not the destination

As CSR initiatives and projects deliver and come to fruition, our DTRT Model will help you to continue to identify new critical areas in your business where you interface with, and have an impact on, society; and where significant opportunities exist for both sides if you can creatively adjust the relationship.

What are the core long-term needs for you and for society that can be addressed as a result?

What resources or capabilities do we need that are proportional to the benefits, and what do we have to offer in realizing the opportunities?

Readers, managers, business owners, organizations! The opportunity to benefit internally and externally from a CSR risk management program using our DTRT Model is yours! Now's the time to get started . . . .

Chapter 6

Reporting and verifying

Pender laughed. "Verify? In this day and age? Who cares about verifying anything? It's all about the speed. Who gets there first defines the truth. You know that as well as any man living."

–David Baldacci, in *The Whole Truth*, 2011, p.65

I can get you as many as 100 stitchers if you need them. Of course, you'll have to pay off their *peshgi*[1] to claim them.

–Pakistani factory owner

Reporting on CSR

Governments recognize that CSR factors are important for an organization's long-term investment and viability. This recognition in the UK was behind the proposal to introduce new reporting regulations, called the Operating and Financial Review (OFR) in 2005. However, later that year, the government decided to repeal these requirements on quoted companies to prepare an OFR, instead requiring them to produce a 'Business Review'. This decision was taken in the context of the government's policy of reducing administrative burdens on organizations and took into account the evidence from consultations on narrative reporting. As David Baldacci suggests, defining the truth may be challenging . . . .

Business review requirements

The requirements for a Business Review were originally added to Section 234ZZB of the Companies Act 1985, and upon the repeal of this, were replaced by the current requirements – Section 417 of the Companies Act (2006). The main requirements are summarized here:

The purpose of the business review is to inform members of the company and help them assess how the directors have performed their duty under section 172 (the duty to promote the success of the company).

The business review must contain:

a   a fair review of the company's business; and
b   a description of the principal risks and uncertainties facing the company.

The review required is a balanced and comprehensive analysis of:

a   the development and performance of the company's business during the financial year; and
b   the position of the company's business at the end of that year, consistent with the size and complexity of the business.

In the case of a quoted company, the business review must, to the extent necessary for an understanding of the development, performance or position of the company's business, include:

a   the main trends and factors likely to affect the future development, performance and position of the company's business;
b   information about:

   i   environmental matters (including the impact of the company's business on the environment);
   ii   the company's employees;
   iii   social and community issues, including information about any policies of the company in relation to those matters and the effectiveness of those policies; and

c   information about persons with whom the company has contractual or other arrangements, which are essential to the business of the company.

If the review does not contain information of each kind mentioned in paragraphs (b)(i), (ii) and (iii) and (c), it must state which of those kinds of information it does not contain.

The review must, to the extent necessary for an understanding of the development, performance or position of the company's business, include:

a   analysis using financial key performance indicators; and
b   where appropriate, analysis using other key performance indicators, including information relating to environmental matters and employee matters.

In the Act, 'key performance indicators' are defined as factors by reference to which the development, performance or position of the company's business can be measured effectively.

Case Study 6.1   Corporation tax dodgers, International

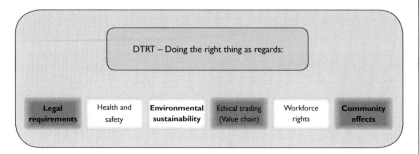

DTRT – Doing the right thing as regards:

| Legal requirements | Health and safety | Environmental sustainability | Ethical trading (Value chain) | Workforce rights | Community effects |

Leading companies avoid tax and act irresponsibility

News reports (Real Business, 2013) claim that approaching half of the UK's leading companies fail to comply with the law by avoiding paying taxes. Over 100 companies listed on the FTSE 350 index have now been accused of tax evasion, with many leading firms hiding profits offshore to avoid paying UK tax. Six organizations alleged to have avoided taxes with a summary of the allegations are:

1 Amazon
2 Apple
3 eBay
4 Facebook
5 Google
6 Starbucks

Amazon

Online super-retailer Amazon has been accused of using Luxembourg as a location to dramatically reduce their tax obligations in the UK. It was found that the company paid just £1.8m in corporation tax in 2011, despite its £3.35bn UK sales. The company justified these figures claiming they only made £74m in profit.

Apple

In the USA, a Senate committee accused Apple of using a complex web of offshore entities to avoid paying billions of dollars in US income tax. Apple says that it is one of the largest US tax payers, having paid $6bn in corporate income tax during 2012. Critics say that due to the size of the company, it could easily be one of the biggest tax avoiders too. Apple was found to have (only) paid a corporation tax rate of 1.9 per cent outside North America.

eBay

Online auction site eBay has also been accused of avoiding paying corporation tax in the UK and Germany. It was found that eBay paid just $1m in tax, despite their sales of over £800m in the UK.

Facebook

Social media company Facebook was found not to have paid any UK corporation tax in the 2012 fiscal year, despite its UK operation reporting a 70 per cent increase in income from the previous year. Figures show that Facebook paid only £1m in UK corporation tax 2007–2014, despite generating sales of £0.5bn in Britain. A Facebook spokesman said that the company pays all the taxes required by UK law.

Google

There was public outrage after it was found that Google had only paid £6m in UK corporation tax in 2011, despite raking in annual profit levels of £2.5bn in Britain. Google's chairman defended the company before the Parliamentary Public Accounts Committee, claiming that the company was fully complying with the law.

Starbucks

Coffee giant Starbucks did not pay any UK corporation tax in 2011, despite making a profit of £380m that year. Starbucks claimed they

(continued)

(continued)

had been making a loss fourteen out of the fifteen years' operating in the UK. Later, investigations suggested that this information was inconsistent with their accounts and not what had been advised to their shareholders. After a public boycott and discussions with HMRC, Starbucks agreed to pay £20m in corporation tax over the next two years.

Responsible behaviour

A recent survey (Ipsos MORI, 2015) shows the dangers to companies when they do not behave responsibly. Nearly half of the British public (45 per cent) reported that they have reconsidered using products or services from a company that has avoided paying tax in this country – see Table 6.1.

There is further evidence of consumers having had enough and taking action that could affect the bottom line. The boycotting of companies or products on the grounds of poor corporate social responsibility (CSR) has increased since 2013, with a seven point increase year on year in the proportion who claim to have boycotted a product in the last 12 months for this reason (up to nearly a quarter; 23 per cent).

Action by the public is set within the context of a high degree of cynicism and distrust in British business, especially banking organizations. Seven in ten people believe that industry and commerce has lost the trust of the general public. A similar percentage (68 per cent) question the motivations of companies' corporate responsibility initiatives, agreeing that 'large companies only invest in the environment and community initiatives to make themselves look better'.

Table 6.1 'I have reconsidered using a company's products and services that has avoided paying tax in this country'.

Strongly agree	= 19%
Tend to agree	= 26%
Neither agree or disagree	= 28%
Tend to disagree	= 13%
Strongly disagree	= 8%
Don't know/no opinion	= 6%

Collected data suggests that distrust in business is (at least in part) under-pinned by the crisis in the financial sector, and casting a negative umbra onto other sectors. Just over half (56 per cent) agree that 'after the financial sector crisis, I generally trust large businesses less', but stories around (perceived?) tax avoidance (even if it is within the law) may have exacerbated this.

The Modern Slavery Act

At the time of writing, The Modern Slavery Act (2015) in the UK is new. This Act of Parliament is designed to tackle slavery and consolidates previous offences relating to human trafficking and slavery in England and Wales. The key areas covered by the new Act are:

- the creation of two new civil orders to prevent modern slavery;
- establishing an Anti-Slavery Commissioner;
- making provision for the protection of modern slavery victims;
- from October 2015, requires larger businesses with total turnover >£36m to disclose what activity they are undertaking to eliminate slavery and trafficking from their supply chains and their own business.

Of interest to these larger businesses will be part 6, which says:

54 Transparency in supply chains, etc.

1   A commercial organisation within subsection (2) must prepare a slavery and human trafficking statement for each financial year of the organization.
2   A commercial organization is within this subsection if it:

   a   supplies goods or services; and
   b   has a total turnover of not less than an amount prescribed by regu-lations made by the Secretary of State.

3   For the purposes of subsection (2)(b), an organisation's total turnover is to be determined in accordance with regulations made by the Secretary of State.
4   A slavery and human trafficking statement for a financial year is:

   a   a statement of the steps the organisation has taken during the financial year to ensure that slavery and human trafficking is not taking place;

      i   in any of its supply chains; and
      ii in any part of its own business.

   Or

   b   a statement that the organisation has taken no such steps.

5   An organisation's slavery and human trafficking statement may include information about:

    a   the organisation's structure, its business and its supply chains;

    b   its policies in relation to slavery and human trafficking;

    c   its due diligence processes in relation to slavery and human trafficking in its business and supply chains;

    d   the parts of its business and supply chains where there is a risk of slavery and human trafficking taking place, and the steps it has taken to assess and manage that risk;

    e   its effectiveness in ensuring that slavery and human trafficking is not taking place in its business or supply chains, measured against such performance indicators as it considers appropriate;

    f   the training about slavery and human trafficking available to its staff.

The bill was introduced to the House of Commons as a draft in October 2013 by James Brokenshire, Parliamentary Under-Secretary for Crime and Security, and sponsored at the Home Office by Theresa May and Lord Bates. It received Royal Assent and became law on 26 March 2015.

> The Act will "send the strongest possible message to criminals that if you are involved in this disgusting trade in human beings, you will be arrested, you will be prosecuted and you will be locked up.
>
> James Brokenshire, MP (Gov.uk, 2015)

> The bill is wholly and exclusively about law enforcement – but it shouldn't be enforcement-based, it should be victim-based.
>
> (Anthony Steen, Chair, Human Trafficking Foundation, The Institute of Employment Rights, 2015)

Verification

Clearly, in an age with almost unrestricted media and freedom for uncensored publication (particularly on the internet), any battle of claim and counter-claim regarding image and claimed and/or supposed performance could go on and on. Therefore, it is probably in everyone's interest that there should be some means of independently verifying organizations' claims about their standards. In the context of this book, this means verifying their claims about their CSR performance.

Management system standards

Specific management system standards (MSS) are designed to bring structured means of control to specific issues; you can read about the origination and evolution of MSS in Chapter 1. Organizations can choose to meet a published set of specific criteria, and then an independently approved auditing body verifies that these standards are indeed met.

SA8000

An example of a CSR-related MSS is SA8000:2008, a global social accountability standard modelled on ISO standards, developed and overseen by Social Accountability International (SAI) (2008). SA8000 is based on the UN Declaration of Human Rights, conventions of the International Labor Organization (ILO), UN and national laws. It spans all industries and corporate social responsibility codes to create a common language to measure social performance. It takes a management systems approach by setting out the structures and procedures that companies must adopt in order to ensure that compliance with the standard is continuously reviewed. Those seeking to comply with SA8000 have adopted policies and procedures that protect the basic human rights of workers by setting standards for decent working conditions. Every facility seeking certification must be audited, and certification provides a public report of good practice.

SA8000 details the following principles:

- no employment of children under the age of 14 (ILO Convention 38);
- no forced labour (exampled in our introductory peshgi[1] comment);
- a safe and healthy working environment;
- the right to form trade unions;
- no discrimination;
- the normal working week must not exceed 48 hours;
- all overtime must be reimbursed;
- rates of pay must meet the legal or industry minimum and be sufficient to meet basic needs and give discretionary income;
- there must be a system in place to manage and review these social issues;
- air pollution: measures must be taken to reduce emissions, particularly of key pollutants, and the organization must seek to go beyond statutory requirements;
- biodiversity and habitats: the importance of biodiversity and significant habitats must be recognized and measures taken to protect and enhance them;
- climate change: measures taken to monitor and reduce greenhouse gas emissions should be highlighted;
- intensity of resource use: resources include energy, water, raw materials and land, and the organization must focus on how efficiently it uses them; this criterion is linked to waste and pollution;

- transport: the organization must consider measures that reduce overall transport requirements and encourage a modal shift away from road transport (for people and freight);
- waste: measures to reduce, re-use and recycle waste;
- water quality: measures to reduce discharges, particularly of key pollutants; a commitment to go beyond statutory requirements; rewarding efforts to meet objectives and targets.

As of September 2014 (the latest data available at the time of writing), 1.9 million workers were employed in over 3400 facilities certified to SA8000, located in 74 countries and in 65 industrial sectors, including clothing manufacture and textiles, building materials and construction, agriculture, chemicals, cosmetics and cleaning services. The countries with the most facility certifications to SA8000 are Italy, India, China, Romania and Pakistan. These five countries together represent over 75 per cent of total global certifications.

At the time of writing, SA8000 was being revised (along the lines described in Chapter 1), and from May 2016, certification will only be available to the new standard, SA8000:2014.

Other accredited management system standards relevant to reporting and verifying CSR include:

- AA 1000;
- ISO 14001;
- BS OHSAS 18001 and ISO 45001;
- ISO 26000;
- Ethical Trading Initiative (ETI) base code.

Accredited MSS provide powerful opportunities for reporting, verifying and reporting upon the effectiveness of CSR (and other) performance. We'll review at each of these now.

AA 1000

The AA 1000 series of standards (three of, see below) consists of principles-based standards to help organizations become more accountable, responsible and sustainable. They address issues affecting governance, business models and organizational strategy, as well as providing operational guidance on sustainability assurance and stakeholder engagement. The AA 1000 standards are designed for the integrated thinking required by the low carbon and green economy, and support integrated reporting and assurance. The standards are applicable to organizations in any sector, of any size and in any region.

The custodian of the standards, AccountAbility, authorizes assurance providers (auditors) around the world. It says that over 150 companies have used or referred to the AA 1000 assurance standards in their reporting to date. These companies include Coca-Cola, British American Tobacco, Vodafone, Royal Dutch Shell and Lego.

The AA 1000 series of standards

1   The AA 1000 AccountAbility Principles Standard (AA 1000APS):
    AA 1000 APA provides a framework for an organization to identify, prioritize and respond to its sustainability challenges.
2   The AA 1000 Assurance Standard (AA1000AS).
    AA 1000 AS provides a methodology for assurance practitioners to evaluate the nature and extent to which an organization adheres to the AccountAbility Principles.
3   The AA1000 Stakeholder Engagement Standard (AA1000SES):
    AA 1000 SES provides a framework to help organisations ensure stakeholder engagement processes are purpose driven, robust and deliver results.

ISO 14001

The ISO 14001 environmental MSS was developed to help organizations to recognize the positive and minimize the negative impacts of their operations on the environment (such as adverse changes to air, land or water) and to provide a mechanism to enable compliance with applicable laws and other standards adopted by the organization.

With its origins in the earliest modern management system standards, ISO 14001 was developed from BS 5750 (quality management) and BS7750 (environmental management), and is now generally regarded as the international specification for environmental management systems. Currently under revision to meet the Annex SL framework (see Chapter 1), it covers:

* requirements for establishing an environmental policy;
* how to determine environmental aspects and impacts of products, activities and services;
* setting environmental objectives and measurable targets;
* implementing and operating programs to meet objectives, targets and significant risks;
* checking and corrective action;
* management review.

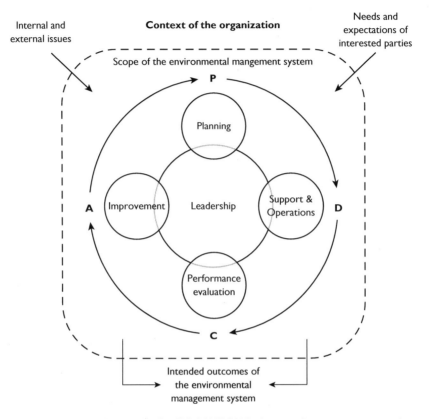

Figure 6.1 High-level structure for ISO 14001:2015, showing the improvement cycle.

ISO 14001:2004 and its revision ISO 14001:2015 are based on the classic 'Deming Wheel' Plan-Do-Check-Act approach, as shown in Figure 1.3

BS OHSAS 18001 and ISO 45001

Called the Occupational Health and Safety Management System, BS OHSAS 18001 specifies requirements for a health and safety management system that enables an organization to identify and control its health and safety risks and to continually improve its performance.

The standard does not give specific health and safety performance criteria, nor does it give detailed specifications for designing a management system, though it is based, like ISO 14001, on the Plan-Do-Check-Act continuum.

BS OHSAS 18001:2007 is the UK's implementation of OHSAS 18001 and has the status of a British Standard. The OHSAS 18001 standard was prepared and published wholly outside of the ISO framework. To avoid confusion, a standard called 'ISO 18000' *does* exist – but it is a radio-frequency identification standard(!).

As noted in Chapter 1, ISO has approved a project to develop its own OH&S MSS, intended to be called ISO 45001. This will replace the BS OHSAS 18001 standard upon its publication in 2016.

At the time of writing, there are over 30,000 external certifications to OHSAS 18001 in the world.

ISO 26000

The International Organization for Standardization (ISO) launched an international standard providing guidelines for social responsibility (SR) in 2010 called ISO 26000, or simply ISO SR. It outlines international recommendations for making an organization more socially responsible. It guides organizations in building and delivering long-term social responsibility strategies, covering a broad area from working practices to environmental policies, sustainable development and the communities impacted.

> This standard will enable businesses to bring together best practice in terms of workforce, customers, neighbours, fair trade and the all-important demands on our natural resources and our climate. Through the BSI standards process we have made an excellent input from UK stakeholders to ensure this is a practical and effective approach.
>
> (Mike Low, Director of Standards, BSi, 2015)

Ethical Trading Initiative base code

The ETI Base Code was founded on the conventions of the International Labor Organization (ILO) and is an internationally recognized code of labour practice, established in 1998. It aims to improve the lives of poor working people around the world. It comprises an alliance of companies, NGOs and trade unions working to promote and improve the implementation of corporate codes of practice which cover supply chain working conditions.

The base code contains nine clauses that reflect the most relevant international standards on labour practices. The base code and principles of implementation have two related functions:

1   They provide a basic philosophy or platform from which the ETI identifies and develops good practice;
2   They provide a generic standard for company performance.

The text and a poster of the ETI base code is available free at http://www.ethicaltrade.org/eti-base-code, and is worth reproducing here in full:

1   **Employment is freely chosen.**

   1.1 There is no forced, bonded or involuntary prison labour.
   1.2 Workers are not required to lodge 'deposits' or their identity papers with their employer and are free to leave their employer after reasonable notice.

2   **Freedom of association and the right to collective bargaining are respected.**

2.1 Workers, without distinction, have the right to join or form trade unions of their own choosing and to bargain collectively.

2.2 The employer adopts an open attitude towards the activities of trade unions and their organizational activities.

2.3 Workers' representatives are not discriminated against and have access to carry out their representative functions in the workplace.

2.4 Where the right to freedom of association and collective bargaining is restricted under law, the employer facilitates, and does not hinder, the development of parallel means for independent and free association and bargaining.

3   **Working conditions are safe and hygienic.**

3.1 A safe and hygienic working environment shall be provided, bearing in mind the prevailing knowledge of the industry and of any specific hazards. Adequate steps shall be taken to prevent accidents and injury to health arising out of, associated with, or occurring in the course of work, by minimizing, so far as is reasonably practicable, the causes of hazards inherent in the working environment.

3.2 Workers shall receive regular and recorded health and safety training, and such training shall be repeated for new or reassigned workers.

3.3 Access to clean toilet facilities and to potable water, and, if appropriate, sanitary facilities for food storage shall be provided.

3.4 Accommodation, where provided, shall be clean, safe, and meet the basic needs of the workers.

3.5 The company observing the code shall assign responsibility for health and safety to a senior management representative.

4   **Child labour shall not be used.**

4.1 There shall be no new recruitment of child labour.

4.2 Companies shall develop or participate in and contribute to policies and programmes which provide for the transition of any child found to be performing child labour to enable her or him to attend and remain in quality education until no longer a child; 'child' and 'child labour' being defined in the appendices.

4.3 Children and young persons under 18 shall not be employed at night or in hazardous conditions.

4.4 These policies and procedures shall conform to the provisions of the relevant ILO standards.

5   **Living wages are paid**

    5.1 Wages and benefits paid for a standard working week meet, at a minimum, national legal standards or industry benchmark standards, whichever is higher. In any event wages should always be enough to meet basic needs and to provide some discretionary income.

    5.2 All workers shall be provided with written and understandable information about their employment conditions in respect to wages before they enter employment and about the particulars of their wages for the pay period concerned each time that they are paid.

    5.3 Deductions from wages as a disciplinary measure shall not be permitted nor shall any deductions from wages not provided for by national law be permitted without the expressed permission of the worker concerned. All disciplinary measures should be recorded.

6   **Working hours are not excessive**

    6.1 Working hours comply with national laws and benchmark industry standards, whichever affords greater protection.

    6.2 In any event, workers shall not on a regular basis be required to work in excess of 48 hours per week and shall be provided with at least one day off for every seven-day period on average. Overtime shall be voluntary, shall not exceed 12 hours per week, shall not be demanded on a regular basis and shall always be compensated at a premium rate.

7   **No discrimination is practised**

    7.1 There is no discrimination in hiring, compensation, access to training, promotion, termination or retirement based on race, caste, national origin, religion, age, disability, gender, marital status, sexual orientation, union membership or political affiliation.

8   **Regular employment is provided**

    8.1 To every extent possible work performed must be on the basis of recognized employment relationship established through national law and practice.

    8.2 Obligations to employees under labour or social security laws and regulations arising from the regular employment relationship shall not be avoided through the use of labour-only contracting, subcontracting, or home-working arrangements, or through apprenticeship schemes where there is no real intent to impart skills or provide regular employment, nor shall any such obligations be avoided through the excessive use of fixed-term contracts of employment.

9　No harsh or inhumane treatment is allowed

9.1　Physical abuse or discipline, the threat of physical abuse, sexual or other harassment and verbal abuse or other forms of intimidation shall be prohibited.

The provisions of this code constitute minimum and not maximum standards, and this code should not be used to prevent companies from exceeding these standards. Companies applying this code are expected to comply with national and other applicable law and, where the provisions of law and this Base Code address the same subject, to apply that provision which affords the greater protection.

Ethical Trading Initiative believes that the labour standards incorporated in its base code constitute the minimum requirement for any corporate code of labour practice. Members of the ETI commit to implement the base code in their supply chains and to report annually on their progress.

Case Study 6.2　Can certification save our forests? Brazil and International

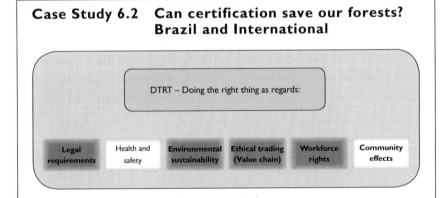

Value chain management is a core focus in CSR management systems. Whoever derives economic or social value from a supply chain – pre-use or post-sale – of a product or service from an organization is at the heart of doing the right thing. In this case study we will review how the concerns for deforestation have led to a range of certification projects to drive the sustainable sourcing of timber, protection of habitats, and even a drive to towards a lower carbon economy. Projects such as the FSC Scheme (Forestry Stewardship Certification) and PEFC

(Programme for the Endorsement of Forest Certification) have formed an important part in verifying the compliance to standards within the forestry management, paper processing and timber supply sectors. But how far can a badge really protect ancient woodlands and support the sustainable long-term viability of our demand for timber? What can be learnt from this model that could be transferred to other sectors to drive CSR to permeate procurement standards as PEFC and FSC have done?

It is estimated that forests cover around a third of the Earth's land area, from Boreal forest biomes of the northern latitudes to tropical rainforests, they are vital to the survival of life on this planet. Forests play an important role in many natural cycles; on a chemical level they provide oxygen production and carbon sinks, but are also vital to water flows and nitrogen cycles, as well as providing extended habitats with a third dimension supporting some of the most biologically diverse places in the world. They also play a critical role in human survival, as it is estimated that 1.6 billion people rely on the benefits forests offer, including food, fresh water, clothing, traditional medicine and shelter (WWF, 2015a). Furthermore forests also have a significant role to place in the global economy. The carbon disclosure project highlights that 'annual exports of primary and secondary wood products from tropical forests have exceeded US$ 20 billion in recent years' and the every year in excess of '3.4 billion cubic meters of wood is extracted from forests, approximately half of which is used for wood fuel (firewood or charcoal), and the remainder is used to make timber and paper products' (Carbon Disclosure Project, 2014), which creates an estimated US$100bn in wood removals and US$18.5bn in other forest products per annum. This is fuelled by over US$64bn in investments annually in forestry related sectors (UNEP, 2011).

(continued)

(continued)

Yet despite timber and pulp being the quintessential definition of a renewable resource, the rate of destruction outstrips its demand: the WWF estimates 58,0000 square miles of forest are lost each year, equivalent to 36 football fields every minute (WWF, 2015).

The complex drivers to the problem are being tackled from a number of different directions, but primarily focus on supply and demand. From the supply side there are a number of projects to directly protect areas of land, such as the WWF ARPA (Amazon Region Protected Areas) campaign, the largest tropical forest conservation project in history according to the charity, which aims to protect 150 million acres of the Brazilian Amazon rainforest. The project has set out the following objectives (WWF, 2015b):

ARPA objectives:

- Establish approximately 283,000 km^2 of new protected areas for strict conservation use.
- Transform approximately 125,000 km^2 of existing but neglected parks by bringing them up to effective management standards.
- Establish approximately 89,000 km^2 of sustainable use reserves in which local communities will have a stake and will benefit from effective stewardship.
- Set up a long-term Protected Areas Trust Fund to ensure the financial viability and integrity of the park system in perpetuity. The funding target is US$220m.

Protection of forest habitats can only ever go a small way to driving a sustainable timber and paper sector. Only when the customer demand includes sustainability principals will the supply chain focus on sourcing from managed sources, but how could this be achieved? The industry responded with schemes such as FSC and PEFC labelling schemes, which highlight to customers that the timber products come from a well-managed source, with a chain of custody certification process to validate the value chain. FSC and PEFC soon became industry standard with paper mills, newspapers and large construction organizations including them in their procurement specifications. Although PEFC and FSC are both focused on using chain of custody processes to assure timber derived products, their approaches have a number of differences.

The FSC Tick and chain of custody processes cover 2,351 certificates and around 1,605,527 ha of forest as of the 7 April 2015

(Forest Stewardship Council, 2015). The organization states that its approach has a number of benefits, which can be categorized into the following areas:

- Valid endorsements: the scheme is endorsed by WWF, Greenpeace and the Woodland Trust, follows ISO Standards on product certification and World Bank assurance principles.
- Global applicability: The FSC standard is the same across the globe; the ten Principles of Forest Management have been developed from an international perspective. This means that where you see the logo you know the standards are the same.
- Consistency: The scheme has a focus on central co-ordination and certification with a core central global office to ensure consistency and assurance of what the 'label' standards for.
- Transparency: FSC requires public summaries of forest management certification reports, controlled wood certification reports, risk assessments and audits; the system also requires a transparent dispute resolution process. This open and public approach encourages trust and open reporting.

However FSC isn't the only scheme. PEFC protects some 264 million ha of forest area, with 15,804 certificates of custody and with in excess of 750,000 forest owners. PEFC use a different approach emphasizing a grass root focus that are each developed independently from a set of core values, adapting to the needs of stakeholders but ensuring minimum standards. PEFC highlights that unique local circumstances requires specific solutions and standards:

> The forest ecosystem is highly complex, and influenced by numerous external factors. Similarly, different forest types in different regions of the world require different sustainable management strategies. This means that criteria for sustainable forest management must be constantly adapted to new circumstances. They must reflect the national context and the specific ecological and environmental conditions, as well as social, economic, political, cultural and spiritual dimensions.
>
> (Programme for the Endorsement
> of Forest Certification, 2015)

The PEFC program does not have a single standard but rather has a process to endorses national schemes that comply with PEFC's Sustainability

(continued)

(continued)

Benchmarks, globally recognized principles, guidelines and criteria developed by international and inter-governmental bodies 'reflecting the national context and the specific ecological and environmental conditions, as well as social, economic, political, cultural and spiritual dimensions' within input and consensus from stakeholders. Currently there are over 35 national schemes under the PEFC umbrella, offering tens of thousands of PEFC-certified products globally. This local-centric methodology allows flexibility in the approach focusing on the needs and threats to forests and does not impose a one size fits all standard.

In recent years the certification process has developed yet further. This is because forests play a critical role in mitigating climate change and as a carbon sink, soaking up carbon dioxide that would otherwise be free in the atmosphere and contribute to ongoing changes in climate patterns. It is estimated that 15 per cent of all greenhouse gas emissions are the result of deforestation. The Carbon Disclosure project in their Global Forests Report (2014) set out a 'Roadmap to deforestation-free supply chains – from commitments to action'. It offers advice to its 240 investors with US$15 trillion in assets, highlighting the links of service sector activities and investments to the impacts of the organizations they support:

- Commitments: The first step for companies is to make a public commitment to remove the commodity-linked deforestation embedded within their global supply chains.
- Targets: Effective implementation of a deforestation commitment requires a roadmap of specific, interim targets.
- Risk assessment: Understanding how your company may be exposed to the risks associated with deforestation is a critical scoping exercise and one that should be reviewed on a regular basis.
- Implementation: Acting to achieve corporate deforestation targets is an iterative process and can differ depending on the company concerned. Typically companies use a combination of certification, supply chain engagement and traceability.
- Leadership: Companies should be striving for leadership in their work towards removing commodity-driven deforestation, which will help unlock the many opportunities available to those working on sustainable commodities.
- The Road Map is a five step approach that that relates not only to driving improvements in carbon management and ensuring organizations minimize their contribution to deforestation, but could also be used as a template for driving change in any value chain.

Public register of corporate responsibility reports

The largest register of corporate responsibility reports past and present is available at www.corporateregister.com. This site provides an interesting insight into the approaches adopted by many some notable organizations; the majority of which are available free of charge – we recommend that you visit this website.

Auditing and verification

The International Register of Certificated Auditors (IRCA) formally approves auditors, and requires an ongoing programme of continuing professional development (CPD) for its registered auditors. Asbury (2013) provides a detailed review of certification and auditor registration bodies, along with an established approach to risk-based auditing.

Auditors provide independent verifications of the effectiveness of management systems used in organizations (activities, processes and services), providing independent assurance to top management. Such verifications can also be used to resolve conflicts of fact in society, the media and elsewhere. These verification processes are well established in the business-to-business procurement sector, but are (almost) unheard of in the end-user retail sector – for example, when was the last time you checked whether the manufacturer of a product you wanted to buy was certified to SA8000, AA1000APS or ISO 14001?

 Test your thinking 12

Nike

Nike Inc. produces footwear, clothing, equipment and accessory products for the sports and athletic market. We think it is the largest seller of such products in the world. Just about all of its products are manufactured by independent contractors, with footwear products, in particular, commonly being manufactured in developing countries.

What are the issues?

Nike has around 700 contracted factories, within which around 20 per cent of the workers are creating Nike products. Conditions for these workers have been a source of heated debate, with allegations made

(continued)

(continued)

by campaigners of poor conditions in which harassment and abuse are commonplace. Nike has sought to respond to these allegations by developing a code of conduct for all of its suppliers. In Indonesia, it was reported that:

> 30.2% of the workers had personally experienced, and 56.8% had observed, verbal abuse. An average of 7.8% of workers reported receiving unwelcome sexual comments, and 3.3% reported being physically abused. In addition, sexual trade practices in recruitment and promotion were reported by at least two workers in each of two different factories, although a subsequent investigation was unable to confirm this. 73.4% of workers are satisfied with their relationship with direct line supervisors, 67.8% are satisfied with management. The main concerns expressed by workers relate to their physical working environment.
>
> (Schanberg, 1996)

Nike's problems also related to a site in Mexico, which had experienced serious problems leading to labour disputes.

In both cases, Nike responded to the audit reports with a detailed corrective action plan.

What do the critics say?

Some critics accuse Nike of abandoning countries as better pay and employment rights are developed, in favour of countries such as China, where these features are presently perhaps less important.

The photograph in Figure 6.2, widely published in 1996, shows a child in Pakistan stitching Nike footballs. Other critics have suggested that Nike should publicize conditions in all its factories and allow independent inspection to verify them. They say that any auditing carried out by Nike should be made public. A lot of focus is given to wage rates paid by the company's suppliers. By and large, audits have found that wage rates are above the national legal minimum, but critics contend that this doesn't actually constitute a fair living wage.

What does Nike say?

Nike accuses critics of peddling inaccurate and old information. It points out that it hasn't 'abandoned countries' and that it remains in Taiwan and Korea, despite the higher wages and better labour rights.

Figure 6.2 Tariq, aged 12, stitching Nike footballs in Pakistan. Photo by Marie Dorigny.

Nike admits that the 1996 photograph documents what they describes as a 'large mistake' when they began to order footballs for the first time from a supplier in Pakistan. They now operate stitching centres that are confirmed not to be using child labour.

Nike believes that sharing factory locations with independent third parties on a confidential basis enables them to monitor their supply chain properly. As for wage rates, the company feels that establishing what constitutes a 'fair' wage is by no means as easy as its critics would have the public believe, and disparages the constant quoting of wage rates in US dollar equivalents, when these are meaningless given the different costs of living in the countries concerned.

Nike is also dismayed at how it has become the principal target of campaigners in this area. The company asks campaigners to look at its competitors as well and find out how many of them have taken the kind of measures that Nike has over the last few years.

This case study raises several questions, which we propose you consider and respond to:

(continued)

(continued)

1   What are the key CSR issues for Nike?
2   Do you think Nike has gone far enough in its supplier auditor program?
3   What else could Nike do in this regard?
4   What are the possible reasons Nike could have for not publishing the reports?
5   If Nike published the reports, do you think that pressure groups would believe them?
6   Why or why not?
7   Do you think pressure groups focus more on companies that claim to be good, rather than those who claim (or seem) to do nothing?

Auditing and validating claims of good deeds and on-the-ground performance is likely to remain an issue for some time. As Sir Winston Churchill said (see below), we are entering 'a period of consequences'. It would help us all to see greater adoption of agreed and common approaches, such as those noted in this chapter, backed up as necessary by a legal framework requiring organizations to maintain similar performance standards overseas as they do in our own country. We continue to look forward to seeing developments in this area in the coming years.

> The era of procrastination, of half-measures, of soothing and baffling expedients, of delays, is coming to a close. In its place, we are entering a period of consequences.
>
> (Sir Winston Churchill (1874–1965),
> later UK Prime Minister, in a speech in 1936)

Note

1   Money owed by workers to their masters from when they were 'bought' from their parents, or from another owner, which binds them to their master. By law, *peshgi* is banned in Pakistan, but the practice remains common. The masters call it an advance against wages, but few workers are ever able to repay the debt (see 'Bonded labour' in Chapter 8).

Chapter 7

The case against CSR

What has never been doubted has never been proven.

–Denis Diderot, 1713–1784

Around the world, some individuals and organizations believe that CSR is a self-serving and unnecessary burden. They believe that the principal reason companies are in business is to make profits for their shareholders, at any cost. They also believe that addressing issues commonly connected to CSR should be the responsibility of national governments and environmental (and other) charities, not private companies. The traditional skeptics' model of CSR either suggests that good business isn't about doing good, or that CSR is only about greenwash. As a CSR practioner we should see this as an exploration, to test our models, as Diderot highlights.

In today's tough financial climate, organizations need to focus on their core activities. As an agent of CSR, you need to be able to understand these arguments and develop strategies to deal with stakeholders' concerns – whether you think they're legitimate or not. Take, for example, the headline 'Recycling row as council pays £2m for SMALLER general-waste bins: Residents attack plan for slim versions to make them recycle more', *Mail Online* or 'Recycling Con' in the *Mail* on 9th February 2013, or the 'Recycling Fiasco' article in the *Mail on Sunday* on 4th January 2009. These outline how councils are having to pay substantial costs for recyclables as their value has fallen on world markets. Stakeholders will rightly question why they should be paying higher Council Tax and business rates to store this material – why can't it just be sent to landfill?

In this chapter, we'll ask you to consider questions and case studies so that you can develop your arguments in favour of doing the right thing.

Test your thinking 13

Consider each of the following arguments against CSR and prepare a positive response:

1   Businesses exist to make profit for their shareholders – not to support society.
2   It's the responsibility of the politicians to deal with all this stuff. It's not up to businesses to get involved.
3   Struggling businesses are just trying to survive hard times – they can't afford to do this.

Here are some key themes and possible responses to these questions.

1. Businesses exist to make profit for their shareholders – not to support society.

CSR is about balancing social, environmental and economic needs. Companies that are aware of the social climate can adapt to it, building customer loyalty and increasing market share. Many CSR factors are also about reducing overheads, such as resource consumption and energy use, and harnessing in-house potential through raising staff morale.

Ethical trading with suppliers and customers will also increase the long-term viability and success of the organization, through more closely aligned objectives, a more secure supply base and bringing the benefits to the whole of your supply chain.

2. It's the responsibility of the politicians to deal with all this stuff. It's not up to businesses to get involved.

Politicians are representatives of the community, including businesses. Many companies spend considerable time and money seeking to influence public policy in their area of interest. That area of interest can range far and wide – from international treaties on climate change, through to domestic policies on health (such as those relating to smoking) or transport. The lobbying activities of companies in these areas show that they do have a role, whether they like it or not.

CSR is not just about obeying the law and paying taxes; it's about managing risk and reputation, and investing in community resources on which you depend.

3. Struggling businesses are just trying to survive hard times – they can't afford to do this

If a company is struggling (and not just whining!), it's even more important to build a competitive advantage. If this same company ignores CSR issues, it's putting itself at an even greater risk – it may end up paying to clean up pollution or damage, being prosecuted and fined, or attracting unwelcome attention from environmental or human rights pressure groups and the media.

Losing or missing out on skilled employees by discriminating on the basis of race, sex, age or sexual orientation isn't good for business either. Well-qualified individuals have a choice about where they earn their living. Will they work for an irresponsible company?

An irresponsible organization also risks losing an increasingly large group of customers who prefer to purchase sustainable goods and services.

All of these negative impacts contribute to the economic and environmental downturn of an area, leading to more recruitment problems. If it doesn't optimize efficiency, the organization also becomes less competitive as it's forced to spend more than it would otherwise have needed on manufacturing, disposal of waste, energy and other resources.

We should now consider each of these arguments in more detail:

Maximizing profits

Firstly that businesses are there to make a profit, failure to maximize profit is not to achieve what the shareholders demand; anything less is technically theft.

As a simple capitalist message, this argument seems plausible, if lacking in morality; but that is of course the point, profit it is argued should be without morals. However this argument comes with a number of flaws; firstly that all games have to have rules. The concept that not maximizing profit is theft highlights that theft could be the best way to maximize profits (not that the authors are suggesting this). Illegal activities could maximize income without significant overheads, however this introduces a risk, in this case of being caught and put into custody, being fined and having assets confiscated under the Proceeds of Crime Act. As we introduced right at the start of this book, CSR should be viewed as a risk management exercise with the potential risks and rewards evaluated. The criminal act would not pass this test as the risk outweighs the reward, and therefore the potential for a profitable reward should always be balanced with risk. So we can see that all markets need rules and regulation if it is not to descend into an anarchic state, with either a lawless Wild West approach or monopolies charging exorbitant prices for basic goods.

This leads into the second issue with the 'maximize profits' concept, that the failure to manage CSR issues is likely to cost your organization over the longer term. Investment in workforce health and safety delivers returns over the longer term, supply chain management helps to secure a stronger supply base, waste minimization and carbon management can directly reduce overheads contributing to the bottom line. CSR programmes can also support marketing campaigns to increase sales (consider Marks and Spencer's Plan A, or Kenco's Gang Culture Initiative). The skill comes in selecting the right material issues and optimizing the balance between minimizing the negative impacts of an organization and maximizing the benefits.

In fact, the term 'material' comes from a material fact that should be disclosed to shareholders to support investment decisions. Consider any of the major incidents: Bhopal, Rani Plaza, Piper Alpha with the benefit of hindsight – was the risk reward balance right? For other shareholders they have invested in a portfolio with CSR claims, their moral compass has guided them to balance economic gains with a social responsibility; it could be argued that not to give these shareholders CSR is mis-selling the product.

Super-capitalism

The second argument is that it is the politician's job to deal with CSR, not organizations, and that companies being encouraged to act as moral beings with social responsibilities diverts public attention from the task of establishing such laws and rules in the first place. Reich (2008) in his paper 'The Case against Corporate Social Responsibility reports that:

> Numerous 'social auditors' now measure how well corporations have achieved it [CSR], and hundreds of companies produce glossy company reports touting the company's dedication to it. Innumerable NGOs – non-government organizations, with full time staffs, websites, newsletters, and funding appeals – have sprung up to develop codes of corporate conduct on aspects of it, and rate corporations on their adherence to it. At least eight hundred mutual funds worldwide say they are devoted to it. The United Nations' Global Compact, launched at Davos in 1999, enumerates goals for it, and by 2006 more than 3,000 firms had signed on. The European Union has established a set of norms for it. Great Britain has a minister for it. Products are now labelled as complying with it.

Most of this is in earnest. Much is sincere. Some of it has had a positive impact. But almost all has occurred outside of the democratic process. To view it as a new form of democratic capitalism is to fail to understand the logic of super-competitive capitalism, what I've termed "super-capitalism." It is also to divert attention from the more difficult but more important job of establishing laws that protect and advance the common good.

Reich argues that CSR of organizations takes the responsibility from the democratic process to make and enforce law on behalf of society, and discusses that in some organizations CSR is 'used' or even abused to meet corporate aims, to make more profit and to quell negative stories. 'Super-capitalism' views the world as being dominated by corporate bodies that influence and lobby governments, setting the agendas in CSR subverting the process in which organizations lead governments, rather than governments setting the rules and leading the people.

This argument places politicians in a different world to the rest of us, why should it be down to a few elected officials to make the difficult choices and how could they possibly develop laws and requirements on organizations that are fair to all and meet the needs of everyone? Organizations are the ones with the most information about the situation, making decisions every day, in health and safety we use the concept of Reasonably Practicable, in environment Best Available Techniques and Best Practicable Environmental Option; even in employment law we use the terms 'unfair dismissal' and 'constructive dismissal'; these require professionals to make judgments based on the nuances of the situations, rather than leaving this to politicians. Politicians have to appeal to the voters, with policies that will get them re-elected within terms of five years or less, whilst many business owners recognize the importance of longer-term strategies if the organization is to survive for the next generation. Every day, consumers vote with their feet as to which products and services meet their needs, the 'buy local' and 'farmers markets' movements highlights the potential of this grassroots super-capitalist approach in action.

Financial burden

The third argument raised was that struggling business cannot afford to invest in 'doing good'. The altruistic model of charitable giving doesn't work for any size of organization, it is rightly seen as a token gesture and throwing money at the problem. The way to maximize benefits for the organization and the community is to focus on those issues that will deliver win-win results. As Corporate Watch (2015) proposes, which of the following statements do not hold to be true for small organizations in-relation to CSR?:

- Times are hard; therefore it is in my interest to pollute more and run an increased risk of prosecutions and fines, not to mention attracting the attention of environmental pressure groups.
- Times are hard; therefore I can afford to lose some of my most talented people – serving or potential – by erecting barriers on the basis of race, gender, age or sexual orientation. And it doesn't matter if employment tribunals occur as a result of my poor employment practices.
- Times are hard; therefore I need to ignore changing values in my customer base towards socially responsible goods and services. I can keep making things just the way I always have.
- Times are hard; so I can ignore the fact that the local communities around my plant are poor living environments with low education achievement, meaning that my best staff won't want to live in them and our future staff will need supplementary training in basic skills such as literacy, which they should be getting at school. Our company can be an island of prosperity in a sea of deprivation.

CSR projects must be carefully identified, planned and monitored. Projects must be an investment with real returns if they are to be sustained, with a marketing plan for a brand or product, a recruitment or promotion process or a new capital investment. These projects would not be viewed as 'doing good', but rather part of business growth; similarly so CSR should be viewed. CSR issues, such as workforce rights, ethical trading or community impacts should be assessed as risks, if a struggling organization does not comply with the law on these matters it may be prosecuted; if the struggling organizations doesn't pay its staff correctly, recruitment, retention and productivity may struggle; if a building contractor does not comply with noise restrictions, the client may receive complaints from the community, making it less likely to use or recommend them.

> Social responsibility is not, in itself, a guarantee of profits. Lack of concerns for the impact of your operations is hardly one either. Badly executed, either approach can destroy value.
> (Mallenbaker.net, 2015b)

Our DTRT Model supports organizations to make decisions to identify, manage and monitor the risks to its organization for long-term benefit. Other texts may look at whether maximizing win-win situations is truly CSR, but if it delivers benefits and minimizes negative impacts in all the significant impact areas, it is a practical place to start.

Case Study 7.1 The Saudi Arabian Oil Company, Saudi Arabia

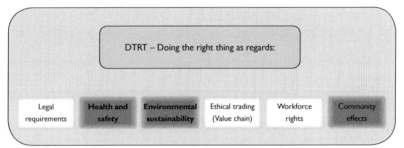

DTRT – Doing the right thing as regards:

| Legal requirements | Health and safety | Environmental sustainability | Ethical trading (Value chain) | Workforce rights | Community effects |

Saudi Aramco

The Saudi Arabian Oil Company Aramco (Saudi Aramco/Aramco) is a petroleum and natural gas company based in Dhahran, Saudi Arabia. Saudi Aramco's value has been estimated at anywhere between US$1.25 trillion and US$7 trillion, making it the world's most valuable company (FT, 2010).

Aramco has both the world's largest proven crude oil reserves, at more than 260 billion barrels, and usually, the largest daily oil production. It owns and operates all energy resources in the Kingdom of Saudi Arabia (KSA). According to a 2015 Forbes report, Aramco is said to be the world's largest oil and gas company.

(continued)

(continued)

Saudi Aramco operates the world's largest single hydrocarbon network, the Master Gas System. Its crude oil production total is 3.4 billion barrels per year, and it manages around 108 oil and gas fields in KSA. Aramco operates Ghawar field, the world's largest onshore oil field, and Safaniya field, the world's largest offshore oil field.

Health and safety management

Aramco has developed its own health and safety management system, comprising 11 management elements and 85 expectations. The 11 management system elements are as follows:

1 leadership and accountability;
2 risk assessment and management;
3 communications;
4 competency and training;
5 asset integrity;
6 safe operations;
7 contractors, suppliers and others;
8 emergency preparedness;
9 incident reporting and analysis;
10 community awareness (off-the-job safety);
11 continuous improvement.

Example health and safety programs

SAFETY AWARENESS CAMPAIGNS

To help foster a culture of safety and amplify the impact of safety knowledge and practices, Aramco conducts safety awareness campaigns at selected locations Kingdom-wide. Through these efforts, more than 2,000 employees, dependents, students and orphans participated in the campaigns, which cover home fire safety, electrical safety, emergency procedures, hand hygiene, fire extinguisher use and driving safety. To enhance safety awareness, demonstrations of first aid and CPR are conducted. Training sessions for contractor employees cover subjects such as safety and behavioral training, heart saver first aid and CPR, hazard communication, and other topics related to firefighting, evacuation, hydrogen sulfide (H_2S) prevention, basic life support, automated external defibrillator use, vehicle safety and arc flash safety training. Aramco completed a total of 5,126 contractor safety sessions in 2014.

SAFETY HOUSE PROGRAMME

Safety houses are facilities that replicate a standard Saudi Aramco house in employee communities. They feature informative photographs, safety statistics and examples of proper and improper furniture placement to demonstrate safety measures within the house. The safety house programme covers fire safety for the entire house in an atmosphere designed to promote learning. Information on first aid procedures for burns is also available. Other safety topics addressed in the safety houses include household chemicals, electrical safety, gas exposure, medication safe practices and CPR training. An estimated 3,200 people visited one of the seven safety houses during 2014.

TRAFFIC SAFETY

Motor vehicle accidents are a major threat to the safety of Aramco employees off the job: Saudi Arabia has one of the highest traffic fatality rates among developing countries. Traffic safety initiatives date back more than 50 years when it was recognized that to change driving habits in the Kingdom, major employers must lead by example. There is still much work to be done, and through the Traffic Safety Signature Program, the company works with its stakeholders to increase the impact of its initiatives in the "four Es" of traffic safety: Education, Enforcement, Engineering and Emergency Care.

CHILDREN

In an initiative to replace unsafe playground equipment, company inspections identified 69 elementary schools that needed new equipment, shade coverings and rubberized flooring in playgrounds. By the end of 2014, it had supported upgrades in 16 schools, were working on 18 more and planning for 11 schools in 2015. The overall program is scheduled for completion in 2018.

Aramco also replaced the fire alarm systems in 89 company-built public schools, with 32 additional schools planned for 2015.

After a successful pilot to improve the traffic flow in the parking areas of four company-built public schools, the company coordinated with local traffic police and concerned municipalities to improve a further 26 school parking areas, and another 30 schools are planned for 2015. This initiative will improve safety as children arrive and depart from their schools.

(continued)

(continued)

FIRE SAFETY

At Aramco facilities, the company applies international fire safety standards in the design, construction, and operation of facilities. Engineering standards, operating and maintenance procedures, and emergency response training and planning all play a critical role in the prevention and control of fires.

The company conducts fire protection outreach programs throughout the year to inspect facilities and buildings for fire hazards and to educate employees and the public about fire safety issues. In addition to a dedicated, annual Fire Protection Week campaign, company fire protection personnel participated in the company's Civil Defense Day and summer programmes.

In 2014, the company's smoke detector campaign reached 800,000 people in nine cities around the Kingdom. Visitors participated in activities related to smoke detector information and skill building and 12,000 smoke detectors were distributed.

Environmental management

Aramco has had an environmental policy since 1963, revised several times with the current edition endorsed in 1999. In February 2011, Aramco published its environmental management system corporate framework. This is very closely aligned to ISO 14001:2004, although external certification of its facilities is not expected or required by the company. Around 250 EMS Coordinators have been recruited and trained to lead implementation, and an Environmental Protection Department (known widely inside the company as EPD) acts as an 'external' assessor (auditor).

Results of EMS implementation assessments are included in the Facility Environmental Performance Index (FEPI), in two categories:

1 Performance;
2 Initiatives.

PERFORMANCE

For Performance, facilities receive a score of 1 out of 5 if their system has been approved by EPD but has not yet been assessed. For each of the 4 achievement levels, the points range from 2 to 5, with Level 1 receiving the highest number of points. These scores will remain the same each year until the next assessment is scheduled (typically 3–5 years).

INITIATIVES

Facilities receive FEPI Initiative points for demonstrating improvements in their system, using the results of the previous assessment as the baseline. They must submit evidence of initiatives planned an implemented along with the assessment results as a FEPI initiative package.

Operational Excellence – OE

In 2014, Aramco embraced a new, integrated management system standard called Operational Excellence; assisted by McKinsey & Co consultants. OE embraces four objectives of cost and profitability, efficiency, reliability and HSE implemented through 13 enabling elements and processes. Environmental management (aligned to ISO 14001) is Element 5.2, and its environmental programs are implemented under authority of this Element.

Example environmental programs

Aramco is establishing a wildlife sanctuary in the Rub' al-Khali near its Shaybah facility, planting hundreds of thousands of mangroves along targeted shores of the Arabian Gulf and establishing artificial reefs.

The company is engaged in promoting the reduction of energy intensity across the Kingdom by advocating responsible policies, public education and energy innovation. A number of the initiatives are in close cooperation with the government.

Advances are made in areas such as reducing the energy intensity of its operations and producing more cleaner-burning natural gas for domestic industry, reduction of flaring, water conservation and recycling.

In residential communities and commercial offices, the company replaced half a million incandescent light bulbs with LED bulbs, saving 30 million kilowatt hours of energy. Millions of Saudis received energy-efficiency tips through its public awareness programmes.

Strategic investments in studying the commercial-scale adaption of renewable sources of energy — primarily solar and wind power — will help grow a clean energy sector in the Kingdom.

Example: CSR risk review – BP risk and reward

BP is a leading petroleum company. Its main businesses are onshore and offshore exploration and production of oil and natural gas, refining and marketing, and petrochemicals. In January 2007, BP Amoco was one of the largest companies in the world, with a capitalization of $232bn. It had a financial turnover that dwarfs that of some small countries. As a petroleum company, it is directly linked to the exploration and production of products from fossil fuels, which in turn are linked to major global environmental challenges.

In 2007, the company had a solar energy business, which was one of the world's largest manufacturers of photovoltaic modules and systems. Recognizing the potential long-term business benefits and in response to short-term pressures, BP achieved a high profile with a major and controversial rebranding to go 'Beyond Petroleum'. In a $200m advertising campaign organized by the advertising firm Olgilvy & Mather, the company transformed its corporate brand insignia from a shield to the more wholesomely natural green, yellow and white sunburst, and it committed to become a sustainable energy company rather than simply a petroleum company. It inspired and impressed some, and irritated others.

Critics at the time pointed out that BP's claim to be a global leader in producing the cleanest-burning fossil fuel (natural gas) is only an incremental improvement over oil at best, and a distraction from getting away from fossil fuels, at worst. BP, they claim, has co-opted the language of the environmentalist without a real commitment to deliver, and with the events in the Gulf of Mexico in 2010 (covered by Case Study 7.2) it would be hard to envisage BP making such a claim today.

As for BP's assertion that was the largest producer of solar energy in the world, they point out that achieving this number one position was trivially easy. It acquired the Solarex solar energy corporation at a cost of $45m – a minute fraction of the $26.5bn it spent on buying Amoco to increase its petroleum capacity. In fact, it's been widely speculated that the company spent more on its new 'eco-friendly' logo than it has so far on solar energy investments! By December 2011, BP announced it would be exiting the solar market.

In a wider context there are very few aspects of how a company behaves as a corporate citizen that don't apply to a company of the size and nature of BP. The most significant of these is the sheer environmental impact. This is felt not only in the extraction of petroleum and the energy used in BP's own operations, but also, and more significantly, through climate change caused by the company's customers using its products.

A company with such extensive operations in developing countries also needs to be careful about its approach to human rights and ethical business practices. BP will have significant impacts on local communities – both as a huge employer and through the nature of its on-the-ground operations. It should seriously expect to seek to reduce any negative impacts there and to invest meaningfully in those communities.

BP, as a global player, is immensely powerful. It has no democratic legitimacy, but is often better able to lead on the social development of the planet than national governments. This is a dilemma it needs to handle carefully.

Figure 7.1 Macondo Well Disaster.

The rebranding was a high-risk plan, as the core of the business was highly impacting in the exploration, extraction and use of its product. But BP was in a culture of taking risks: in the aftermath of the Macondo Well Disaster reporters investigated BP's approach, and in her article 'In BP's Record, a History of Boldness and Costly Blunders' Lyall (2010) reported:

> The problems at Thunder Horse [a BP drilling platform] were not an anomaly, but a warning that BP was taking too many risks and cutting corners in pursuit of growth and profits, according to analysts, competitors and former employees. Despite a catalogue of crises and near misses in recent years, BP has been chronically unable or unwilling to learn from its mistakes, an examination of its record shows.
>
> 'They were very arrogant and proud and in denial,' said Steve Arendt, a safety specialist who assisted the panel appointed by BP to investigate the company's refineries after a deadly 2005 explosion at its Texas City, Tex., facility. 'It is possible they were fooled by their success.'
>
> Indeed, there was a great deal of success to admire. In little more than a decade, BP grew from a middleweight into the industry's second-largest

company, behind only Exxon Mobil, with soaring profits, fat dividends and a share price to match.

From its base in London, the company struck bold deals in politically volatile areas like Angola and Azerbaijan and pushed technology to the limit in the remotest reaches of Alaska and the deepest waters of the Gulf of Mexico — 'the tough stuff that others cannot or choose not to do,' as its chief executive, Tony Hayward, once put it.

The company also led an industry wave of cost cutting and consolidation. It took over American competitors like Amoco and Atlantic Richfield and eliminated tens of thousands of jobs in several rounds, streamlining management but forcing the company to rely more heavily on outside contractors.

For a long time, BP's strategy seemed to pay off. But on April 20, the nightmare situation occurred: the Deepwater Horizon drilling rig exploded, killing 11 workers and sending millions of gallons of oil gushing from BP's Macondo well like so much black poison.

(Lyall, 2010)

Test your thinking 14

Find out more for yourself by looking at the two following sources of information, and then answer the questions beneath.

1   BP's website dealing with key CSR issues can be found at http://www.bp.com/en/global/corporate/sustainability.html.
2   There's an alternative perspective on BP's profits and environmental costs start at https://en.wikipedia.org/wiki/BP and then explore further, thinking about the source, legitimacy and reliability of the authors.

1   What do you consider to be the key CSR issues for BP?
2   What do you think where the key motivating factors behind BP's rebranding?
3   How has the incidents that BP has been involved with changed your image of BP?
4   Why did BP see the risk reward balance, differently to how we might view it now?
5   Do you think that BP had identified the right CSR issues to tackle?

6   Do you think companies such as BP are a net contributor or consumer in society?
7   What evidence is there that BP have learnt the lessons, since 2011?
8   With the benefit of hindsight, if you could go back to 2007 what advice would you give BP?

This time, we haven't provided any sample answers, because there are few right or wrong ones! The idea of the exercise is to encourage you to elaborate your thoughts and ideas on CSR. (The following Case Study 7.2 provides additional perspective on BP).

We also urge you to look at other organizations from a similar perspective – perhaps starting with your own. We think that a competent practitioner should know the arguments against, CSR as well as for it.

Case Study 7.2   When risk and reward fall out of balance, Macondo, Gulf of Mexico

In April 2010, 11 people lost their lives when the Macondo oil rig burst into flames, in the Gulf of Mexico. Yet it is not the loss of Jason Anderson, Dale Burkeen, Donald Clark, Stephen Curtis, Roy Wyatt Kemp, Karl Kleppinger, Gordon Jones, Blair Manuel, Dewey Revette, Shane Roshto and Adam Weise that will be remembered, it will be the size of the spillage; a disaster movie script the media played out in real time, as BP, Transocean and Halliburton tried to stop the release of oil from the failed pressure relief valve. This case study reviews that fateful incident, and draws lessons in risk management, value chain management and media relations, with an insight into international politics when disaster strikes.

Building on the Deepwater Horizon oil rig commenced in December 1998 in Ulsan, South Korea, by Hyundai Heavy Industries Shipyard, and was delivered in February 2001 at a value of $560m dollars. A decade later in January 2011, the Presidential Report, 'Deep Water', stated:

On April 20, 2010, the 126 workers on the BP Deepwater Horizon were going about the routines of completing an exploratory oil well—unaware of impending disaster. What unfolded would have unknown impacts shaped by the Gulf region's distinctive cultures, institutions, and geography—and by economic forces resulting from the unique coexistence of energy resources, bountiful fisheries

(continued)

(continued)

> and wildlife, and coastal tourism. The oil and gas industry, long lured by Gulf reserves and public incentives, progressively developed and deployed new technologies, at ever-larger scales, in pursuit of valuable energy supplies in increasingly deeper waters farther from the coastline. Regulators, however, failed to keep pace with the industrial expansion and new technology—often because of industry's resistance to more effective oversight. The result was a serious, and ultimately inexcusable, shortfall in supervision of offshore drilling that played out in the Macondo well blowout and the catastrophic oil spill that followed.
>
> (National Commission on the BP Deepwater Horizon Oil Spill and Offshore Drilling, 2011)

Deepwater drilling is a complex operation and the Deepwater Horizon rig was at the cutting edge. In August 2009, the media reported that the rig had drilled to a new record depth of 35,050 feet vertical depth in 4,130 feet of water; but working at the boundaries of technology comes with higher risk, not only in the risk you knowingly take, but also in the risk of the unknown. The immediate cause of the incident was a lack of pressure containment in the well, releasing hydrocarbons into the marine ecosystem above. Operating at such great depths represented a range of challenges to contain those pressures, but the cement in the well, the drilling muds and the blowout preventer had been designed and constructed specifically for it. However, the risks associated with each element had been under appreciated and additional controls had not been fully considered and therefore not implemented. In addition to this, due to the working environment at sea bed, meant that once a pressure failure had occurred, stopping the flow was no easy task. The Presidential report concluded that there was evidence of:

- Limited formal, disciplined analysis of risk factors of the cement job.
- Insufficient communication that there should be elevated vigilance of the containment control measures.
- A lack of understanding of the relative difficulty of the cementing plan before, during, or after the job, or recommending any post-cementing measures.

Once the incident occurred the media played out the story in real time and the owners, operators, regulators, Prime Ministers and Presidents were drawn into a disaster movie script. They were under significant pressure to act, to stop the flow of oil, to blame others and to demonstrate leadership. Below is an edited timeline from a UK national newspaper, it is reproduced here not to agree or disagree on the events or opinions expressed by any of the parties involved, but to ascertain the potential for CSR issues to escalate from one organization's issue to an international incident.

- **22 April**: Deepwater Horizon rig sinks in 5,000ft of water. Reports of a five-mile-long oil slick. Search-and-rescue operations by the US National Response Team begin.
- **23 April**: The US coast guard suspends the search for missing workers, who are all presumed dead. The rig is found upside down about a quarter-mile from the blowout preventer.
- **26 April**: BP's shares fall 2 per cent amid fears that the cost of cleanup and legal claims will hit the London-based company hard.
- **28 April**: The coastguard says the flow of oil is 5,000bpd, five times greater than first estimated, after a third leak is discovered.
- **29 April**: President Obama says BP is responsible for the cleanup.
- **30 April**: An Obama aide says no drilling will be allowed in new areas until the cause of the Deepwater Horizon accident is established. Safety inspections of all 30 deepwater drilling rigs and 47 deepwater production platforms are ordered.
- **2 May**: US officials close areas affected by the spill to fishing. Obama visits the Gulf coast to see cleanup efforts first hand.
- **4 May**: BP executives face Congress in a closed session, as the White House backs a Senate proposal to increase the limit on liability payouts from $75m to $10bn (£6.5bn) for the cost of a spill.
- **6 May**: Toxic, pink, oily seawater washes ashore on the Chandeleur Islands off the Louisiana coast, an important nesting and breeding area for many bird species. Hayward tells the BBC that the blow-out preventer owned by Transocean was at fault for the leak. BP, he said, 'will be judged not on the basis of an accident that, you know, frankly was not our accident'. Analysts put the cost of the spill for BP at £15bn.
- **11 May**: At a hearing before the Senate committee Halliburton, which cemented BP's well, claims to have met BP's stated requirements for the task and cites the failure of Transocean's blowout preventer. Transocean's CEO says the blowout preventer was successfully tested a week before the accident; he also blames BP and Halliburton for the inadequate cementing believed to have led to the explosion. BP's president says that Transocean, as owner/operator of the drilling rig, is responsible for safety.

(continued)

(continued)

- **14 May**: Obama complains: 'I did not appreciate what I considered to be a ridiculous spectacle during the congressional hearings into this matter. You had executives of BP and Transocean and Halliburton falling over each other to point the finger of blame at somebody else . . . it is pretty clear that the system failed, and it failed badly'.
- **18 May**: As the spill continues to spread, the no fishing zone is doubled to 19 per cent of the Gulf waters.
- **20 May**: Experts testifying at the congressional hearing put the figure at 20,000–100,000 barrels per day.
- **3 June**: BP faces political flack over its decision to pay out more than $10bn (£6.8bn) in dividends to shareholders, despite the deepening crisis.
- **6 June**: BP announces the containment cap is capturing 10,000 barrels of oil a day; approximately half the total amount being leaked.
- **11 June**: David Cameron, the UK Prime Minster, calls BP's chairman, Carl-Henric Svanberg, to a meeting at Downing Street to discuss the oil disaster.
- **14 June** – Obama compares the BP oil spill to 9/11.
- **16 June**: BP agrees to a $20bn (£13.5bn) down payment towards compensation for victims of the oil spill.
- **18 June**: BP's credit rating is downgraded by Moody's after expressing concern at the escalating cost of the cleanup and the potential cost of litigation claims.
- **19 June**: One of BP's partners, Anadarko Petroleum, refuses to accept any responsibility for the Deepwater Horizon explosion, despite owning a quarter of the well. Its chief executive, Jim Hackett, says BP's actions probably amounted to 'gross negligence or willful misconduct.'
- **25 June**: BP shares hit a 14-year low of 304p after the cleanup bill reaches $2.35bn.
- **28 June**: Russia's top energy official says he expects Hayward to step down soon. Protesters disrupt Tate Britain's party celebrating ten years of BP sponsorship, throwing molasses over the steps of the gallery.
- **5 July**: BP announces the cost of the oil spill has now risen to over $3bn. The company asks its partners, Anadarko and Mitsui Oil Exploration, to contribute almost $400m.
- **15 July**: Hillary Clinton pledges to looks into claims BP lobbied for the release of the Lockerbie bomber [a terrorist incident that killed over 250 people].

- **15 July:** BP stops the flow of oil for the first time in 87 days.
- **21 July:** BP admits to using Photoshop to exaggerate the level of activity at the Gulf oil spill command center. The picture, posted on the company's website, shows staff monitoring ten giant video screens. In reality, three of the screens were blank.

(The Guardian, 2010)

The spill was the largest accidental release the oil sector had known, with estimated four million barrels of oil being discharged. US Courts have fined BP a record $1.25bn in criminal fines, two BP employees have been indicted on manslaughter charges and a BP executive has been indicted on charges that he lied to authorities about his work estimating the Gulf spill rate. The scale of the environmental and social impact is hard to estimate, but the scale of the economic impacts provides a degree of insight. According to BP'S own figures it has spent more than $14bn on the cleanup, with over 70 million personnel hours cleaning up the impact of the spill. This can be more than doubled for other costs, as illustrated in the table below:

Table 7.1 BP's payments related to Gulf Coast recovery

Activity (as at 31 December 2014)	Funding
Response and cleanup	$14 billion+
Claims, advances and settlements	$13.1 billion
Funding for the natural resource damage assessment process	$1 billion+
Early restoration projects *(approximate cost of approved projects)*	$698 million
State-led tourism campaigns	$179 million
State-led seafood marketing programmes	$48.5 million
State-led seafood testing	$25.3 million

(BP, 2015a)

However this is not the complete picture, as these figures come from BP. As a Louisianan court 2014 found that BP was 67 per cent responsible for the accident, additional costs have also been incurred by the rig owner Transocean (which was found to be 30 per cent responsible) and Halliburton, which manufactured the cement that failed as a critical barrier in the well (3 per cent responsible).

The social costs to the region can be linked to the range of claims that have been received, which include: seafood fishing losses, business

(continued)

(continued)

losses in sectors such as tourism, individual economic loss, loss of subsistence, vessel physical damage, costal and wetlands property damage, as well as property sales losses.

With hindsight it is easy to see the risk-reward balance was incorrect, but the culture in the sector was wrong and the regulatory process was not keeping pace with technology. As the demand for oil and gas continues, so more ecologically and socially sensitive environments will be explored; sufficient risk management of the known and potential impacts need to be carefully evaluated if the correct balance is to be achieved. The Deep Water Horizon incident highlights how organizations will be held criminally and socially accountable when incidents occur, and as the Board that investigated the loss of the Columbia space shuttle noted, 'complex systems almost always fail in complex ways' (U.S House Committee on Science and Technology, 1986).

In the years 1846 to date, the ten hottest years on record have been in the last 14 years.

(*An Inconvenient Truth*, 2006)

Chapter 8

Opportunities in the supply chain

> With great power, there must also come great responsibility!
> –Spider-Man (attributed to Lee, S., and Ditko, S., 1962)

The core principle of CSR concerns managing our relations with others to minimize the negative and maximize the positive. As stated in Lee and Ditko's Spider-Man, 'with great power comes great responsibility.' One of the most direct ways that any organization can interact with others is through its supply chain (aka value chain).

A supply chain is all the links in a product's life cycle that bring the product or service to the customer. This includes the raw materials consumed by your organization, all the manufacturing and quality control processes, delivery to the point of consumption and subsequent disposal. This supply chain creates a 'cradle-to-grave' continuum. All organizations in a supply chain are linked, and they depend on one another in order to operate. The managers of these relationships should focus on two key directions:

1 Purchasing or procurement; looking upstream.
2 Sales and customer service, concentrating on the downstream processes.

In this chapter, we'll look at how suppliers and customers could choose – or be influenced – to interact in positive ways with your organization, and how their decisions can be associated with positive or negative outcomes. We'll consider the responsibilities your organization has within its supply chain and the benefits of promoting CSR among your supply chain contacts.

The essence of business

Organizations generally exist to provide goods and services. Businesses aim to make a profit from doing this. Providing goods and services involves interactions between two or more parties, where money (or other reimbursement) is exchanged as payment for the supply of the goods or services. Organizations usually need to buy a wide range of goods and services to operate – e.g. raw materials, electricity and water. However, as this provision could be open to abuse, the concept of a contract or legally binding promise – bound by the rules of offer, acceptance and consideration – has been developed and enforced through the ages. The principle of a contract is that a supplier of goods or services agrees to deliver products of the right quantity and right quality at the right time in exchange for the agreed right price.

> In my culture . . . a good agreement is self-enforcing because both parties go away smiling and are happy to see that each of us is smiling. If one smiles and the other scowls, the agreement will not stick, lawyers or no lawyers.
>
> (Handy, 1994)

This pure capitalism has to have its boundaries. We should remember that individuals will try to gain profit at the expense of others – some legally but others illegally – even within this framework of contract and ownership. There is often significant potential for one party to gain an upper hand over another, and you should question whether your organization abuses its purchasing power.

Let's consider what is, for most people, the most abhorrent trade – slavery. In Chapter 2, we outlined the abolition of slavery in the UK and then in the British colonies in the nineteenth century. It's also prohibited by:

- the Universal Declaration of Human Rights, 1948;
- the UN Supplementary Convention on the Abolition of Slavery, 1956.

But slavery is still practiced. In bonded labour, workers are deceived into taking a loan for immigration, transit or medical care. They're then forced to work long hours, seven days a week, for up to 365 days a year. They receive basic food and shelter as 'payment' for their work, but may never pay off the loan, which can be passed down for generations. Forced labour affects people who are illegally recruited by individuals, governments or political parties and forced to work – sometimes under threats of violence or other penalties.

In slavery by descent, people are either born into a slave class or are from an ethnic, economic or other group that society views as suited to being used as slave labour.

Trafficking involves the transport and/or trade of people from one area to another for the purpose of forcing them into slavery, including the sex trade. While we trust that it's unlikely that anyone reading this book will be involved in trafficking women into bonded prostitution, your organization may be supporting other human or environmental bad practices through your supply chain selections. Think about these questions:

- Do you drink coffee? Was the price you paid for it fair to the producer?
- How, and by whom, were the clothes you're wearing now made?

Figure 8.1 Would you want your brand showing here?

- Are you wearing jewellery? In what conditions was the gold mined?
- Does your paper come from recycled or sustainably managed sources?
- What are working conditions like in your suppliers' premises? Are they safe and healthy?
- Are your suppliers or customers causing pollution?

Case study 8.1 relates to the issue of supply chain management. The Rani Plaza disaster is a classic example of the need to engage with the supply chain. Other case studies, such as BP, Macando (Case Study 7.2) and the link between consumers to growers relating to the coffee sector (Case Study 9.1) also offer practical lessons in the importance of supply chain management.

Case Study 8.1   Rani Plaza disaster, Bangladesh

In April 2013, a structure in Bangladesh collapsed, killing more than 1100 workers. The building contained a garment factory that supplied clothes to international high street fashion brands. The incident demonstrated how globalization had shrunk the world, linking some of the poorest communities on the globe to consumers in some of the wealthiest. The collapse raised questions not only about the operations of the

(continued)

(continued)

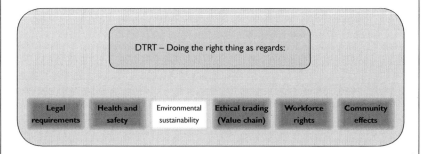

high street names, but also the responsibilities and standards they apply in sourcing goods. The world of fashion inherently has a high turnover in styles, and the complexity of the situation highlights that companies would have done more harm than good if they choose not to engage with the factories and just walk away. So what can be learnt from the public attitudes, media attention and shareholders responses to this incident?

The Rani Plaza building was located in the city of Dhaka, Bangladesh with around 4000 other clothing factories supporting Bangladesh's trade in garment manufacture, one of the world's largest exporters of apparel and clothing, employing over four million people in the country. The factories inside the building made outfits for a broad range of global brands, including Walmart, Matalan, Primark, Monsoon and Benetton, and similar surrounding factories supplied many other brands as well, providing clothing for the global demand in high turnover fashion. The Rana Plaza itself housed over 5000 textile workers in converted factories in a structure originally designed for offices and schools. The upper four floors had been adapted into factories without a permit, with diesel generators supplying the power, which created vibrations the structure was not designed to withstand.

To compound the issues of the four-storey extension, the original structure had been reportedly built on sub-standard foundations, either on a water course or on areas backfilled with refuse. It has also been suggested that the materials used in the construction where alleged to have been of substandard quality. On the days before the incident took place, operatives and managers noticed large fractures in the building, but despite the concerns of staff, they were compelled to go inside, with threats that failure to turn up for work would result in losing a whole month's pay. After a second review of the cracks it was deemed that the building was safe to use, in contrary to the initial report.

Unsurprisingly these factors came together to create a tragedy.

At 8.57am on the morning of 24th April 2013, the building collapsed with an estimated 3122 workers inside. Shortly before the collapse, the power had gone out and the generators on the roof had started up, creating vibrations that acted as shock waves to the already stressed and fractured structure. A pillar in one corner of the building gave way with a thunderous shudder, initiating a domino of storey collapses, as each level weighed heavy on the fragile supporting structure below. In a scene similar to an earthquake, the toll of this man-made disaster is counted – 1130 lives lost, many more injured and uncountable numbers of dependents in Bangladesh's hand-to-mouth existence affected.

In the aftermath of such an event, what should the international clothing sector response be? The initial response, to those who do not understand the complexities, is to disengage with this value chain. As the customer, we have a duty of care not to use contractors and suppliers who use disreputable practices, but CSR is more nuanced; what will the impact on the local communities in a least developed nation if multinationals disinvest?

Over the past two decades, the textile industry has been the main driver for sustained economic growth in Bangladesh, which has seen poverty reduce from 60 per cent to 30 per cent of the population. The value chain supports around 40 million jobs indirectly (as quote in *The Guardian*, 2013a). Disinvestment in Bangladesh would have a greater impact than continuing to support it, hurting the people who we're trying to protect the most.

(continued)

(continued)

One organization heavily associated with the incident was Primark, a high street fashion retailer, as one of its suppliers, New Wave Bottoms, were based on the second floor of the Rani Plaza. Within less than a month of the incident, Primark signed an industry accord to remain in Bangladesh and provide financial support to a range for measures including:

- a programme of safety inspections and funding for remediation measures;
- fire safety training in supplier factories;
- payments to workers and their families directly within the organizations supply chain;
- contributions to a Rani Plaza Donors Trust to support other workers.

Primark reported that the total aid payment was in the region of $12 million. A spokesman said:

> Primark is very pleased to support this initiative. The company has consistently believed that the collaborative approach facilitated through this agreement was the most likely initiative to bring effective and sustainable change for the better to the Bangladeshi garment industry.
>
> The company was the first brand to acknowledge that its suppliers were housed in the Rana Plaza complex. The company was the first brand to commit to paying compensation to workers and their dependents. And the company was the first UK brand to sign up to the Accord on building and fire safety.
>
> The company is now extending help to workers who made clothing for its competitors. And the company is working as fast as possible to devise a scheme to provide long-term, secure assistance to workers in its supplier factory. The company has consistently said it will meet its responsibilities in full in this matter.
>
> (Primark, 2015)

Peter McAllister, Director of the Ethical Trading Initiative, said:

> Primark is doing the right thing by offering immediate support for the victims and families of the Rana Plaza disaster. We're pleased that Primark has also confirmed its commitment to providing long-term compensation and support, which it is developing with credible labour representatives. This is a welcome move, and we encourage the other brands that sourced from Rana Plaza to follow suit.
>
> (Primark, 2015)

This sector-wide collaborative approach extended to international trade relations recognizing the role governments have in international commerce. In the European Union, as a Least-Developed Country, Bangladesh benefited from Trade preferences in textiles; this has now been more closely linked to CSR requirements, driving Bangladesh to show sustained progress in improving its labour rights and working conditions in line with core ILO conventions. One such programme is the 'Compact for Continuous Improvements in Labour Rights and Factory Safety in the Ready-Made Garment and Knitwear Industry in Bangladesh' (European Commission, 2013), which lists commitments to act within deadlines on issues such as:

- Reforming the Bangladesh Labour Law to strengthen workers' rights, in particular regarding freedom of association and the right to collective bargaining, and to improve occupational health and safety. The ILO will monitor the effective enforcement of the new legislation.
- Recruiting 200 additional inspectors, as part of the efforts to ensure regular visits to factories and assess them in terms of working conditions, including occupational safety and health, and compliance with labour laws.
- Improving building and fire safety, especially structural safety of buildings and fire safety in ready-made garment factories. The ILO will help to coordinate efforts and mobilize technical resources.

On the Second Anniversary of the event, Federica Mogherini, High Representative of the European Union for Foreign Affairs and Security Policy and Vice-President of the Commission said:

> The Rana Plaza disaster will remain a dark page for Bangladesh and the international community. The Sustainability Compact has tried to bring together all partners – public and private - necessary for quick and effective action. Some progress has been achieved, but the full implementation of the Compact remains indispensable to promote labour rights and to ensure safe working conditions in Bangladesh. At a time when the Country is confronted with severe political and social challenges, the Sustainability Compact has the potential for setting an example on how to address the basic needs and legitimate expectations of the people of Bangladesh. It is essential that this potential is brought to fruition.
>
> (EU Delegation to the UN, 2015)

Example: Farmers accuse Tesco of putting them out of business

Consider the allegations made by farmers against Tesco supermarkets:

At a Tesco annual meeting, a farmer from Lincolnshire said he was losing 2p on every litre of milk that left his farm due to low prices imposed by supermarkets. 'We need a fair farm gate price for milk so that farmers could get a fair return on their investment,' he said.

The Tesco Chief Executive said the company was doing all it could in the circumstances to help farmers to be successful because the company had a vested interest in keeping a healthy supply chain.

He said Tesco tried to source products from local domestic markets instead of imports wherever possible. But the firm's actions were at least partly governed by factors outside its control such as exchange rates, government policy and movement in global agricultural prices.

The UK government has since introduced a code of conduct for large supermarkets after it was shown that they were distorting the market. This demonstrates that even (or especially) the largest organizations need to consider their responsibilities to supply chains.

Price

Traditionally, many organizations have focused on obtaining goods and services for the cheapest possible price. Profit is basically derived by the formula:

Profit = value of sales – cost of purchases

However, many organizations established that the cheapest price and the best price are two different things – that price wasn't the sole ingredient in a good contract. Value and cheapest price are two different parameters. Consider a t-shirt that is made using child labour, cheap cotton and polluting dyes, manufactured in sweatshop conditions and sold for 99p, but which shrinks and fades after the first wash. Is this good value? Several pressure groups recognize that much of our consumption is fuelled by our lifestyles and suggest that it is the responsibility of large multinational companies to drive change into their supply chains wherever they're located. As consumers, we must consider the price, manufacturing standards, environmental good practice and quality when we assess good value.

Value is not only a factor for the consumer; international standards such as ISO 14001:2015 are broadening the concept of the supply chain to the term 'value chain'. The standards require organizations to consider the life cycle costs and impacts of their products, activities and services looking at the effects on parties that provide value. This could include suppliers, outsourced workers, contractors and others, together with parties that receive value, including shareholders, employees, supplier, customers, consumers, members and other users. Together all interfaces between these groups create a Value Chain, which ISO 14001:2015 (International Organization for Standardization, 2015) defines as an 'entire sequence of activities or parties that provide or receive value in the form of products or services'.

This value chain concept is broader than the traditional supply chain model, as it extends the focus of an organization both upstream and downstream. Take, for example, wastes created during the manufacture of a product – traditionally this might not be seen as part of the supply chain, but we accept the concept of the 'duty of care for waste' in its disposal. Further, we see that others could obtain a value from that waste through reuse by a charity or recycling of the materials, but if we examine it further we could also consider the waste generated by the disposal and use of the product. Only by broadening the focus can we see the whole value chain.

The recognition of the responsibility of multinationals to supply chains helped to develop the 'UN Global Compact', which incorporates ten core principles of CSR. The table on the next page summarizes each of these principles.

Test your thinking 15

Consider your organization's suppliers and contractors, their conduct and your procurement processes.

1   To what degree does your organization actively uphold, enforce and promote each of the UN Global Compact ten principles listed in Table 8.1?
2   If not completely, how could your organization go further towards adopting them?

We'll now look at some issues that may influence your answers to these questions.

Choosing suppliers

In addition to value for money, will you seek to further your corporate responsibility objectives through your purchasing activity and supplier relationships? Will you use ethical criteria to exclude or positively discriminate in favour of certain suppliers? Will you support initiatives that aim to increase the number of diverse (e.g. ethnic-minority owned, women-owned)

Table 8.1 A summary of the principles of the UN Global Compact.

Human rights principles

| Principle 1 | Businesses should support and respect the protection of internationally proclaimed human rights. |
| Principle 2 | Businesses should ensure that their own operations are not complicit in human rights abuses. |

Labour principles

Principle 3	Businesses should uphold the freedom of association and the effective recognition of the right to collective bargaining.
Principle 4	Businesses should uphold the elimination of forced or compulsory labour.
Principle 5	Businesses should uphold the effective abolition of child labour.
Principle 6	Businesses should uphold the elimination of discrimination in respect of employment and occupation.

Environment principles

Principle 7	Businesses should support a precautionary approach to environmental challenges.
Principle 8	Businesses should undertake initiatives to promote greater environmental responsibility.
Principle 9	Businesses should encourage the development and diffusion of environmentally friendly technologies.

The anti-corruption principle

| Principle 10 | Businesses should work against all forms of corruption, including extortion and bribery. |

businesses that supply goods and services to your organization? You may also wish to consider measures to make sure that small businesses are given fair consideration.

Conduct during procurement

This refers to the way your staff conduct business – how goods and services are bought on behalf of the organization. Are your staff encouraged and supported to act with integrity, and in line with your organization's ethical values when establishing and maintaining supplier relationships? Do you insist that your suppliers' bills are paid on time, or that offers of gifts and hospitality are registered? How do you prevent conflicts of interest? If you work for a large company, are you concerned to be judged as a fair customer by your suppliers? Do you have policies on dependency, or on transparency regarding tendering, or on engagement when contract terms are not met, changed or are being wound down?

Your supplier's practices

Are you clear about the extent of your organization's responsibility down and across the supply chain? What do you expect of your suppliers? Do you impose social and environmental standards on them? Do you seek to influence their policies and practices or offer them assistance to improve?

Case Study 8.2   Carbon management within a supply chain, UK

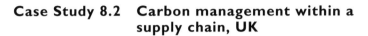

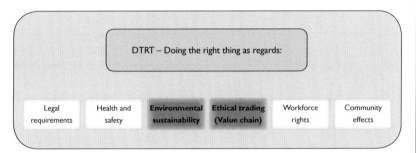

Sustainability in the service sector is very different to other 'higher risk' sectors such as the chemical, manufacturing or retail sectors (as discussed earlier in this book). The service sector doesn't tend to consume large amounts of raw materials or produce a product that could have potential environmental or social impacts across the full life cycle. However, customers of organizations within the service sector still have expectations that these businesses will operate in a responsible way. It is also quite typical that the higher risks from the services provided are associated with activities within from their supply chain.

The Innovation Group Plc. operates within the wider Insurance Sector. A Sector where the impacts of climate change are costly and the expectations from consumers to be environmentally and socially responsible are high.

Innovation Group is a software and services company, helping to manage four million insurance claims a year across the world on behalf of customers in the motor and property insurance sectors, fleet sector and motor manufacturing sector. It is clear that climate change is now having a noticeable impact on these areas, as claim costs are increasing in relation to changes in the frequency and severity of weather-related events. As a result, the Group's customers are concerned about climate change and expect Innovation Group to understand and manage the

(continued)

(continued)

environmental risks and opportunities within their supply chain, as well as their own business.

Innovation Group's own environmental and social impacts amount to only a small proportion of the overall impact of the whole supply chain. However, Innovation Group has a dedicated strategy to reduce the impact of its own operations and in particular has a target to reduce the intensity of its Scope 1 (direct emissions) and Scope 2 (purchased electricity) carbon emissions. The Group's global carbon intensity reduction target is to reduce carbon emissions per full time employee (tCO_2e/FTE) by 6 per cent by the end of the 2015 financial year against the 2013 Financial Year base year. It also plans to extend this to 15 per cent reduction by the end of the 2020 financial year.

In addition to the direct impacts from Innovation Group's own operations, the Group identified that its extensive global network of suppliers, which is an essential component of the Group business, has the potential to have a far greater negative impact on the climate.

Working over a two-year period the CarbonFix Foundation suggested and developed a carbon management Supply Chain model for Innovation Group. The CarbonFix Foundation initially visited over 50 suppliers at their premises and held a series of regional workshops to help explain the reasons behind evaluating carbon footprints and the use of the SmartCarbon software. An e-learning course was provided in addition to these workshops, which allowed the learners to explore the science of climate change and methods for carbon reporting at their own pace.

This model enabled the supply-chain companies to assess and understand their carbon footprint and report this to Innovation Group. The CarbonFix Foundation also assisted Innovation Group procurement team to ensure that carbon management and annual reporting was part of their supply-chain contracts. Once the model was operating, it was then passed to Innovation Group to expand throughout their organization.

This 'Approved Carbon Managed Supplier (ACaMS)' programme was initially piloted through the UK Property Division of the business, but the Group has since published targets to extend this programme across their supply chains globally by 2020.

By supporting and enabling suppliers to measure and manage their carbon emissions, Innovation Group is able to bring the long-term benefits of reduced energy and material usage to its clients, suppliers and shareholders. In addition to the obvious environmental benefits, this system demonstrates market leadership and provides a strong message of the Group's commitment to acting on Climate Risk. The Group have stated that its clients see this capability as a differentiator. The programme also provides an opportunity to build stronger relations with clients and suppliers.

In addition, the scheme provides all companies engaged on the ACaMs Network with recognition that they have been trained to calculate, report and manage their carbon emissions. As well as a logo to recognize individual levels of progress for each company (see table below), all supply chain members also receive a report of their own carbon performance and advice to help to develop a Carbon Abatement Plan for their business. The UK Property Division of Innovation Group has been awarded the Carbon Fix Foundation Level 4 Carbon Managed status.

Carbon Managed	Level 4: + Supply Chain
	Endorsed by Carbonfix.it Nov 14

What ACaMS members say about the programme

It is exciting for us as a business to be part of a bigger project, which raises the profile of all contractors on this network that will hopefully make a difference to the bigger environmental issue so we can all do our bit.

(Liam Hanlon, Forshaw Group)

I'm excited that we were invited to be part of this programme. It is an opportunity to be part of something that is going to make a difference. If we can teach our employees about sustainability, they can take it away and use it in their lives.

(Mark Robinson, Lanmarc Ltd.)

The project is really interesting . . . it also makes you think about issues and what you can do as an individual and a company. Bringing individuals and companies together, highlighting what we can all do enables us to come up with ideas that we can put in place.

(Laura Baybutt, Hawthorn NW)

Recognition for supply chain members

Table 8.2 The Carbon Fix Foundation four-phase certification scheme.

Phase of Carbon Management	Logo as displayed in e-mail footer/website/letterhead	What this means
Phase 1: Aware	Carbon Managed | Level 1: Aware Endorsed by Carbonfix.it Nov 13	This organization has completed an advanced Carbon Accounting E-learning course. This is based on the GHG Protocol and takes around 7–10 hours to complete.

(continued)

(continued)

Table 8.2 (continued)

Phase of Carbon Management	Logo as displayed in e-mail footer/website/letterhead	What this means
Phase 2: Report	Carbon Managed | Level 2: Report Endorsed by Carbonfix.it Nov 13	This organization has completed phase 1 above and in addition has entered 12 months of emissions data onto the SmartCarbon™ web-based portal in order to calculate and report at least one year's GHG Emissions.
Phase 3: Act	Carbon Managed | Level 3: Act (Offset + 20%) Endorsed by Carbonfix.it Nov 14	This organization has completed phases 1 and 2 above and in addition has taken action to reduce their emissions. This may include implementing a carbon reduction plan and/or investing in a certified and Carbon Fix Foundation endorsed Carbon Offset project. The % of total footprint offset will be shown if applicable.
Phase 4: + Supply chain	Carbon Managed | Level 4: + Supply Chain Endorsed by Carbonfix.it Nov 14	This organization has completed phases 1–3 above and in addition has engaged with their supply chain members to support them to also manage their carbon emissions by following the same model.

Sustainable procurement

The concept of incorporating CSR into the purchasing process is called 'sustainable procurement'. Sustainable procurement is the inclusion of environmental, social and economic factors in purchasing decisions, so that the long-term viability and maximum value of the goods or services can be obtained for the organization, the community and the environment. It involves reviewing the organization's procurement policies to widen the scope from purely best price or best quality to include elements from the CSR agenda.

Sustainable procurement seeks to recognize and emphasize that as the buyer, you have a huge degree of discretion over your choice of suppliers. This discretion not only includes your choice of the people and organizations you trade with, but also goes beyond this first-tier supply into the whole supply chain – how and where they obtain their resources. Sustainable procurement highlights that it's not just your choice but also your responsibility to make sure that your supply chain is well managed and operates on a socially and environmentally sound basis, not purely an economic one.

The purchasing decision should include gathering information on the impact of the organization's suppliers, including their areas of environmental impact and their record on employment rights and ethical trading. There are numerous benefits for organizations that promote environmental issues in the supplier chain:

- Cost savings: if you encourage suppliers to reduce waste, use fewer resources and be more energy efficient, they can produce goods at a lower cost. One organization implemented a returnable packaging scheme, eliminating 21,720 cardboard cartons with annual savings of £7,000 and 15 tonnes of waste.
- Supplier loyalty: developing partnership working reduces costs and CSR impacts, builds the relationship with suppliers and helps in all sectors.
- Minimizing corporate risk: if you've verified that your suppliers are suitable, it minimizes the chance that a major social or environmental incident or prosecution will affect the supply.
- Demonstrating good management: developing the supply chain well illustrates that the organization is well managed and encourages shareholders to invest. It also tells you what your suppliers' management style is, demonstrating how forward thinking and adaptive they can be.
- Accreditation and certification: SA 8000, ISO 14001 and Global Compact each require organizations to identify their aspects and their controls, including contractors and suppliers. They should develop improvement objectives for significant impacts[1]. If an organization wants to gain accreditation, it will generally need to include a supplier development programme.
- Competitive advantage: CSR provides opportunities to increase market share and to open new markets. Customers and shareholders alike are increasingly aware of organizations' CSR credentials, and base their buying decisions on what they find out. This may include the impact of the life cycle of the product.
- Brand protection: For some organizations, CSR is a component of the brand. For example, Innocent Smoothies highlight the health benefits of their product together with the social benefits of its supply chain, Café Direct emphasizes the direct link to the farmers. For others, bad publicity on CSR issues could affect the brand image – for example, Coca Cola has experienced bad publicity about its alleged consumption of scarce water supplies in India.[2]
- Ethical duty: particularly for public sector organizations, CSR management demonstrates that the organization considers the needs of its community in its procurement policy.

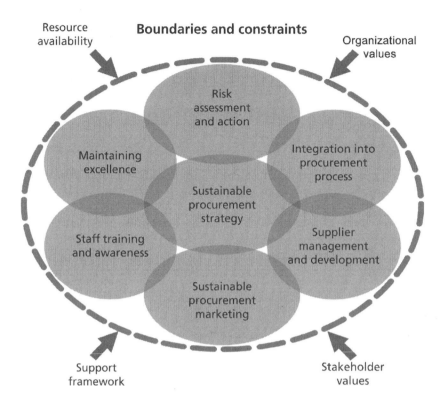

Figure 8.2 Sustainable procurement guide adapted from the Environment Agency (Environment Agency, 2003).

The Environment Agency in the UK has developed a sustainable procurement strategy focusing on six key elements, as illustrated in the figure above.

The first stage of this sustainable procurement strategy is to understand your aspects and impacts. As with any risk management system, the initial milestone is to be aware and assess the magnitude of the effects your organization is having socially, environmentally and economically, on a local and global scale. The scale and nature of your organization's operation will determine the depth, approach and comprehensiveness of your review. In this chapter, we're focusing on supply chain issues, but this could also include the impacts of the operations and outputs of your organization.

If any system is to be embedded in the operations and culture of an organization, right from the start you should consider how it would be integrated into the current structures and procedures of the organization.

If sustainable procurement is to become part of considerations at the purchasing stage, you need to review how you currently assess your suppliers, and how much weight you'll give to CSR over (say) price or reliable delivery. In developing your procurement strategy, you need to strike the right balance. If CSR is weighted too lightly, this will not bring about the significant change you want to encourage.

Supplier management can be tackled in two key ways. The first is to incorporate CSR considerations at the specification level, where appropriate, using a scoring method to include the benefits to the environment and communities in the selection process. The second is to encourage suppliers to improve the CSR footprint of the goods or services they supply to you. It's important to consider our approach with our suppliers – do we expect them to change overnight? Most people think not – this wouldn't be a reasonable approach to CSR, however desirable it might be. Instead, we probably need to nurture them over time to gain sustained benefits.

One of the best methods is to support a dialogue with the intention of identifying 'win–win' situations. Try not to work on a 'stick' approach – focus on the positives that improved CSR will bring to both organizations. Highlight why you're doing it, and the pressures and benefits. Many organizations operate a scored procurement process. CSR can be integrated into this process with an appropriate weighting. Suppliers can be moved onto a supplier development list and supported if they're significant for your organization. If your organization doesn't have a formal procurement process, then this could be an ideal time to find out what the right strategy would be for you. Would a little more time spent at the purchasing stage save problems further down the line?

Other methods of supplier management include:

- questionnaire samples to ascertain suppliers' current status;
- developing a code of conduct;
- developing purchasing checklists;
- making a positive effort to support voluntary and charity organizations through, for example, buying goods and services from them;
- benchmarking your supplier chain against those of other suitable organizations.

Sustainable procurement marketing – how can we make the most of the good work we're doing?

It's important to celebrate your successes and show others the benefits of a sustainable procurement policy. Initially, the approach of introducing a policy is critical, rather than dictating the process. You need to show how this will be useful to others' organizations and demonstrate the range of advantages. You need to show a partnership approach, remembering that suppliers are as entitled to benefit from the principles of CSR just as much as the general community. By negotiating with, and influencing them, you're more likely to champion change.

Clearly there comes a situation where a supplier organization must either comply with your core principles, or not be used.

> It is a mistake to isolate 'greening the supply chain' as something completely different. It should be presented and received as one of the many customer expectations (in addition to price, performance, quality, etc.). If you treat it as a new and separate conversation, it may look more difficult than it needs to be. Given the natural tendency to resist change, there is no need to make this any larger than it needs to be as long as you are able to get the performance improvements you are after.
>
> (Ben Packard, Director of Environmental
> Affairs, Starbucks; Hitchcock and Willard, 2006)

Staff competence

If you're to ask staff to develop in their roles and to incorporate CSR into their working life (and home life – see Chapter 9), you need to make sure that they have an understanding of the key concepts, the benefits and their individual roles in the organization's approach to CSR.

While on one level, the basic concepts are welcomed by many, incorporating it into work-based decisions can be more of a challenge. Ensuring an effective sustainable procurement strategy needs specifiers, influencers, budget holders, buyers and senior management all to understand their roles and the impacts their decisions can have on CSR.

Maintaining excellence

Once you've set your policy, taken a benchmark and assessed your suppliers, how can you continue to improve and promote your CSR goals? The first stage is to verify your current position through auditing; this is dealt with in more depth in Chapter 6.

Once an audit programme is in place, the next stage is to consider how and to what extent your organization should support improvements in your supply chain. This will clearly depend on a wide range of factors, including:

- public or private sector;
- size of organization;
- policy or belief in CSR;
- resources available;
- significance of risks or impacts;
- market sector;
- competition;
- media interest;

- supplier base;
- good practice information availability.

It's important to recognize the wider benefits of the supplier development programme so that all the costs can be considered. Hosting a supplier development workshop may also build better relationships to aid the understanding of operations from both the supplier and client's perspective. This is a simple event or series of events that encourage communication and sharing of ideas to solve problems that are common to the supply chain, such as logistic or manufacturing issues.

Typical improvement ideas for suppliers can include:

- knowledge exchange workshops (where best practice is shared), training and information;
- shared ideas and common goals;
- practical solutions, such as shared waste minimization programmes, energy efficiency, returnable packaging systems, transport solutions, life cycle assessment, fair trade concepts, shared sustainable product research;
- long-term partnership planning to support the viability of all organizations in the supply chain.

Once you've established your strategy, remember to bring it to the attention of your current and prospective clients.

Test your thinking 16

Consider your own organization and the suggestions outlined in the sustainable procurement strategy model, and answer these questions:

1   Who are your key suppliers?
2   Which of these suppliers is most likely to have a major CSR impact?
3   How could CSR be integrated into your current purchasing polices?
4   Who makes or influences purchasing decisions in your organization?
5   What information, skills and training would these people need to incorporate CSR principles into the decisions they make?
6   How could you market a sustainable procurement strategy to your suppliers?
7   What are the main barriers to starting now and how could you overcome them?
8   How could you help your suppliers improve their CSR performance?

Whether you work with a large company or public sector body with direct impacts, or a small- to medium-sized enterprise within a supply chain, the pressure is on you to ensure good practice throughout your lives. The point of CSR is to get you to consider your impacts on others and the environment. After your own operations, the contractors and suppliers you select are the most direct influences you have. Health and safety legislation and product liability regulations recognize the duty you have for your supply chain; when will you acknowledge your responsibility for the purchasing decisions your organization makes?

Notes

1 The terms 'aspect' and 'impact' are used here in the meanings given in ISO 14001:2015 (International Organization for Standardization, 2015). An aspect is 'an element of an organization's activities, products or services that can interact with the environment', while an impact is 'any change to the environment, whether adverse or beneficial, wholly or partially resulting from an organization's activities, products or services'.
2 For more information, see www.corpwatch.org/article.php?id=7508.

Chapter 9

Personal social responsibility

> No man is an island, entire of itself . . . . Any man's death diminishes me, because I am involved in mankind; and therefore never send to know for whom the bell tolls; it tolls for thee.
> —John Donne (1572–1631), Devotions Upon Emergent Occasions, *Meditation XVII*

So far in this book, we've looked at the role of the organization in examining its responsibilities to stakeholders and developing a programme to mitigate its negative effects. However, as society and organizations are made up of individuals, we should consider how our personal decisions affect the wider society. Our purchasing decisions are one of the strongest powers we have, whether in our home life or at work. The selection we make at the checkout is the ultimate demonstration of the level of respect we have for workers we may never meet, the ethics we support and supply chains we condone. And it's not just what we choose to buy – our other actions, such as how much we recycle and what we turn off, also have an impact on the world around us.

Personal social responsibility (PSR) is an important component in any CSR programme as it recognizes that, as individuals, we're usually the end users of the products or services we've been discussing so far in this book. It's important that we take individual responsibility for the impacts associated with those products and services. When we buy something, we're supporting and implicitly approving of all of the actions in the supply chain that brought that product to us. If that product or service used child labour, forced people to work in poor conditions or caused significant pollution, hasn't that all been done on our behalf for our purchase, to satisfy our needs and desires?

In this chapter, we consider what an individual can do to minimize their personal social impact, and we highlight how an individual can become an agent for change within their own sphere of influence. We can all live behind the theory that it's somebody else's job; complain that our own actions won't make a significant difference; and point to others who are worse than us.

But change requires action! Action requires individuals to make a conscious effort to alter their current behavioural patterns. History reminds us of the individuals who have made a difference for good or bad – Nelson Mandela, Mahatma Gandhi, Mother Teresa, Bob Geldof, Bill Gates, Adolf Hitler or Osama bin Laden. All have changed our world to a greater or lesser extent. You too can be the agent for change in your life, household, organization or community.

If you're to make a difference, you need to understand how to instigate and sustain change. It's easy to get enthusiastic about a new project at the start, but how can you make sure that it results in lasting changes over the longer term, and that you don't return to your old ways when the novelty wears off? Being an agent for change, either in your own life or in other people's behavior, requires effort, tenacity and ardour. Seven simple and logical steps can support effective change:

1   Focus on what you can change, not what you can't. At the start, or when times get tough, it's easy to get distracted by focusing on areas that you have little or no control over. You need to be realistic and spend your efforts on your own sphere of activity and influence.

2   Identify barriers. With any programme of change, there are always challenges to face. By identifying them early on, and by considering your options and coping strategies, they don't have to derail your progress if or when they crop up.

3   Set realistic targets. We all work better when we have something to aim for and to plot progress against. By considering what you need or want to achieve, you can make sure you channel your time and effort in the right direction. And don't be too optimistic about what can be achieved.

4   Easy wins. Good news motivates us all! A sense of achievement can come from building in attainable milestones early in the plan. This helps to develop momentum more quickly, reinforce behaviour change and support your progress towards the long-term objectives.

5   Monitor your progress. It's important to develop some simple monitoring measures to make sure that progress is kept on track.

6   Look for the positives. Many people concentrate on the things they could have done better. This can create a negative outlook, reinforcing past behaviour patterns. Look at what you have positively achieved and how the new plan is making a difference.

7   Celebrate each success! When targets are achieved, reward yourself.

The fact that you're reading this chapter shows your commendable desire to make that change. So – ask yourself now: what practical steps can you take right away to make a difference?

Celebrate success

Look for positives

Monitor progress

Easy wins

Target setting

Identify barriers

Focus

Figure 9.1 Seven steps to PSR change.

Test your thinking 17

Considering the influence you have in your personal life, at work and in your community, what can you do to optimize your personal social responsibility? Use the list below as a guide:

1   Your personal life
   • What do you buy?
   • How do you live?
   • What do you use?
   • How do you travel when you go shopping? To work? On holiday?
   • What do you tell your children?
   • What do you tell your friends?
   • What do you learn?
   • What do you throw away?

(continued)

(continued)

2 Workplace
- What decisions do you make at work?
- Who can you influence?
- Which decisions can you influence?
- What do you use in your work?
- What do you throw away?

3 Community
- Do you vote?
- Who do you vote for?
- Do you do any formal or informal voluntary work?
- How can you help with the skills you have (or could learn)?
- Who do you talk to and network with?
- Who do you know who is active in your community?
- What could you do right away (see our 100 actions on pages 249–254 for ideas)?

These ideas are all possibilities. Not every suggestion will apply to everyone, but we can all do more than we do now.

Get informed – make sure that you're aware of what you're buying, and what the current issues are.

While there's a confusing amount of information on CSR issues, the simple test is to buy products that you believe, in all good faith, have been produced with the aim of reducing the negative impact on those who produce and supply them, wildlife and the environment.

Use labels to choose products that have a lower impact on the environment – for example, fair trade products, energy efficient appliances and cars, and sustainable fish. Using labels to buy sustainable wood and peat-free compost will protect important natural habitats that help balance climate change effects. If you're unsure, the information age means it's easy to find out!

Case Study 9.1 Coffee Bean links consumers to growers, Latin and Central America

Derived from a simple bean of the Genus coffee, the Arabica and Robusta varieties of coffee bean have developed into an international commodity and become the second most consumed drink after water.

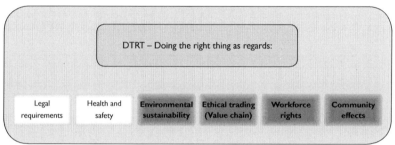

The products bear names from across the continents including Java, Columbia and Kenya, reflecting that coffee plants are cultivated in over 70 countries around the globe. The trade supports subsistence farmers and major international brands including Kenco and Nestle to the ubiquitous Starbucks and other coffee houses. In this case study we will review the brands behind the stories and the interactions it has created in schemes such as Fairtrade and Rainforest Alliance certification, to work with gang cultures in South America.

The first origins of Coffee drinking is not clear, but it is thought that Coffee was introduced to Yemen from Ethiopia in the fifteenth century by Ali Omar Al-Shadili. (It is reported that he operated in a small port on the Red Sea called Muza or Mocha, and was the leader of the Sufi sect earning him the name 'Saint of Mocha' (Bennett, 2001)). From these beginnings, an estimated 141.9 million 60kg bags of coffee where produced in 2014–2015, and nearly 150 million 60kg bags were consumed, drawing on reserve stocks (International Coffee Organization, 2015a).

(continued)

(continued)

The first drivers towards industrial sustainability initiatives in the sector came from an economic perceptive. As early as 1906, the State of São Paulo, Brazil had developed an agreement to challenge the problems of oversupply, driving down prices affecting subsidence farmers (International Coffee Organization, 2015b). This economic focus continued throughout the 20th Century with tax and trade arguments, such as the USA–Brazil soluble coffee dispute, as outlined by the International Coffee Organization in their report 'International Coffee Organization: 1963–2013':

> A major factor in this dispute was that it involved the world's biggest producer and the world's biggest consumer. Essentially the USA complained that Brazilian soluble coffee exporters had access, through tax concessions, to cheaper coffee than did US manufacturers. Brazil countered that it had a right to process its own raw materials and protect a fledgling industry. The dispute was referred to a legal panel with inconclusive results. Eventually the two parties reached agreement in bilateral talks which allowed Brazil to export a set amount of soluble coffee to the USA.
>
> (International Coffee Organization, 2015b).

This juxtaposition between consumers in more developed nations and producers in developing nations encourages us to review where the 'added value' is in the supply chain. Financially retailers, roasters and exporters are seen as higher value-adding processes rather than the growers, leading to an imbalance between the top consuming countries, such as the EU and US, and the top exporting countries, such as Brazil, Columbia, Vietnam, Indonesia and Ethiopia. One way to add value at the source of the supply chain is to incorporate sustainable management practices, which can be offered at a premium price to consumers, with a financial benefit to the growers.

In additional to financial balancing, CSR programmes can also bring win-win benefits to communities and organizations. 'The 'Nestlé concept of corporate social responsibility as implemented in Latin America' (2006) highlights the value chain benefits of a CSR programme through a framework entitled 'creating shared value' and illustrated in the table below:

Within the sector as a whole, this approach was adopted at the International Coffee Agreement 2007, which encouraged members of the International Coffee Organization to develop a sustainable coffee sector in economic, social and environmental terms. This is reinforced

Table 9.1 The value chain benefits of a CSR programme through a framework of 'creating shared value'.

	Agriculture and sourcing	Manufacturing and distribution	Products and consumers
Value Chain Impacts	**Purchasing practices** Sourcing for quality and sustainability; Research and development for better yields.	**Environmental, labour and safety practices** Food safety through improved standards of operations; Labour practices for mutual benefit; Improved environmental standards.	**New/renovated products for nutrition, health and wellness** Research for consumer benefit; Consumer nutrition, health and wellness.
Building a context for growth	**Agricultural and supplier development** Knowledge transfer and farm assistance; Partnerships for sustainable agriculture.	**Better food safety standards and workforce development** Risk management for food safety; Creation of employment opportunities in the community.	**Increase knowledge and awareness for healthy nutrition and lifestyles** Knowledge and education for healthy nutrition and lifestyles.
Value for society	**Access to raw materials at specified quality and foreseeable price**	**Premium food manufacturer**	**Profitable growth from superior product benefits**
Value for Nestlé	**Higher food output using fewer resources**	**Higher food production standards**	**Wider access to food, and improved nutrition and health**

Source: Nestlé, 2006.

by Article 36, within the agreement, which refers to the principles and objectives on sustainable development contained in Agenda 21 adopted at the United Nations Conference on Environment and Development and those adopted at the World Summit on Sustainable Development. Other initiatives included the Fairtrade scheme, which is discussed later in this chapter. Beside the direct economic benefit to many coffee growers, sustainable coffees provide additional intended benefits at the producer level in the field that go beyond a market advantage. These can include:

(continued)

(continued)

1   improved natural resource management and biodiversity conservation;
2   crop resilience to weather and climactic risk;
3   on-farm diversification and fewer external input costs reduce financial exposure;
4   community or organizational development and increased use of rural labour;
5   fewer health risks due to misuse of agrochemicals.
(International Coffee Organization, 2015c).

Over the past decade, these CSR strategies have expanded beyond management of coffee farms and Fairtrade. Mondelēz International, the world's second-largest coffee company under its Kenco brand has a major campaign called Coffee Made Happy. This $200m programme 'wants to make coffee farming a sustainable, productive and respected profession by helping one million coffee smallholder farmers become successful entrepreneurs by 2020' (Kenco, 2015).

One part of this is the Coffee vs. Gangs programme in Honduras. The programme draws together what to most would be seen as two separate worlds, but they exist in one location. Coffee is an important part of the legal economy in Honduras, however as a country it is also the murder capital of the world; in a 2013 United Nations' report Lemahieu and Me found found 90 homicides per 100,000 people in 2012. Gang culture draws in much of the Honduran youth, with tragic impacts on the availability of labour for the industry. Kenco have developed a programme to support its business and local society by developing young peoples' skills to become coffee farmers away from the pressures of gang culture. The choice may be tough pulling them away from their local communities but provides a secure way to earn a living, without the threat of violence, of joining a gang or being killed.

Martin Andreasen, Marketing Manager: Coffee, UK at Mondelēz, says:

> Consumers expect more, we have to be open and we have to be transparent. This is taking a big step into the unknown and the ad is just the kickstart to the campaign. We are trying not to do things that are just a badging exercise it's about trying to do what is right. Consumers are looking for brands that are there for a reason, linked to a real purpose.
>
> (Kemp, 2014)

It is not only the project that is groundbreaking; the marketing has a transparency as well. The project is being advertised as a story around 20 young people involved in the project, with a commitment to follow their lives over the coming years. This gives the strategy a credibility, as the organization does not know if the programme will be a success or not.

> The project has elevated the role of marketing within our business and pulled our people and agencies together and shifted the conversation away from 'what is your marketing budget this year' to being a genuinely galvanizing force.
>
> > (Emad Nadim, Brand Manager
> > at Kenco; Kemp, 2014)

The simple coffee bean links the globe from coffee drinkers to growers and highlights how CSR can be developed to support organizations to stand out from the competition and drive up CSR standards through market pressures.

Labelwise

In order to help you with this process you need to get 'labelwise'. Logos and labels are there to help us to quickly recognize those products that meet a certain standard. At an organizational level, it may be that the company is certificated to an accredited standard (see Chapter 6). But what about the everyday consumer? What information is on the label, and what do these labels mean?

Labelling

Fair trade

> Fair trade is about better prices, decent working conditions, local sustainability and fair terms of trade for farmers and workers in the developing world. By requiring companies to pay sustainable prices (which must

Figure 9.2 Fairtrade logo.

never fall lower than the market price), Fairtrade addresses the injustices of conventional trade, which traditionally discriminates against the poorest, weakest producers. It enables them to improve their position and have more control over their lives.

(Fairtrade Organization, 2015)

For more information, contact the Fairtrade Foundation, www.fairtrade. org.uk.

Organic

To many people, 'organic' means made without man-made chemicals. However, within the EU, in order for a product to be marketed as organic it must meet particular certification standards. These are implemented in the UK under the Organic Products Regulations 2004, through the Compendium of UK Organic Standards.

The Soil Association has added to these standards and developed a logo that is widely used. The product showing the label must meet a range of agricultural, environmental, food processing and social principles.

The Soil Association's agricultural principles are to:

- produce food of high quality in sufficient quantity;
- work within natural systems and cycles throughout all levels from the soil to plants and animals;
- maintain the long-term fertility and biological activity of soils;
- treat livestock ethically, meeting their physiological and behavioural needs;
- respect regional, environmental, climatic and geographic differences and (appropriate) practices that have evolved in response to them.

Its environmental principles are to:

- foster biodiversity and protect sensitive habitats and landscape features;
- maximize use of renewable resources and recycling;
- minimize pollution and waste.

Figure 9.3 Soil Association Organic Standard logo.

Its food processing principles are to:

- minimize processing, consistent with the food in question;
- maximize information on processing methods and ingredients.

Its social principles are to:

- provide a fair and adequate quality of life, work satisfaction and working environment;
- develop ecologically responsible production, processing and distribution chains, emphasizing local systems.

Rainforest Alliance Certified

This logo indicates that the product contains ingredients sourced from forests or farms certified by the Rainforest Alliance as meeting the Standards for Sustainable Agriculture. This Standard sets out ten key principle themes which the organization should be following. The themes relate to:

- social and environmental management systems;
- ecosystem conservation;
- wildlife protection;
- water conservation;
- fair treatment and good working conditions for workers;
- occupational health and safety;
- community relations;
- integrated crop management;
- soil management and conservation;
- integrated waste management.

The alliance supports an online learning platform at www.sustainableagriculturetraining.org/, which includes interesting free training resources

Figure 9.4 Rainforest Alliance Certified logo.

Figure 9.5 The 'Möbius loop'.

and tests. If you wish to learn more about sustainable agriculture practices around the globe we recommend you try it for yourself, PSR in action.

Recycled vs. recyclable

Many products show the 'three chasing arrows' recycling logo, called the 'Möbius loop'. There are a number of similar recycling logos, and it's important to understand the difference between them:

This symbol denotes that the material is able to be recycled. It may be produced from virgin material but, as the consumer, you can recycle it. Until you do, there's little benefit to the environment.

If you buy recyclable materials, it's vital that you do indeed recycle them in order to achieve the intended benefits of reducing resource use and cutting landfill waste.

The recycling symbol with a single figure inside (i.e. without a per cent sign) indicates a plastic recycling classification to help in sorting material after collection and before processing. The figure on the opposite page explains the numbers and abbreviations.

Items made from recycled materials are usually labelled with a different 'Möbius loop' marking. This time, it has a percentage figure inside. This indicates the percentage of the product's material that has been recycled, demonstrating obvious environmental benefits. These items can also themselves be recycled.

Figure 9.6 'Möbius loop' with markings to show the item is made from recycled materials.

Figure 9.7 'Crossed-out wheelie bin' symbol for recyclable electrical products complying with EN 50419.

The 'crossed-out wheelie bin' symbol means that the electrical product carrying it complies with EN 50419, and is recyclable. If you bought it after 13 August 2005, you can take it back to the store where you bought it for recycling. (You're responsible for appropriately disposing of electrical appliances bought before this date, but some retailers will accept these older products for recycling, especially if you're buying a replacement from them.)

Forest Stewardship Council

Products displaying this mark are made from wood that comes from well-managed forests and has been certified according to the Forest Stewardship Council standards by independent organizations.

This mark may be displayed with a percentage figure to show how much of the materials come from recycled sources. But unlike with the standard recycling symbol, products without the percentage figure can also be considered as having a lower environmental impact.

PEFC –Programme for the Endorsement of Forest Certification

Figure 9.8 Forest Stewardship Council logo.

Figure 9.9 PEFC Certified and PEFC Recycled logos.

The PEFC logo and label on a product communicates to customers that the wood or fibre has been responsibly sourced. The PEFC Standards are an umbrella standard that approves national agreements focused on local issues, rather than representing a global set of requirements. To ensure that the all of the national standards deliver a degree of consistency, PEFC assesses each application to its global sustainability benchmarks. PEFC criteria, regulations and guidelines also include provisions for standards development and implementation and define requirements for stakeholder engagement in standard setting and scheme development; regional and group certification, certification and accreditation procedures, chain of custody, logo use, and complaints and appeals mechanism.

The PEFC standard also includes logo use standards, which differentiate between products that are PEFC Certified (which indicate that over 70 per cent of the material comes from PEFC sources or recycled materials) and PEFC Recycled (where over 70 per cent of the material comes from recycled sources). In both cases up to 30 per cent of the material may come from non-certified or traceable sources.

Other symbols

A common symbol on packaging in the UK is the green dot (*der grüne Punkt*). This has no direct environmental significance but indicates the manufacturer has paid into a packaging recovery system in Germany.

Figure 9.10 Plastic recycling classifications.

Figure 9.11 The green dot (*der grüne Punkt*).

Personal actions

However, it's not all about the labels. There are also simple steps you can take to reduce the impact of the items that you buy, such as buying from local suppliers where possible, buying fresh and in-season food only, and buying only what you need.

Consider what you use

It sounds really obvious, but think about where you use your energy, water and resources, and how you could be more efficient.

CONSIDER RESOURCE USE, CLIMATE CHANGE AND WASTE

To tackle climate change:

Figure 9.12 An energy rating label for a washing machine.

- save energy at home – 'turn down, switch off, unplug';
- buy energy-efficient products – look for the Energy Saving Recommended label or a European energy label rating of A;
- switch to an energy supplier with a lower carbon footprint or a renewable energy tariff;
- improve your home insulation;
- try to reduce your car use – walking, cycling or taking the bus or train will help to reduce local air pollution and climate change;
- tackle the environmental impact of flying by considering options for reducing your travel – for example taking fewer, longer breaks if possible instead of several short ones, holidaying in your home country or travelling to nearby countries by rail or sea. At work, consider video-conferencing rather than travelling long distances for meetings;
- consider food miles and low-carbon products;
- review your footprint and action plan at www.actonco2.co.uk.

TO REDUCE WATER USE:

- turn off taps properly and fix them if they leak;
- install water-efficient products – low flush volume toilets, water-efficient shower heads and aerating heads on washbasin taps help to reduce your water use, as does fitting a 'hippo' or other water-saving device;
- collect rainwater in water butts and use it for watering your garden.

Driving

We all know we should use our cars less, but what about when we're in them? Is there anything we can do? The following advice is provided by the UK Automobile Association (2015):

BEFORE YOU GO

- Regular servicing: get the car serviced regularly (according to the manufacturer's schedule) to maintain engine efficiency.
- Tyre pressures: check tyre pressures regularly and before long journeys. Under-inflated tyres create more rolling resistance and so use more fuel. Getting tyre pressures right is important for safety too. Refer to your car's handbook, as pressures will normally have to be increased for heavier loads.
- Lose weight: extra weight means extra fuel, so if there's stuff in the boot you don't need on the journey take it out and leave it at home.
- Streamline: roof racks or boxes create extra wind resistance and so increase fuel consumption. If you don't need it, take it off; if you do, pack it carefully to reduce the extra drag.

- Don't get lost: plan unfamiliar journeys to reduce the chance of getting lost.
- Combine short trips: cold starts are inefficient, so it pays to combine errands, such as buying the paper, dropping off the recycling or collecting the kids into one trip, rather than making multiple short trips.
- Consider alternatives: if it's a short journey (a couple of miles or so), consider walking or cycling rather than taking the car. Fuel consumption is worse when the engine is cold, and pollution will be greater too until the emissions control system gets up to normal temperature.

ON THE WAY

- Leave promptly: don't start the engine until you're ready to go. This avoids fuel wastage due to unnecessary idling and ensures that the engine warms up as quickly as possible. In winter months, scrape ice off the windows rather than leaving the car idling for a long period to warm up.
- Easy does it: drive smoothly, accelerate gently and read the road ahead to avoid unnecessary braking.
- Decelerate smoothly: when you have to slow down or stop, decelerate smoothly by releasing the accelerator in good time, leaving the car in gear.
- Rolling: if you can keep the car moving all the time, so much the better. Stopping then starting again uses more fuel than keeping rolling.
- Change up earlier: change gear as soon as possible without labouring the engine. Try changing up at an engine speed of around 2,000 rpm in a diesel car or around 2,500 rpm in a petrol car. This can make such a difference to fuel consumption that all cars in the future are likely to be fitted with gear shift indicators that light a lamp on the dashboard to indicate the most efficient gear change points.
- Cut down on the air con: air conditioning increases fuel consumption at low speeds, but at higher speeds the effects are less noticeable. So if it's a hot day, it's more economical to open the windows around town and save the air conditioning for high-speed driving. Don't leave the air-con on all the time – but you should run it at least once a week throughout the year to maintain the system in good condition.
- Turn it off: any electrical load increases fuel consumption, so turn off your heated rear windscreen, demister blowers and headlights when you don't need them.
- Stick to the limits: drive within the speed limit – the faster you go the greater the fuel consumption and the greater the pollution too. According to the Department for Transport, driving at 70 mph uses up to 9 per cent more fuel than at 60 mph and up to 15 per cent more than at 50 mph. Cruising at 80 mph can use up to 25 per cent more fuel than at 70 mph (see the Figure 9.13 on page 206).
- Don't be idle: if you do get caught in a queue, avoid wasting fuel by turning the engine off if it looks like you could be waiting for more than three minutes.

Figure 9.13 Fuel savings from reduced speed.

Consider what you throw away

TACKLE WASTE

Look at what you throw away and consider the 'seven Rs':

1   Remove: can you eliminate the waste you create? Take bags with you when you go shopping, rather than using new ones. Consider whether you need a new item – can you repair or modify one you've got already? Think about the quality of the item you buy – how long will it last?
2   Reduce: think about what and how much you buy – do you waste some of it?
3   Re-use: pass things on to friends, family and charities if you no longer need them.
4   Repair: can it be fixed rather than just replaced?
5   Recycle: can you give recyclables to support charities? Most councils run doorstep recycling collections for paper, glass and plastics, but local refuse sites often accept many other things, including wood, shoes, textiles and TVs.
6   Recover: consider composting – many local councils offer subsidized compost bins or home collection for kitchen and garden waste.
7   Responsibility: take ownership of your waste – make sure it doesn't litter the environment.

Tackle your health

PSR isn't just about your impact on others – you need to look after yourself, too. You can make a big difference by:

- tackling your smoking;
- reducing your alcohol intake;
- eating healthily, e.g. five portions of fruit and vegetables a day;
- taking more exercise;
- practicing safe sex.

Cancer Research UK highlight that:

> In the UK, more than 1 in 2 people will develop cancer at some point in their lives. Every year, more than 331,000 people are diagnosed with the disease. But experts estimate that more than 4 in 10 cancer cases could be prevented by lifestyle changes, such as:
>
> - not smoking;
> - keeping a healthy bodyweight;
> - cutting back on alcohol;
> - eating a healthy, balanced diet;
> - keeping active;
> - avoiding certain infections (such as HPV);
> - enjoying the sun safely;
> - occupation (avoiding cancer risks in the workplace).
>
> (Cancer Research UK, 2015)

Be smart in the sun by remembering the 'SunSmart' message, provided by Cancer Research UK:

- Spend time in the shade between 11 and 3;
- Make sure you never burn;
- Aim to cover up with a t-shirt, hat and sunglasses;
- Remember to take extra care with children;
- Use factor 15+ sunscreen;
- Also, report mole changes or unusual skin growths promptly to your doctor.

Tackle your community

You can influence your local community by:

- challenging discrimination wherever you find it;
- considering action – voluntary work, involvement in pressure groups or standing for election as a local councillor;
- treating others as you'd like to be treated yourself;
- being an 'agent of change';
- trying to be a net contributor to life in general;
- supporting charities.

Tackle your work

In every other chapter of this book except this one, we've intentionally focused on the organizational level. Now you know what is needed, you can start to influence your organization to take action:

- Recommend a management systems approach such as SA 8000 or ISO 14001 (see Chapter 6). Even if your organization decides against external certification, you can still apply the framework.
- Develop (or contribute to) a process for setting objectives and targets.
- Review your success. You don't need a fully accredited approach to be able to make more ethically considered decisions.
- Help shape a vision of what type of organization you'd like to work for and strive to get others to consider how CSR helps meet their aims.
- Develop an implementation plan to establish your CSR impacts, mitigations, monitoring and reporting.
- Encourage your organization to measure performance and report. Establish key performance indicators for CSR issues.
- Role shift: look at how you can develop your role to include CSR and influence others.
- Tackle issues in your business linked to CSR – social, environmental, supply chain management, ethical trading, fair trade and engagement with all stakeholder groups.

Case Study 9.2   Ethics Adviser resigns over 25,000 deaths, India

In January 2012, the Sustainability Commissioner and Ethics Adviser for the London 2012 Olympic games resigned live on the BBC's flagship news program *Newsnight* due to the connections of the proposed supplier of external sheeting and sponsor to the main Olympic stadium to an incident that occurred 28 years earlier. The company that wished

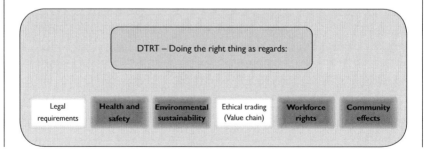

DTRT – Doing the right thing as regards:

Legal requirements | Health and safety | Environmental sustainability | Ethical trading (Value chain) | Workforce rights | Community effects

to supply the materials was part of larger organization that had previously owned the Union Carbide India Limited pesticide works in the town of Bhopal, India.

Meredith Alexander stated into TV cameras; 'By coming on air tonight, I'm taking the decision to resign my position and stand up for my principles . . . I feel that I was part of a body that has been used to legitimize Dow's involvement in the games.' She went on to state that while Dow Chemicals have an 'army of PR people', she hoped that her resignation could bring some attention to the continuing plight of victims in Bhopal (Bhopal Medical Appeal, 2012).

What was it about an incident that occurred nearly 30 years before that pushed a sustainability professional to give up a once-in-a-lifetime opportunity to be part of an Olympic Host City? The incident that drove Ms Alexander's decision lies less with the initial incident – horrific in scale and nature though it was – it is her feelings in relation to the ongoing response, aftercare and lack of support the then and subsequent owners failed to provide. How far should professionals take personal stances in relation to the decisions of the organizations as a whole?

The initial incident occurred just after midnight on the 3rd December 1984, when 27 tonnes of Methyl Isocyanate (MIC) was released from a pesticide manufacturing plant, located in the Madhya Pradesh region of India. MIC is a highly reactive material and the design of the plant required significant quantities to be stored. In the EU the maximum recommended storage quantity is half a tonne; on that night 67 tonnes were stored in tanks on site.

The details of the incident are still hotly disputed by both sides, with Union Carbide Corporation (UCC) stating that it was by direct sabotage, while the Indian Authorities, and those affected suggest that six safety systems where not operational; citing unproven technology, inadequate safety systems and giant storage as being a cocktail for disaster (Bhopal Medical Appeal, 2012).

What is not in dispute is that a significant volume of water entered the MIC storage tank, causing a reaction that forced the pressure release valve to open and allowed the release of toxic gas. As the gas spread from the plant, it covered the nearby shanty towns before enveloping the streets and homes of those sleeping in Bhopal. Those that did wake – coughing, choking and rubbing their stinging eyes – found that not all the effects where instantaneous, as in the years to come they reported effects including cancers, blindness, extreme difficulty in breathing, gynecological disorders and birth defects. Early

(continued)

(continued)

estimates, from one set of disputed official Indian Government figures, put the death toll on that night at 3,800 deaths and 11,000
disabilities, as quoted on the Dow Chemical's website, who purchased Union Carbide in 2001 (acquiring it's assets and liabilities)
(Browning, 1993). While other groups put the figures nearer 25,000
deaths and 120,000 people still suffering from ailments caused by
the accident and the subsequent pollution at the plant site (Bhopal
Medical Appeal, 2012).

The dispute about the cause, scale and nature of harm, have been
further complicated by the fact that the site was a partially state
owned and part private organization, set up in another country.
The impacts of the imbalance of a multinational corporation versus
individuals with disabilities who have lost many family members,
have only added to the delays in investigations, resolutions and
compensation.

The following edited timeline is taken from the Union Carbide
Website, which represents their version of the events and is used here
to illustrate the complexity of the case:

> Union Carbide India Limited (UCIL) was established in 1934,
> when Union Carbide Corporation (UCC) became one of the first
> US companies to invest in India . . . the Bhopal plant was built in
> the late 1970s

> **1984**

> Dec 3   The Bhopal Gas Tragedy

> Shortly after midnight, methyl isocyanate (MIC) gas leaks from
> a tank at the UCIL Bhopal plant. According to the state govern-
> ment of Madhya Pradesh, about 3,000 people die and several
> thousand other individuals experience permanent and partial
> disabilities.

> Dec 4   Immediate Action

> Word of the disaster is received at Union Carbide headquarters
> in Connecticut. Chairman and CEO Warren Anderson, together
> with a technical team, depart to India to assist the government in
> dealing with the incident. Upon arrival, Anderson is placed under
> house arrest and urged by the Indian government to leave the
> country within 24 hours.

Union Carbide organizes a team of international medical experts, as well as supplies and equipment, to work with the local Bhopal medical community.

The UCC technical team begins assessing the cause of the gas leak.

Dec 14 Warren Anderson testifies before Congress. He stresses UCC commitment to safety and promises to take actions to ensure that a similar incident 'cannot happen again.'

1985

Feb Interim Relief

Union Carbide establishes a fund for victims of the tragedy – the (UCC) Employees' Bhopal Relief Fund that collects more than $120,000.

Mar Bhopal Gas Leak Act

Government of India (GOI) enacts the Bhopal Gas Leak Disaster Act that enables the GOI to act as the legal representative of the victims in claims arising from or related to the Bhopal disaster.

Cause of the Incident UCC

Technical team reports that a large volume of water was introduced into the MIC tank and triggered a reaction that resulted in the gas release. Independently, a committee of experts for the Indian government arrives at the same conclusion.

Apr Union Carbide Offers $7 Million Interim Relief UCC offers $5 million in relief for victims before the U.S. District Court, bringing the total to date to $7 million.

1986

Mar Union Carbide Proposes $350 Million as Settlement for Victims and Families

Union Carbide proposes a settlement amount of $350 million that will generate a fund for Bhopal victims of between $500-600 million over 20 years. Plaintiffs' U.S. attorneys endorse amount.

May Bhopal Litigation Transferred to India

(continued)

(continued)

U.S. District Court Judge transfers all Bhopal litigation to India. Decision is appealed.

1987

Jan   U.S. Court of Appeals Affirms Transfer of Litigation to India

The court rules that UCIL is a separate entity, owned, managed and operated exclusively by Indian citizens in India.

Aug   Union Carbide Announces Humanitarian Relief

Union Carbide offers an additional $4.6 million in humanitarian interim relief for immediate rehabilitation of Bhopal victims.

1988

Jan   Litigation in India

Throughout 1988, arguments and appeals take place before the Indian Courts regarding compensation for the victims. In November, the Supreme Court of India asks the Government of India and UCC to reach a settlement, and tells both sides to 'start with a clean slate'.

May   New Evidence on Causation

Independent investigation by the engineering and consulting firm Arthur D. Little, Inc., concludes that the gas leak could only have been caused by sabotage; someone intentionally connected a water hose to the gas storage tank and caused a massive chemical reaction.

1989

Feb   Final Settlement at $470 Million

The Supreme Court of India directs a final settlement of all Bhopal litigation in the amount of $470 million, to be paid by March 31, 1989. Both the Government of India and Union Carbide accept the court's direction. UCC pays $425 million; UCIL pays the rupee equivalent of $45 million (including $5 million of interim relief previously paid).

1991

Oct   Supreme Court Confirms the Settlement and Closes Legal Proceedings

The Supreme Court of India upholds the civil settlement of $470 million in its entirety and sets aside portion of settlement that quashed criminal prosecutions that were pending at the time of settlement. The Court also:

- Requires Government of India to purchase, out of the settlement fund, a group medical insurance policy to cover 100,000 persons who may later develop symptoms;
- Requires Government of India to make up any shortfall, however unlikely, in settlement fund;
- Gives directions concerning the administration of settlement fund;
- Dismisses all outstanding petitions seeking review of settlement; and
- Requests UCC and UCIL to voluntarily fund capital and operating costs of a hospital in Bhopal for eight years, estimated at approximately $17 million, to be built on land donated by the state government.

UCC and UCIL agree to fund the hospital, as requested.

1992

Apr   Union Carbide Sets Up Trust Fund

UCC establishes charitable trust to ensure its share of the funding to build a hospital in Bhopal and fund operations for up to eight years.

1995–1999

Charitable Trust Builds Hospital

Hospital charitable trust begins facility construction in October 1995.

UCC provides approximately $90 million from the sale of all its UCIL stock.

By 1999, the trust has $100 million. Building is completed and physicians and medical staff are being selected. The hospital will have facilities for the treatment of eye, lung and heart problems.

2004

July   Supreme Court of India Orders Release of Remaining Settlement Funds to Victims

(continued)

(continued)

Fifteen years after reaching settlement, the Supreme Court of India orders the Government of India to release all additional settlement funds to the victims. News reports indicate that there is approximately $327 million in the fund as a result of earned interest from money remaining after all claims had been paid.

U.S. District Court Says Union Carbide Not Liable in Jagarnath Sahu 2007 case

Judge John Keenan of the U.S. District Court in New York rules that Union Carbide is not liable for any on-going pollution form the Bhopal chemical plant.

2005

Apr   Supreme Court of India Extends Deadline For Release of Remaining Settlement Funds

The Supreme Court of India grants a request from the Welfare Commission for Bhopal Gas Victims and extends to April 30, 2006, the distribution of the rest of the settlement funds by the Welfare Commission. News reports indicate that approximately $390 million remains in the fund as a result of earned interest.

2006

Aug   U.S. Court of Appeals Upholds Dismissal of 8-Year-Old Bano Case

The Second Circuit Court of Appeals in New York upholds the dismissal of the remaining claims in the case of Bano vs. Union Carbide Corporation, thereby denying plaintiffs' motions for class certification and claims for property damages and remediation of the Bhopal plant site by Union Carbide. The ruling reaffirms UCC's long-held positions and finally puts to rest – both procedurally and substantively – the issues raised in the class action complaint first filed against Union Carbide in 1999 by Haseena Bi and several organizations representing the residents of Bhopal, India.

Sep   Bhopal Welfare Commission Reports All Initial Compensation Claims, Revised Petitions Cleared

Indian media report states the 'registrar in the office of Welfare Commissioner . . . said that all cases of initial compensation claims by victims of the 1984 Bhopal gas tragedy have been cleared . . . With clearance of initial compensation claims and revision petitions, no case is pending'.

Oct   Madhya Pradesh State Government To Prepare Drinking Water, Healthcare, Environmental Rehabilitation Plan

Indian media report says the state government of Madhya Pradesh will 'chalk out an action plan in the next two months for providing drinking water, adequate healthcare and economic and environmental rehabilitation to survivors of the Bhopal gas tragedy'.

2007

Mar   New Class Action Lawsuit Filed in New York Federal Court

Jagarnath Sahu et al. v. UCC and Warren Anderson seeks damages to clean up six individual properties allegedly polluted by contaminants from the Bhopal plant, as well as the remediation of property in 16 colonies adjoining the plant. Suit has been stayed pending resolution of appeal in Janki Bai Sahu case. (See decision in June 2013 below.)

2013

June   U.S. Court of Appeals Upholds 2012 Ruling Union Carbide Not Liable in Janki Bai Sahu Case

The Federal Second Circuit Court of Appeals upholds a 2012 judgment of the district court that Union Carbide was not liable for any environmental remediation or pollution-related personal injury claims made by residents near the Bhopal plant site in India.

2014

July   U.S. Court Rules UCC Not Liable for Property Damage Claims in Jagarnath Sahu Case

A U.S. Federal court concludes in the Jagarnath Sahu et al. v. UCC case (Sahu II) that neither Union Carbide nor Warren Anderson could be sued for ongoing contamination from the Bhopal chemical plant. This suit was originally filed in 2007, but hearings on it were stayed pending resolution of the Janki Bai Sahu case (Sahu I), which was dismissed in 2013. An appeal is pending in this case.
                    (www.bhopal.com/ Published by Dow Chemicals)

The legacy that continues to this day is the battle surrounding the compensation and liabilities relating to the incident, as demonstrated by

(continued)

(continued)

the Sustainability Commissioner's resignation on live television. Union Carbon Corporation maintain that the cause of the incident was 'undeniably sabotage' Jackson Browning report (1993), however regardless of the disputed cause of the incident, they go on to comment:

> The sheer scope of the Bhopal incident made it an extremely complex public communications problem. Ron Wishart, summoned by Chairman Anderson from a government relations assignment in Washington to aid him in directing the Bhopal crisis team, put it very succinctly: 'The problems raised by the tragedy spanned two companies, two governments, two continents, and two cultures.' As our chief outside counsel put it, 'There were three tragedies at Bhopal – the gas leak, the reaction to it by the Indian government, and the consequent inability to get relief to the genuine victims.'
>
> (Browning, 1993)

Public Records show that Warren Anderson was the CEO of Union Carbide at the time of the Bhopal Incident, he died on 29 September 2014. He was arrested in the days following the incident, paid bail and left India. He was officially labelled a fugitive, and a judge called him an 'absconder'. He died, as many thousands of others, with a legacy of the Bhopal incident unresolved.

How can PSR affect CSR?

Better organizations have already recognized that it's only through personal behavioural changes that the highest levels of CSR performance will be achieved. Some have proposed and implemented voluntary personal commitments for each member of staff to pledge to meet CSR and sustainability objectives, believing that this will result in a more positive outcome than compelling staff to comply.

Here is an example of a PSR initiative proposed to the employees of Salford University in Manchester, UK.

Sustainability charter for personal action

Your commitment   I am committed to this charter for personal action and will undertake one or more of the actions below.

Please tick as appropriate:

✓   Switch off all lights in a single-occupancy or empty office when leaving it for more than an hour. If we all did this, it would save five per cent of our overall electric budget.

✓   When printing, do you need a hard copy? If so, re-use the back of old paper. For reports, always print double sided and use recycled paper where possible. Last year, the organization spent £x with paper suppliers – help reduce this next year.

✓   When in the office, especially during summer months, check whether you need all the lights on. If we all turned unnecessary lights off, it would save five per cent of our overall electricity budget.

✓   Find a partner to share your drive to work with each day, cutting down on single car occupancy. This saves you money, and reduces emissions and congestion. Never drive around with your boot full, and never fill your tank to the top – it's a car, not a fuel tanker. A full tank is equivalent to an extra passenger in weight.

✓   Where possible, switch off your computer and monitor before leaving the office for the day. If we all did this, it would wipe 10 per cent off our electric energy bill. Small-powered equipment, copiers, and printers account for most of our base load [30 per cent].

✓   Use public transport if possible. One day a week can save you money, and society benefits from reduced congestion and emissions.

✓   Report any dripping taps or water leaks to your facilities department. A dripping tap fills a bath of water every week.

✓   Work with your organization on sustainable development activities in the local community.

✓   Remember the three Rs – reduce, re-use (plastic carriers, bottles and boxes) and recycle (glass, cans, plastic bottles, paper and computers).

✓   Tell a friend! We need everyone to get involved in this campaign. Remember: not only do we help to save the planet, but all money we save can help to pay for other organizational initiatives, such as enhanced staff benefits or improved and updated equipment.

A possible criticism of this approach is that while the organization is taking a positive lead, it falls short of requiring staff to meet any set standards. Should the organization ask staff to volunteer to pledge to and follow these principles, or should it be part of the organization's mandatory procedures that must be followed? If staff don't choose to make this pledge, what then? However, in the true spirit of CSR, and as each employee is themselves a stakeholder, we need to engage and encourage them to make a difference in their area of responsibility. The idea that 'one volunteer is better than ten pressed men' is a good starting principle from which to help build consensus, and encourages staff to take action where the organization has no direct control or influence, such as at home.

As an agent for change, you should consider what you have direct influence over. What can you change? Start with yourself, and then look around you. Whether or not you decide to start (or continue) taking a CSR approach to your whole life, we've presented this chapter to give you practical ideas to get you thinking about what you can do to become a more socially responsible individual. As Walter Lippman (1914) highlights, 'We have changed our environment more quickly than we know how to change ourselves.' The problem is that, as with Newton's third law of motion, every action has an equal and opposite reaction. For everything we buy, use and throw away, we alter the balance of the earth's resources. The question is to what extent we as individuals are willing to compromise our present desires for society and future generations.

PSR is only a start, but it should bring significant benefits to you, your family and your community. After all, everything you do affects everything and everyone else – 'no man is an island'.

Chapter 10

Learning from London

Citius, altius, forties
(Swifter, higher, stronger)

–Olympic motto

While an ancient Greek myth tells of the Olympic Games being founded by Hercules, son of Zeus and king of the gods, the earliest written documents of the earthly games tell that a single event, the 'stade' – a run of approximately 192 metres – was held as part of a religious festival to Zeus. The records, dating back to 776 BCE, detail the first Olympic champion as Coroebus, who, along with all the other athletes, completed the event naked. These games were accompanied by a truce, allowing Greek Olympians to travel between warring city-states in a time of conflict. The popularity of the original games continued to grow, being held every four years for nearly 1,200 years, until they were outlawed by the Roman emperor Theodosius I, a Christian, who abolished the games because of their pagan influences (International Olympic Committee, 2015).

The competitive arena of the ancient Greek games held in the eigth century BC may seem a strange place to start the last chapter of this book. The idea of being the best in a gladiatorial battle, of excelling in a competitive event, of being swifter, higher and stronger that your adversaries, would not appear the natural home for altruistic gestures and the ideals and concepts of CSR that we've already covered. But on closer inspection, the concept of fair play and sportsmanship that is quintessential to the Olympic spirit mirrors the philosophy of CSR. As we saw in earlier chapters, CSR is about playing by the rules, not exploiting others, and reaping the rewards in the long run. In sport, only by beating your competitors fairly and within the rules can you leave no room for doubt that you're a world-class athlete, the best in your field and a worthy champion.

In this chapter, we'll look at how the Olympic organization has become an exemplar in trying to incorporate CSR into its own core goals. We'll also discuss what your organization could learn from the London 2012 sustainability goals of the Olympic Delivery Authority, either to help in winning direct tenders, delivering benefits or to use the example of the games to make the changes in your business that will build a legacy of success for many years to come.

Approximately 2,500 years after the first Greek games, a Frenchman named Pierre de Coubertin began the modern Olympic Movement, which established the modern games. The games of the first Olympiad were held in 1896 in Athens, with nine events. The games were always intended to be more than a pure quest for sporting excellence, as shown through the original goal of the Olympic Movement:

> To contribute to building a peaceful and better world by educating youth through sport practiced without discrimination of any kind and in the Olympic spirit, which requires mutual understanding with a spirit of friendship, solidarity and fair play.
>
> (IOC, 2008)

This goal has been developed over the intervening century and incorporated into six principles of Olympism that follow the concepts of CSR and PSR:

1   Olympism is a philosophy of life, exalting and combining in a balanced whole the qualities of body, will and mind. Blending sport with culture and education, Olympism seeks to create a way of life based on the joy of effort, the educational value of good example and respect for universal fundamental ethical principles.
2   The goal of Olympism is to place sport at the service of the harmonious development of man, with a view to promoting a peaceful society concerned with the preservation of human dignity.
3   The Olympic Movement is the concerted, organized, universal and permanent action, carried out under the supreme authority of the International Olympic Committee, of all individuals and entities who are inspired by the values of Olympism. It covers the five continents. It reaches its peak with the bringing together of the world's athletes at the great sports festival, the Olympic Games. Its symbol is five interlaced rings.
4   The practice of sport is a human right. Every individual must have the possibility of practicing sport, without discrimination of any kind and in the Olympic spirit, which requires mutual understanding with a spirit of friendship, solidarity and fair play. The organization, administration and management of sport must be controlled by independent sports organizations.
5   Any form of discrimination with regard to a country or a person on grounds of race, religion, politics, gender or otherwise is incompatible with belonging to the Olympic Movement.
6   Belonging to the Olympic Movement requires compliance with the Olympic Charter and recognition by the IOC.

(International Olympic Committee, 2007)

These principles have been transferred into the host city selection process. Hosting the games is a costly venture, and only if long-term legacy planning maximizes the benefits can a worthwhile return be seen on the investment.

London 2012

London 2012 represented an opportunity for the whole of the UK not only to be associated with the games, but also to capture the essence of the Olympic ideal. Whilst many were doubtful in a typically British way that the games could or would succeed, the games delivered in vision, as a sporting event on the world stage, and demonstrated how CSR could be delivered as part of the games.

At the core of the London bid was the concept of legacy, and this drove CSR and a programme of sustainable development as part of the delivery of the Olympic event. The construction phase, the games themselves and the legacy were viewed as an opportunity for the UK to tackle issues such as sustainable construction, climate change, waste management, social inclusion, obesity and community cohesion. Those who viewed the games only as a sporting event missed the core values of the Olympic Movement.

With an event of this scale there where many different organizations, in this chapter we focus on the work of London Organising Committee of the Olympic and Paralympic Games (LOCOG), which was the organization responsible for overseeing the planning and development of the 2012 Summer Olympic and Paralympic Games and Olympic Delivery Authority (ODA), which was a non-departmental public body of the Department for Culture, Media and Sport, responsible for ensuring the delivery of venues, infrastructure and legacy.

The London 2012 ODA developed a sustainability plan that invited those who wanted to be involved to be more inspired on sustainability issues to act to make a difference, as illustrated in this extract:

Making a real difference

We want to use the Games to illustrate the capacity of major events to influence behaviour and develop knowledge.

We want the Games to inspire people to:

- recycle more;
- use more public transport, walk and cycle more;
- lifestyle choices – preferences for environmentally efficient homes/ work places, sustainable food, and/or greener products;
- more sustainable corporate practices.

After the Games we want people to know more about:

- new methods of environmental management, monitoring and reporting;
- demonstration of new, 'green' technology;
- development of 'green' businesses.

We also want to use the Games to showcase the sustainable approach and influence the way future major events are managed.

(LOCOG, 2009)

The ODA included legacy planning from day one, as illustrated in Figure 10.1 below. Your organization can start to consider its own CSR journey today by considering each of the ODA sustainability plan goals, and using these as drivers for change in your professional and personal life. The 12 key sustainability objectives are:

1   minimizing carbon emissions;
2   efficient water use, re-use and recycling;
3   protecting and enhancing biodiversity;
4   prioritizing walking, cycling and the use of public transport;
5   optimizing the reduction of waste through design;
6   creating new, safe, mixed-use communities;
7   environmentally and socially responsible materials;
8   creating a highly accessible Olympic Park and venues;
9   optimizing land, water and air quality and minimizing noise;

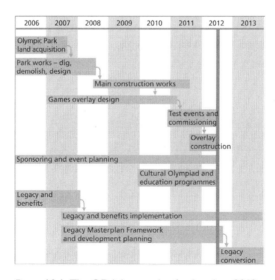

Figure 10.1 The ODA legacy plan for London, 2012.

10   creating new employment and business opportunities;
11   providing healthy lifestyle opportunities;
12   involving the community.

Clearly, for a publicly funded event to justify spending millions of pounds of taxpayers' money, it had to deliver benefits at many levels. But why should your organization consider these goals as part of its business objectives? Apart from jumping through a metaphorical hoop in order to gain a contract, what's in it for you?

Test your thinking 18

For each of the 12 sustainability objectives, consider the benefits to you, your organization and your community from pursuing that objective.
   A few of the key benefits are:

Minimizing carbon emissions

Carbon management and energy efficiency have a range of benefits to the individual and organization. Reducing use of fuel, electricity and transport will directly save money. In terms of CSR effects, lower carbon emissions collectively across civilizations will help to control the effects of man-made climate change, including sea level change, the frequency of severe storms, the spread of infectious diseases, disruption to food, water and infrastructure and population movement caused by climate change. As we have seen in Chapter 2, more and more governments' are incorporating Carbon Management into legal frameworks, such as the EU Emissions Trading Scheme; organizations need to respond either directly to applicable legislation or to monitor and manage the risk of increased regulations in the future.

Efficient water use, re-use and recycling

Water management links directly to energy use, so all the benefits and problems above also apply here. Water is a resource for wildlife habitats, and we also need clean drinking water for general use, so the more we waste, the less we as a society have to use on the things we need. Water also costs money, and most businesses and an increasing number of domestic customers are charged for the amount they use.

(continued)

(continued)

Protecting and enhancing biodiversity

Biodiversity is important as the variety and the number of species reflects the genetic health of our ecosystem. As the climate changes, and human needs change, we need a diverse range of species to maintain supplies of essential products of the biosphere, such as oxygen. Biodiversity also provides a genetic resource for medical, agricultural and technological developments for the future. Wildlife, nature reserves and green spaces also have an amenity value.

Prioritizing walking, cycling and the use of public transport

For the individual, this can help to reduce transport costs and increase exercise and personal fitness. For business, it means less demand for car parking, and for society it means reduced congestion and less air pollution.

Optimizing the reduction of waste through design

If we use resources inefficiently, we're not only wasting the material in question, but we're also increasing the pollution and environmental degradation caused in the extraction, manufacture, transport, packaging and disposal of that material. This affects you as an individual through air pollution and land contamination from landfill; it affects your organization since it not only has to buy the materials you throw away but must also pay to dispose of them; and it affects the community, which has to provide landfill, incineration and recycling facilities.

Creating new, safe, mixed-use communities

We all want to live in safety. We can't create all-new communities, but we can all do more to support the community we live in. As individuals, supporting and engaging in our community – by helping a neighbour or supporting voluntary work – brings a range of benefits including personal satisfaction, a greater sense of community and a larger social network. For the business, this can bring benefits including increased staff morale, productivity, good publicity and marketing opportunities. Safer communities are more likely to have reduced crime figures, which reduces the costs of neighbourhood policing.

Environmentally and socially responsible materials

Purchasing power is one of the strongest freedoms we have (see Chapter 9). By choosing environmentally and socially responsible materials, we have the ability to change multinational organizations. Why would Tesco stock fair trade coffee or ASDA-Walmart offer organic chocolate if people didn't want to buy them? For the individual, the purchasing decision helps to demonstrate to the world that they're willing to pay for more ethical practices and a better environment, and thus become an agent of change. For the organization, more environmentally friendly products and materials may be cheaper in the long run, will increase your energy security, could open new markets and offer a competitive advantage.

Creating highly accessible venues and access to services

According to the Department for Work and Pensions, there are over 11 million people with a limiting long-term illness, impairment or disability (Department for Work and Pensions, 2014). For someone with a disability, getting access to your organization's services brings the simple benefit of being able to interact in society as an able-bodied person can. For your organization, it brings the benefit of a market of an additional at least £80bn, based on 2002 (the estimated annual purchasing power of people with disabilities, Family Resources Survey 2002/03. This figure is now ten years old and the DWP say they have no plans to update it, suggesting that the current figure is likely to be much higher), along with the possibility of access to committed and skilled employees, and avoiding court actions for discrimination. For society, the more the barriers to disability are removed, the easier it is for individuals to contribute to the community.

Optimizing land, water and air quality and minimizing noise

If we optimize land, water and air quality, individuals will benefit from a higher standard of living through less pollution. This reduces the risk of pollution-related medical conditions (such as asthma), causes less stress from noise and creates a more pleasant environment in which to live. Organizations benefit from not paying for waste or raw materials they don't need, and society will benefit from lower healthcare costs.

Creating new employment and business opportunities

New employment and business opportunities help individuals become more affluent, have greater job satisfaction and improve their standard of living. Organizations can thrive, grow and become more profitable, and therefore pay higher taxes to support community programmes.

(continued)

(continued)

Providing healthy lifestyle opportunities

A commitment to healthy lifestyles links educating staff, from choosing good diets and taking more regular exercise to managing health and safety at work. For the individual, a healthy lifestyle will reduce the risk of illness (such as heart disease, cancer and diabetes) and improve their length and quality of life, while health and safety at work will reduce the likelihood of work-related disability. Organizations benefit as staff have fewer accidents, are off sick less often and have fewer work-related health problems. This supports the retention of skills and experience within the organization, reduces civil and criminal liabilities, and increases productivity and profitability. In society, lower rates of illness will lead to more revenue from taxation, lower incapacity benefit payments, less of a burden on the national healthcare service and more productivity – this in turn contributes to a higher GDP.

Involving the community

A community is a collective of consenting individuals. The basic premise of CSR is to run your organization in a way that does not exploit the individuals, society or environment it comes into contact with. Involving communities benefits the participating individuals through social networking, a sense of achievement and support. The organization benefits from good public relations, a higher media profile and improved staff morale, and society benefits from increased inputs, such as taxation.

As we have seen, many of the ODA's sustainability objectives could bring tangible benefits to you, your organization and your community. All the organizations in the London 2012 Olympic supply chain were required to contribute towards these goals. Organizations which were not involved in CSR may be at a distinct disadvantage. as they may not have the same competitive edge and may have less motivated staff with higher sickness absence rates, lower productivity and retention rates and be less profitable. As intended, the Olympics 'raised the bar'. Is your organization training now to achieve gold?

The question for any organization is how to deliver these sustainability objectives while meeting the concurrent objective of running an organization (in the case of the ODA, this was the feat of hosting successful Olympic and Paralympic Games). ISO 14001:2015 starts to provide an answer, as it drives organizations to see sustainability issues as a strategic risk and opportunity for the organization resilience, that environmental issues should be considered as an integral business risk and our DTRT model extends this to all areas of CSR.

Within the sustainability plan, the ODA focused on five key themes of climate change, waste, biodiversity, healthy living and inclusion. In each area, it planned a range of initiatives to help minimize its environmental impact and maximize the social and economic benefits in the construction, event and legacy phases.

This extract is from the London 2012 Sustainability Plan (LOCOG, 2009):

Climate change

As far as possible, we will ensure that everything that is being constructed can be used and improved on in the future. For example, we are planning so that the communities that remain in and around the Olympic Park after the Games will be able to access local renewable energy sources as new, low/zero carbon fuels become available.

After the Games, at least 20 per cent of energy requirements will be supplied by on-site renewable energy sources.

The close proximity of the Park to transport connections and the creation of new footpaths and cycle routes will help reduce car dependency among the local community.

Waste

Through the education campaigns we run before and during the Games, we will encourage people to reduce, reuse or recycle waste. We hope that the 2012 programme will aim to help change people's habits for good – and inspire other major events in the future to be more sustainable.

The Games will act as a catalyst for the development of new waste processing facilities in east London, which will provide a lasting facility.

Biodiversity

The Olympic Park Masterplan provides for 102 hectares of open space. The Park will be the largest new urban green space in Europe and the area will benefit from:

- enhanced water and land habitats;
- open water and wetlands; and
- species-rich grasslands.

The types of plant used will be native to south-east England (and ideally of locally-grown stock), which are suited to predicted future climates.

This will help the whole site be better adapted to climate change, through its ability to cope with heavy rainfall events as well as providing greenery to provide shade.

Healthy living

The legacy of a new parkland designed to promote walking, cycling and provide sporting facilities for the elite athletes and the community has excellent health benefits for the area. In addition, permanent buildings will be converted into service buildings that will support the community. These include:

- the Aquatics Centre will be available for use by local residents; and
- the Polyclinic (which will offer medical services to athletes during the Games) will be transformed by Newham Primary Care Trust into a new primary care centre for local people.

Sport programmes will continue to be developed as a result of the London 2012 Games across London and the UK.

Inclusion

To make London 2012 'Everyone's Games', the UK Government and the Mayor of London have prepared delivery plans to ensure that benefits and participation can be spread as widely as possible. The Government published 'Our Promise for 2012' in June 2007, and is planning to publish a detailed legacy action plan in 2008. The Mayor published 'Your 2012', summarizing its delivery plans, in July 2007.

London 2012 is committed to working closely with local authorities and communities, in order to maximize the benefits that the Park can deliver after the Games, in terms of:

- re-integrating communities on either side of the Lower Lea Valley;
- creating housing (including affordable housing) and jobs for local people;
- creating parkland and legacy venues that will benefit local communities, as well as supporting elite sports; and
- enabling social cohesion, and social, economic and environmental regeneration in one of the most underdeveloped parts of the UK.

(LOCOG, 2009)

The Olympic Games are not unique. Every organization needs to look at its own social, economic and environmental impacts and develop an appropriate CSR management programme to maximize the benefits to its stakeholders.

Test your thinking 19

We'd like you now to consider the five key themes of the ODA's sustainability plan. How does your organization affect its stakeholders in these areas? What CSR action could your organization take to optimize the benefits in these five theme areas?

1   climate change;
2   waste;
3   biodiversity;
4   healthy living;
5   inclusion.

Here are some possible answers and 34 ideas for action.

Climate change: ten ideas

1   Identify all sources of direct and indirect greenhouse gas releases from your organization's operations. Consider electricity use, direct burning of fossil fuels (e.g. mains gas boilers) and other releases of greenhouse gases (e.g. air conditioner refrigerants, transport).
2   Measure and establish monitoring methods for each of your releases, and establish a benchmark from which improvements can be verified.
3   Turn off anything not in use or on standby.
4   Help your staff to grasp the issues with posters, emails and briefings.
5   Change your energy supplier to one with a renewable tariff or with a lower carbon dioxide generation mix.
6   Research best practice – visit the Carbon Trust website (www. carbontrust.com) for support and information.
7   Buy energy-efficient equipment and include energy use as a criterion in your purchasing policy.
8   Promote energy efficiency among your suppliers.
9   Develop your processes and products to be more energy-efficient.
10   After reducing your energy use, consider carbon offsetting (see the figure below).

(continued)

(continued)

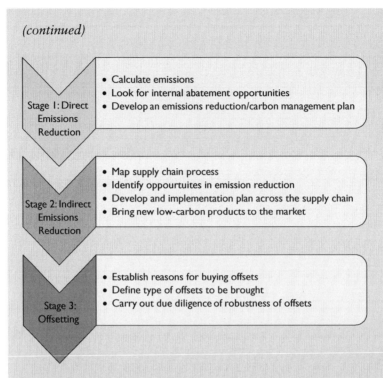

Stage 1: Direct Emissions Reduction
- Calculate emissions
- Look for internal abatement opportunities
- Develop an emissions reduction/carbon management plan

Stage 2: Indirect Emissions Reduction
- Map supply chain process
- Identify oppourtuites in emission reduction
- Develop and implementation plan across the supply chain
- Bring new low-carbon products to the market

Stage 3: Offsetting
- Establish reasons for buying offsets
- Define type of offsets to be brought
- Carry out due diligence of robustness of offsets

Figure 10.2 The Carbon Trust three-stage approach to developing robust offsetting strategy.

Waste: ten ideas

1 Classify all your waste streams, establishing what is produced, how much there is of it and where it's currently disposed of. This could be linked to an awareness programme, such as 'record what you bin today'.

2 Establish regular monitoring for each waste stream. Calculate the annual waste footprint, including the amount sent for recycling or landfill. Include this in management reports and information to staff, including the cost of waste disposal and the items being disposed of, if possible.

3 Review legal compliance requirements in relation to the waste management duty of care, including controlled and hazardous waste, waste electrical and electronic equipment, and packaging.

4 Get commitment from key influencers, appoint champions and set targets to aim for. Develop action plans to implement waste minimization or reduction measures and assign responsibilities.

5   Investigate waste reduction options. Review all of your organization's processes – start with packaging waste. Also consider your purchasing policy so that you can be sure that you're buying the correct stock to prevent waste in the first place.

6   Review your processes. Consider lean production and quality control principles, such as smaller batch sizes to reduce the amount of waste you create.

7   Consider your outputs. Is your product as energy-efficient, minimally packaged and eco-designed as it could be?

8   From the thorough process review in ideas 5, 6 and 7, apply the waste hierarchy (see Figure 10.1) in relation to each waste stream. Ask these questions in turn:

   o   can the waste be eliminated completely?
   o   can the volume, weight or hazardous content be reduced?
   o   can the item be re-used or repaired either in house or by others?
   o   can the material be recycled?
   o   can the material be used for energy recovery or composting
   o   are you using licensed carriers and disposal methods (i.e. responsible disposal) to get rid of any remaining waste?

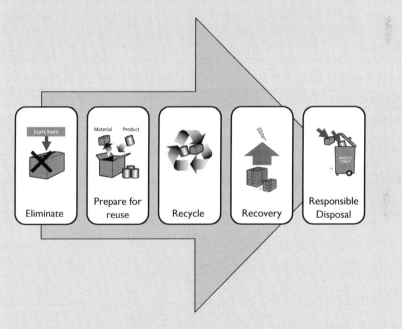

Figure 10.3 The waste hierarchy.

(continued)

(continued)

Also consider:

- o including waste and recycling monitoring in inspection reports;
- o contacting suppliers to encourage them to use minimum or returnable packaging;
- o encouraging paperless systems where feasible;
- o monitoring ordering amounts and maintaining good stock control;
- o researching best practice on websites such as WRAP (www. wrap.org.uk);
- o providing information on how to reduce waste, e.g. next to printers and photocopiers;
- o considering product shelf life and disposal methods at the purchasing stage.

9 Provide training to staff, and explain how important it is to eliminate, reduce, reuse and recycle. Emphasize the volume and cost of waste, and the cost of replacing the item you're throwing away. Implement a staff suggestion and/or reward scheme.

10 Spread the news. Include information on waste recycling schemes, reductions and cost savings in reports, internal communications and company newsletters.

Biodiversity: four ideas

1 Consider nature conservation in your procurement policy, and make sure paper and timber is from Forestry Stewardship Council certified sources. Make sure no items you use are on the CITES lists – see Chapter 9 for more details on labelling and markings.

2 Consider your landscaped areas, and maximize their wildlife value. Rather than having just mown grass, investigate the possibility of:

- o choosing plant species suitable to the local environment – use native species where suitable;
- o planting ground cover in some areas to provide habitat for birds, small mammals and invertebrates;
- o planting dense shrubs to provide safe nesting sites, and plants that bear berries to provide food for wildlife;
- o choosing plants that flower and fruit in different seasons to create year-round food sources and visual interest;
- o selecting nectar-producing varieties of flowering plants and avoid F1 hybrids known not to produce pollen and nectar;

- o replanting with native species where non-native trees are due for replacement;
- o retaining crevices, slots and holes for invertebrates in wooden fences and on buildings and similar structures;
- o reducing use of mowers and leaf clearing machines that remove invertebrates and organic material;
- o installing nest boxes and bird baths;
- o installing insect nesting boxes in suitable locations;
- o reviewing and, if necessary, modifying use of horticultural chemicals;
- o using peat-free compost and manure on flower beds;
- o using only organic fertilizers;
- o providing information boards at the entrances to your grounds explaining what you're doing to improve biological diversity.

(This list is based on information provided by the Westminster Biodiversity Partnership 'Local Biodiversity Action Plan' (Westminster Biodiversity Partnership, 2007)).

3 Review pollution and spillage control to ensure the protection of local watercourses, especially those leading to local natural reserves or Sites of Special Scientific Interest.
4 Support local nature conservation groups, voluntary workers and wildlife trusts.

Healthy living: five ideas

1 Make sure your workplace occupational health management system is implemented as intended.
2 Promote offsite health and safety to staff – employees injured at home in DIY or sporting accidents have an impact on your organization. Consider promotional literature to give staff guidance on good practices.
3 Promote a healthy lifestyle through good nutrition and regular exercise. Investigate reduced membership fees for people wanting to use a gym – or open one on site if you have the space and funds.
4 Positively support a healthy work–life balance. Staff who are less stressed are more productive, take less time off work and will stay in their job longer. Review the kinds of flexible work patterns that are feasible for your organization. Respond positively when your staff ask for flexibility.

(continued)

(continued)

5   Provide supportive information: this could be leaflets or web addresses of groups to help with childcare, debt relief or benefits, or more resource-intensive initiatives, such as providing a counselling and employee assistance programme (sometimes known as an 'EAP'), or private health care.

Inclusion: five ideas

1   Review the accessibility of your site, seeking external advice if necessary. Consider the needs of customers and employees.
2   Review your recruitment, promotion and retention policies. Consider where you advertise, what skills or abilities are actually needed for the job, and whether the current policies reflect best practice and legal standards.
3   Review your products and services. How do they meet the needs of people with disabilities or individuals from a range of social backgrounds? Is there an opportunity to develop the product or service to gain access to these markets?
4   Consider open days and educational activities to support local schools, and give talks or work experience opportunities.
5   Support the rehabilitation of staff following long-term absence.

Did the London 2012 Games achieve its goals?

The memories of the London Olympics live on, from those that saw the Olympic torch visit a town near them, sitting down to see the opening ceremony, watching the games in person or watching three gold medal winners on Super Saturday, the Olympics delivered images that will stay with the nation for decades to come. Furthermore, the event delivered a world-class event without realizing any of the doom-mongers' fears of traffic congestion, overspends or flops. It was part of a cultural awakening of the UK's strength to deliver projects on a world stage, which linked with projects such as Heathrow Airport Terminal 5, royal events such as the Diamond Jubilee and Wedding of the Duke and Duchesses of Cambridge, sporting successes in the Tour de France and at Wimbledon for Andy Murray and Formula 1 World Championships for Lewis Hamilton, gave the British a new found optimism. Has your organization achieved such as positive cultural revolution?

Case Study 10.1   Electrical sport sells electric cars, China, Malaysia, Uruguay, Argentina, USA, Monaco, Germany, Russia, UK

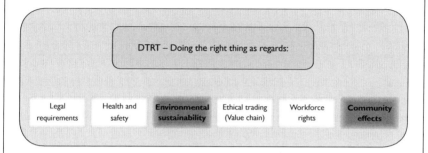

Formula E

> This is the start of the future. Fifteen years from now, all new cars will be clean.
>
> –Sir Richard Branson, speaking to the crowd at the inaugural London Formula E event, 27 June 2015

Formula E is a new FIA single-seater championship, and is the world's first fully electric racing series. Beginning in September 2014 and running through until June 2015, the championship competed in the heart of some of the world's leading cities, including Beijing, Miami, Moscow and London. For the inaugural season, ten teams, each with two drivers, went head-to-head creating a unique and exciting racing series designed to appeal to a new generation of motorsport fans. It represents a vision for the future of the motor industry over the coming decades, serving as a framework for R&D around the electric vehicle, accelerating general interest in these cars and promoting sustainability.

> This spectacular series will offer both entertainment and a new opportunity to share FIA's values for clean energy, mobility and sustainability. The FIA is definitely looking to the future!
>
> (Jean Todd, President of the FIA)

(continued)

(continued)

> We expect this championship to become the framework for research and development around the electric car, a key element for the future of our cities.
>
> (Alejandro Agag, CEO Formula E Holdings)

We attended the first London race, and it was a real spectacle. It was 'sold out' with over 30,000 spectators present, and with a host of new technologies on display and in use. We're pleased to promote it here and share an overview of this new CSR-friendly sport.

From season two (2015–2016), Formula E will be amended to operate as an 'open championship', allowing teams and manufacturers the opportunity to showcase their own electrical energy innovations. Working to the technical specifications set out by the FIA, teams will focus their efforts on improving and developing battery technology in the belief that this will filter into the everyday electric vehicle market.

The championship centres around three core values of Energy, Environment and Entertainment, and is a fusion of engineering, technology, sport, science, design, music and entertainment— all combining to drive the change towards an electric future.

Figure 10.4 The Formula E racing car.

The Formula E car

The Spark-Renault SRT_01E racecar was the first vehicle to be homologated by the FIA. Using the very latest technology, the zero emission SRT_01E aimed to stretch the boundaries of what is currently achievable in electric motorsport, whilst ensuring a balance between cost-effectiveness and sustainability, in addition to coping with the demands of racing entirely on street circuits.

It was built by new French company, Spark Racing Technology, led by the renowned Frédéric Vasseur, together with a consortium of some of the leading companies in motorsport. Italian firm Dallara, which boasted more than 40 years' motorsport experience, constructed the monocoque chassis, aerodynamically designed to aid overtaking. Made from carbon fibre and aluminium, the chassis is both super lightweight and incredibly strong and fully complies with the latest FIA crash tests – the same used to regulate Formula One.

Providing the electric powertrain and electronics is McLaren Electronics Systems, a world leader in high-performance technology for motorsport. Meanwhile, Williams Advanced Engineering, part of the Williams group of companies that includes the world-famous Williams F1 Team, will supply the batteries producing 200kw, the equivalent of 270bhp (horsepower). This will be linked to a five-speed paddle shift sequential gearbox, supplied by Hewland, with fixed ratios to help reduce costs further.

Overseeing all the systems integration will be the Championship's Technical Partner Renault, a leader of electric vehicles and an expert in motorsport thanks to its Renault Sport Technologies and Renault Sport F1 programs. Specially designed 18-inch treaded tyres will be supplied by Official Tyre Partner Michelin, capable of providing optimum performance in both wet and dry conditions.

Rules and regulations

The 2014–2015 FIA Formula E Championship was contested over eleven rounds on ten city-centre circuits around the globe (the final two rounds were held in London). All rounds were one-day events with practice, qualifying and the race taking place in a single day in order to reduce costs and minimize disruption to the host city.

Practice

All events opened with a 45-minute practice session followed by a further 30-minute session, giving drivers opportunities to experience the

(continued)

(continued)

Figure 10.5 Spaces for charging electric vehicles at the Marriott/NCP car park in Bristol, UK.

circuit. They will have up to two cars available to them giving them the option to change cars should they wish. Full power (200kw/270bhp) will be available throughout.

Qualifying

The qualifying session is a straight fight for the fastest lap time and determines the order for the day's race. The session will last 55 minutes (40 minutes track) and sees the drivers divided into four groups of five cars, with each group having ten minutes to set their best time. Full power (200kw/270bhp) will be available throughout with drivers only able to use one car. The driver setting the fastest time will be awarded three points.

ePrix

Races begin by standing start and last for approximately one hour with drivers making one mandatory pit stop in order to change cars. Power will be restricted to 'race mode' (150kw/202.5bhp) but for those drivers with 'FanBoost' (see below), the power output can be temporarily increased to 180kw/243bhp for five seconds per car. Points will be awarded using the standard FIA system, with the driver setting the fastest lap also receiving two additional points.

FanBoost

Fans can give their favorite driver an extra speed boost by voting for them prior to the race. The three drivers with the most votes will each receive a five second 'power boost' per car, per driver, temporarily increasing their car's power from 150kw to 180kw. Votes are cast online to increase fan engagement, and voting closes a short time before the start of the race.

Championship

The FIA Formula E Championship will consist of both a drivers and a teams' championship. A driver's end of season total is made up of his or her best results less one. A team's total is made up by counting all scores during the season.

Champion driver in the first season was Nelson Piquet Jr, and the champion team was eDAMS-Renault.

Pit stops/Car changes

During races, drivers are required to make one mandatory pit stop in order to change cars. This must take place in their 'pit box' and be observed by an FIA steward to ensure all safety equipment is correctly applied. A minimum time period for the stop (determined on the day) was also enforced. Tyre changes, unless a puncture, are not permitted during this pit stop.

Points and prizes

Drivers scored points using the standard FIA system of: 1st = 25pts, 2nd = 18pts, 3 = 15pts, 4th = 12pts, 5th = 10pts, 6th = 8pts, 7th = 6pts, 8th = 4pts, 9th = 2pts and 10th = 1pt. Three points are awarded to the driver securing pole position, whilst the driver setting the fastest lap received two points. The top three drivers in each race receive a trophy presented on the podium. Trophies are also presented to the driver and team champions at the end of the season. All receive prize money.

Testing

Teams/drivers were entitled to participate in nine official test days; five pre-season, two in-season and two post-season. Private testing in any way was not permitted. No other running was allowed to take place unless for promotional use.

(continued)

(continued)

Tyres and allocation

The Official Tyre Supplier for the FIA Formula E Championship was Michelin. Each driver was supplied five new front tyres and five new rear tyres per event. Those must last for the entire race event – practice, qualifying and race. One front tyre and one rear tyre must come from the previous event (except for the first race where obviously only new tyres were available).

Licence

All drivers, competitors and officials participating in the championship must hold current and valid licences with a minimum requirement of Grade B FIA International driver's licence and a specific FIA 'eLicence'.

Car charging

Charging of the Formula E cars is not permitted during any practice, qualifying or race session or at any time prior to the completion of post-qualifying or post-race scrutineering (which means checking that the cars comply with the rules). Charging in the pits is only permitted using equipment complying with FIA safety regulations. Charging of all 20 cars from flat to full was designed to take 50 minutes.

Drivers

A total of thirty-five drivers from around the world (many ex-F1), from ten teams, competed in the 2014/2015 FIA Formula E Championship.

Social responsibility

One of the most unique aspects of the FIA Formula E Championship is its commitment and promotion of clean energy and sustainability. Using entertainment, Formula E continues to aspire to drive the change towards the greater use of sustainable mobility. In short, it wants to improve the image and perception of electric vehicles and to encourage more people to buy and use them. Of course, Formula E can't do this alone, but it can act as a catalyst between motor car and component companies, leaders, experts, cities and policy-makers to spread the idea and feasibility of an alternative electric future. How exactly does Formula E intend this? By increasing the sales and uptake of electric vehicles (EVs) which in turn helps reduce pollution levels and improve people's health . . . not to mention save many millions of barrels of oil and create many new jobs. By showing people that EVs don't have to be 'uncool' or 'slow' and by improving the infrastructure, costs and technology available – such as battery life – Formula E hopes to achieve this goal.

In 2013, Formula E commissioned a report, by leading global professional services firm Ernst & Young, to assess the global value of Formula E to the EV market over the next 25 years (2015–2040) and its wider economic, environmental and social impact, in addition to delivering a sustainable legacy. It was shown that Formula E can help sell an additional 77 million EVs worldwide, save 4 billion barrels of oil and help make savings of 25 billion euros on healthcare (Ernst & Young, 2013).

However in addition to the core activity, the games also delivered in many other ways. The *London 2012 Post Games Sustainability Report – A Legacy of Change*, (LOCOG, 2012) stated:

> There is a lot to pass on to future Games and the wider world of events and businesses generally. We are enormously proud of what we have managed to do but we know this has only been a start.

In more detail it highlighted:

> This report provides the final results of the key strands of our sustainability programme, many of which will set a benchmark for the future. But overall, how were the Games delivered in a sustainable way? When we published our Sustainability Guidelines for Corporate and Public Events (first issued in July 2008 and updated in May 2010 and February 2012), we set out a definition of what we meant by a sustainable event. This identified eight key attributes, which I think are a good way of looking at how we performed:

> **1   Provide an accessible and inclusive setting for all**
> The detailed planning in the early years to ensure we designed our venues and services to be as accessible as possible really bore fruit during the Games, complemented by the highly successful Games Mobility service. Our food services provided sufficient options to cater for diverse dietary, ethnic, cultural and practical needs; we provided affordable options, access to free drinking water and people could bring their own food into LOCOG venues. Above all, the warm welcome provided our volunteer Games Makers from all walks of life helped to make everyone feel part of the Games.

> **2   Provide a safe and secure atmosphere**
> Thankfully there were no major safety or security incidents during the Games. The screening of visitors into venues was efficient, friendly and

even fun. This was due in large part to the marvelous professionalism of the armed forces and police and their positive engagement with the public. Behind the scenes, the work of the security and emergency services all contributed to the overwhelmingly relaxed and secure atmosphere at the Games.

3   Have minimal negative impacts on the environment
The Games inevitably consume a large amount of resources, but through our planning, procurement and operational choices we have massively avoided waste, we have made substantial carbon savings, sourced environmentally friendly products and taken care to protect the natural and cultural heritage found on our venues. From the natural planting of the Olympic Park to the detailed surveys and ecological management at Greenwich Park and Box Hill, and the partnerships we initiated, we made important contributions to biodiversity conservation.

4   Encourage healthy living
The inspirational power of sport clearly shone through during the Games. Since then, clubs up and down the country have reported a surge in participation in so many different sports. For the Games we instigated the Active Travel Programme, which not only enabled spectators and workforce to cycle or walk to venues, but it formed a huge part of managing the background travel demand across London. We addressed air quality concerns by ensuring we had a low-emission vehicle fleet, maximizing use of public transport modes and fitting particulate filters to several of our temporary power generators. Finally, let's not forget the health and wellbeing benefits of creating a major new parkland in east London, providing vital open space for recreation and enjoyment of the natural environment.

5   Promote responsible sourcing
Staging the Games required a vast amount of goods and services, more than £1 billion-worth in value, all of which had to be sourced sustainably. We put huge effort into our procurement programme, in which sustainability was an integral part of our definition of value for money. This gave us a diverse supplier base, of which 70 per cent of companies were small and medium-sized enterprises (SMEs) and represented all nations and regions of the UK. In 2011, we were certified to the globally recognized standard of the Chartered Institute of Purchasing and Supply for our effective processes, strategies, policies and procedures.

We always knew there would be challenges, particularly in the area of labour standards, which is why our ground-breaking Sustainable Sourcing

Code introduced the innovative concept of a Complaints and Dispute Resolution Mechanism, something we understand other companies are looking to emulate.

6   Deliver excellent customer experience
When people feel valued they appreciate what you have done. All our client groups, from athletes to spectators, gave us excellent feedback on their Games experience. Their appreciation of the quality of service, of the venues and landscaping, of the transport and security services and the friendliness of the volunteer Games Makers made for an especially memorable occasion. Attention to detail had been a vital factor in achieving this, and sustainability was a key component.

7   Encourage more sustainable behaviour
One thing that came through loud and clear from the Games was that people respected the quality of the venues. So many remarked on how clean and litter-free they were, and how easy it was for them to recycle their waste. Respect for place was also important, whether at the newly created Olympic Park, on the sensitive chalk grasslands of Box Hill (part of the Road Cycling route), or on the grassy cliffs overlooking Weymouth Bay (our Sailing venue).

Through many of the Inspire projects, our Get Set education programme and the local initiative Changing Places, we engaged thousands of people in sustainability projects and activities which we hope will continue for a long time to come.

8   Leave a positive legacy
Although ultimately legacy is a long-term perspective, we can already see numerous examples where our work is being carried forward: among our partners, BT and Coca-Cola have adopted and adapted our carbon footprint methodology to look at their business areas; the Food Legacy Pledge (managed by Sustain) is attracting widespread support; the Waste and Resources Action Programme (WRAP) is taking forward many of the learnings from our zero waste Games vision; and we have been instrumental in the development of the new international management system standard for sustainable events, ISO 20121: 2012.

The assurance statement highlighted the Commission had received 235 recommendations and that it had less than 10 per cent either not been achieved, show no progress yet, or are at significant risk of having not been achieved, demonstrating that they were open to criticism and continue improvement in-relation to meeting its commitments.

Setting a legacy standard

The games set the benchmark in a diverse range of CSR areas, it was completed on time, within budget and in health and safety it achieved an accident frequency rate on site of 0.16 per 100,000 hours worked – in comparison to the construction sector average of 0.55, and the all industry average of 0.21. (HSE, 2012) You can read more about this at www.crsrisk.com, HSE News blog: April 2015, in the article we wrote exploring the matter. There were no work-related fatalities on the whole London 2012 construction programme, when the prevailing sector rate would have expected three lives to have been lost, the first Olympic build to achieve this in history. But not all recent major infrastructure projects have been equally as successful . . .

Case Study 10.2   FIFA Soccer World Cup 2022, Qatar

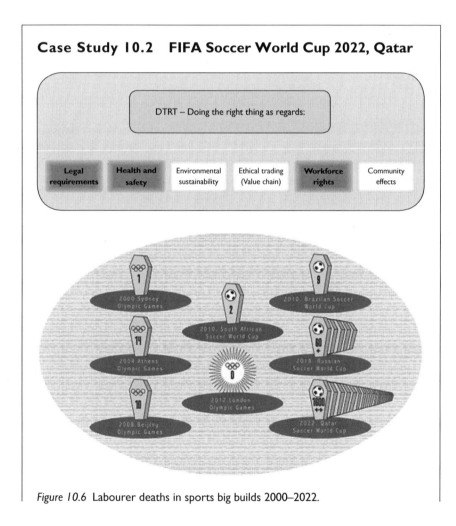

DTRT – Doing the right thing as regards:

| Legal requirements | Health and safety | Environmental sustainability | Ethical trading (Value chain) | Workforce rights | Community effects |

Figure 10.6 Labourer deaths in sports big builds 2000–2022.

FIFA and events in 2015

Founded in 1904, and based in Zurich, Switzerland, the Fédération Internationale de Football Association (FIFA) is the governing body of football (soccer). It is responsible for the organization of the game's major international tournaments, including the four-yearly World Cup and the Women's World Cup.

Journalists had linked senior FIFA officers with corruption, bribery, and alleged vote-rigging pursuant to the re-election of President Joseph 'Sepp' Blatter, and the decision to award World Cups to Russia in 2018 and to Qatar in 2022. These allegations led to indictment of nine top FIFA officials and four executives of sports management companies by the US Department of Justice on charges of money laundering, fraud and racketeering. On 27 May 2015 Swiss authorities arrested several of these officials. These authorities were also initiating a separate criminal investigation into how the organization awarded the 2018 and 2022 World Cups.

President Blatter resigned from his position on 2 June 2015, but announced that he would remain in his position until an election could be held to appoint a his successor. Blatter and the UEFA President (and his once-likely successor) Michel Platini were banned from all involvement in football-related activities by FIFA's ethics committe on 21 December 2015.

Safety in big builds and the FIFA World Cup 2022

> The Arabic world deserves a World Cup. They have 22 countries and have not had any opportunity to organize the tournament.
> – Sepp Blatter, FIFA President, April 2010

On 2 December 2010, it was announced that Qatar would host the 2022 FIFA World Cup. Massive infrastructure projects like constructing stadiums, accommodation and transport systems for any global event like this can cause workers to be injured or killed. The table below shows fatal accidents reported for a sample of recent major 'big builds' (as they are commonly known):

- 2000: Sydney Olympic Games = 1
- 2004: Athens Olympic Games = 14
- 2008: Beijing Olympic Games = 10
- 2010: South African soccer World Cup = 2
- 2012: London Olympic Games = 0
- 2014: Brazilian soccer World Cup = 9
- 2018: Russian soccer World Cup = 60 by summer 2015; event forthcoming

(continued)

(continued)

For labourers working in construction for Qatar's 2022 World Cup, construction safety seems to have been very different. Desert heat, dehydration, poor working conditions and limited labor protection will cause this World Cup to be the deadliest work zone for a sporting event in modern history. And at the time of writing, there are still *seven years* to go before the football kicks off . . . .

While it's near impossible to get exact numbers – as the government of Qatar does not publish them – current estimates presented by the Washington Post suggest more than 1,600 labourers have died so far during World Cup-related construction, including over 1,400 deaths between 2012–2014 and approximately 200 deaths so far in 2015. The extraordinary level of construction activity in Qatar ahead of the 2022 World Cup is on course to cost the lives of at least 4,000 migrant workers before a ball is kicked, the International Trade Union Confederation (ITUC) has claimed (Guardian, 2013b).

Compare that to the figures in the table above to see how appalling this appears to be. Russia's upcoming 2018 games have documented 60 worker deaths so far – clearly, this is disastrous when compared to equivalent builds in South Africa and Brazil, and to Olympic Games builds, but a mere fraction of what Qatar's workers have experienced to date.

It is important in reviewing this case study to note that the original Washington Post blog article (27 May 2015), entitled 'The human cost of FIFA's corruption', has been subsequently amended to say 'This story has been updated to reflect the fact that figures include total migrant worker deaths in Qatar, not just World Cup-related' (Washington Post, 2015).

In Occupational Health and Wellbeing it developed a 3W approach focusing on the Workers with clinical inventions, the Workplace through ill-health prevention, and a comprehensive health promotion to drive Well-being. The prevention lead approach started with a clear design focus, skilling the design team to recognize health implications and involve occupational hygienists to eliminate up to an estimate 50 per cent of hazards at the design stage. Following this the residual risk mitigation and RAMS reviews ensured the control of health hazards was communicated as a clear priority equal to the traditionally emphasizes safety hazards. This programme was supported through education, engagement and involvement of all workers but especially of first line management to ensure the correct focus is given to occupational health hazards on a daily basis. A well-defined strategy of monitoring and leading indicator data collection of health impact frequency ratings gave the team a clear picture of the effectiveness of current control measures supporting risk review and continuous improvement.

The legacy concept has also inspired a website of lessons learnt at http://learninglegacy.independent.gov.uk/themes/ with information in ten learning legacy themes:

1 Archaeology;
2 Health and safety;
3 Design and engineering innovation;
4 Procurement and supply chain management;
5 Equality, inclusion, employment and skills;
6 Project and programme management;
7 Master planning and town planning;
8 Systems and technology;
9 Sustainability;
10 Transport.

Beyond the Olympics

The Olympics have always embodied the ideal of Olympic virtue and the CSR principle of being the best you can be (without this being at the expense of others). This ideal is not new; consider the Victorian philanthropists who saw that social reforms, such as relocating workers to out-of-town developments, benefited not only workers but businesses as well. Accordingly, their legacy formed companies such as Cadbury, Rowntree and Lloyds Bank (see Chapter 2). But what about after 2012? Was CSR just 'the new black' – just another fashion?

204 National Olympic Committees participated in the opening ceremony of the London Olympic Games in 2012. With every nation having many organizations that affect and are affected by CSR, it's more than probable that responsible competitiveness will only continue to grow and evolve as we learn more about the interactions between organizations and the earth and its inhabitants. The importance of responsible competitiveness will continue to present an opportunity for organizations to demonstrate their abilities to stand above the marketplace, and to demonstrate their integrity to their customers.

Pascal Lamy, the Director-General of the World Trade Organization, said:

> Responsible competitiveness is an essential ingredient for effective global markets. It blends forward-looking corporate strategies, innovative public policies, and a vibrant, engaged civil society. It is about

creating a new generation of profitable products and business processes underpinned by rules that support societies' broader social, environmental and economic aims.

(Quoted in AccountAbility, 2007)

Summary

It's clear that social reform isn't a new business concept. In an environmentally aware, image-conscious and global market, the stakes are higher than ever. In this chapter, we've reviewed how your organization could follow the Olympic ideal for CSR. You should aim to be swifter at meeting the needs of your stakeholders, reach higher to be more successful and be a stronger organization to overcome the risk in an external context of ever greater complexity that lies ahead.

Throughout this book, we've encouraged you to look at the many interactions between your organization and society. As you've worked through the 'Test your thinking' exercises and reviewed the case studies, you'll have realized that organizations are not like islands, standing on their own, but that they have positive and negative impacts on the communities they serve and interact within. Stakeholders of a organization can apply a range of pressures which can represent an opportunity not only for companies, but also for individuals. CSR also needs to extended into the personal sphere, where each of us accepts the true price of the goods and services we buy, and the broader impacts of the purchasing decisions we make.

If we expect companies to take CSR seriously, consumers need to drive the market. Only then will organizations see the opportunity that CSR represents. As a result, business and society will get the benefits of a more ethical, less environmentally damaging, more socially focused economic system, with the potential to give everyone better quality of life.

Endnote

We hope genuinely that you've enjoyed reading our second book about CSR and PSR, and testing your own thinking as you've progressed. We want you to do something for the Earth right now. Believe that you personally can make a difference. We're worried that humans have become a parasite that can kill its host. We are worried too, that a lack of active risk management can (and has) kill businesses. There's nothing at all extraordinary in Earth's history about extinctions of species, nor in the business environment of the extinction of unprepared companies. Drastic and immediate action is needed. Every journey starts with a single step, and today is your day to take that first step. Good luck in all that you do to help us all.

One small step for man, one giant leap for mankind.

(Astronaut Neil Armstrong,
20 July 1969, from the surface of the Moon)

Appendix I

100 CSR actions

Here is our fresh and updated, ready-to-go list of possible CSR-related actions that you could choose to use and get started right away. Together, these comprise a selection of activities to help you and your organization to quickly and substantially improve its credentials. Of course, no list can be absolutely definitive, and we welcome comments and suggestions from our readers. These, if used, will be credited in future editions of this book.

Management

1 Always start at work by seeking support for your ideas from management. (Almost) anything can be achieved with senior support.
2 Draft, adopt and communicate a CSR policy for your organization. We've included an example for your use in Appendix 2. Feel free to use or amend it to suit your own requirements. Keep records of everything you do under the policy commitments.
3 Identify your key stakeholders. Let them know what you're doing. Assess their interest, and tell them of your broad intentions. Staff and customers (and possibly others) will ask questions. Be ready to answer their questions promptly.
4 Conduct a baseline review. Use the guidance in this book to identify the significant CSR-related impacts in your organization.
5 Prioritize your initial action plan. Focus on (say) five key issues, and set objectives and shorter-term milestone targets.
6 Implement your plans. Keep on top of changing circumstances internally and externally, and the changing expectations of your stakeholders.
7 Promote CSR in your supply chain. Suggest to your suppliers and clients that they may like to join you on your journey.
8 Monitor progress, perhaps against appropriate key performance indicators.
9 Make sure that top management is involved in a regular senior review – say six-monthly (or at least annually).
10 Decide whether external certification (e.g. ISO 14001, SA 8000) is appropriate.

Community

11 Think of ways to engage with your organization's neighbours – the people who live nearby. For example, hold an open day or invite them to a 'town hall meeting'.

12 Consider and write down your organization's impacts on the local labour market and the local environment.

13 Be ready to provide external support to the local and regional community (when you can) following loss of essential services such as water or electricity, or when there is flooding.

14 Select a charity of the year and help with fundraising activities for it. Perhaps your organization could match the funds raised by your staff?

15 Tell your staff that you'll provide an agreed amount of time to support voluntary and charitable organizations. How about a volunteer scheme, say one day per employee per year to provide your organization's specialist skills? How about reading mentoring to a local school? Or work experience/placement?

16 Look again at your purchasing policy. Are the payment terms and cancellation charges as fair as they should be?

17 Promote car sharing. Offer incentives and benefits (convenient parking spaces, leave five minutes earlier), or make small donations in kind to a nominated charity.

18 Support local teams – football, cricket, Scouts, Brownies.

19 Buy from local vendors.

20 Prepare a regular newsletter and circulate it widely. Good communications are an important part of any new initiative. And you'll soon have good news to share.

Environment

21 Always promote the prevention of pollution. Tell staff how important this is, whether it's litter or an oil slick.

22 Purchase recycled, low-energy, low-environmental impact equipment. Look for the energy labelling. And return electrical equipment to the store where you bought it when it's no longer usable.

23 Reduce, re-use, recycle at every opportunity. Ask your staff for suggestions, and reward good ideas.

24 Promote environmental initiatives among your staff and reward good ideas.

25 Measure your carbon footprint – get someone to help if necessary. Reduce what you can, offset what you can't reduce. Offsetting your carbon footprint isn't expensive.

26 Always be on the lookout for leaks. Include this on regular inspection checklists and site tours. Minimize leaks of water, from air lines, as well as other spillage.

27 Develop an emergency plan for foreseeable events. This will help a lot if things go wrong – the first hour is usually critical, and knowing what to do and in which order gets you back on the road to recovery quickly. And don't forget to practice so that you're sure that your plan works reliably.

28 Sort out a transport policy for the organization. Minimize unnecessary trips, plan for return loads and help drivers with route-planning. Set out your organization's long-term vision, and discuss it with your staff.

29 Include hybrid cars in the fleet and avoid 'gas guzzlers'. Use published data on CO emissions to guide you.

30 Don't use or buy anything included on the CITES list (endangered wild animals and plants).

Ethics

31 Review your employment policies, specifically looking for any form of discrimination.

32 Establish fair grievance procedures, and hear any cases that are raised quickly and independently.

33 Develop and publish an ethical procurement policy.

34 Invest in ethical funds.

35 Make clear to all your staff that bribery and corruption in any form are completely unacceptable. We suggest that you give relevant examples of unacceptable practices – e.g. excessive entertainment, large gifts, or any financial inducements.

36 Don't engage in any anti-competitive practices (anti-trust). Take legal advice if necessary.

37 Vow never to take advantage in times of crisis (e.g. if you sell generators, don't increase the price when there's a power cut).

38 Consult as early as possible as market conditions change, e.g. with employees and suppliers.

39 Take all steps necessary to confirm there is no child labour in your supply chain.

40 Take responsibility for your actions in the marketplace. We suggest the following examples make great starting points:

- pay suppliers on time in accordance with the agreed terms
- undertake responsible labelling and marketing
- acknowledge patents, property and copyright
- pay a fair rate for work, goods and services
- recall defective products promptly.

Human rights

41 Take all steps necessary to confirm there is no illegal labour, and no bonded labour or slavery anywhere in your supply chain.

42 Audit and review your business practices and premises for access for people with disabilities – it's the law!

43 Promote life-long learning and continual development among your staff.

44 Maintain a policy of equal pay for equal work.

45 Support staff who want to participate in civic duties, e.g. as elected councillors, special constables, or members of the Territorial Army.

46 Treat people who complain about your products or services with respect. Investigate the problem and understand their point of view.

47 Support staff who may be victimized, e.g. because of educational difficulties, their sexuality or disabilities.

48 Actively fight racism, inform staff of your company policy, and never let racist comments (sometimes called 'jokes') go unchallenged.

49 Don't tell discriminatory jokes – and don't forward them (e.g. by email or text).

50 Don't buy counterfeit products – they indirectly support illegal practices.

Workforce

51 Communicate with your workforce transparently, promptly and accurately.

52 Moderate your expectations for working hours – employees have lives outside of work!

53 Consider the feasibility of flexi-time and family-friendly policies.

54 Conduct regular staff development reviews.

55 Workers generally come to work to do their best, but they'll sometimes make mistakes. Recognize this, and be humane with them when they do.

At home

56 Turn TVs and other electrical items off – don't leave them on standby.

57 Fit energy-efficient light bulbs.

58 Insulate your home, block drafts and close off unused rooms.

59 Choose a fuel-efficient vehicle (or a bicycle).

60 Use public transport where possible.

61 Live near where you work – don't over-commute. This way, you'll see more of your family, too.

62 Consider the impact of your holidays on the environment.

63 Turn the tap off when you brush your teeth.

64 Talk to your kids about CSR – it's in the UK National Curriculum!

65 Improve biodiversity in your garden. Plant native species, keep woody offcuts where possible to encourage wildlife and try not to use too many chemicals.

66 Grow your own vegetables (zero food miles!).

67 Eat more vegetarian meals – meat involves more greenhouse gases, land, water and chemicals to produce.

68 Boycott bottled water – drink tap water.

69 Take showers, not baths.

70 Re-use shopping bags. In Wales, and now in England, they always charge for them!

PSR – personal social responsibility

71 Consider what you buy at the shops.

72 Consider what you use at home and in the garage and garden.

73 Tackle climate change – measure your energy consumption and take steps to reduce it.

74 Reduce water use – turn taps off when not using them, and don't fill the bath to the top.

75 Reassess your car – plan to buy a cleaner one next time, and consider alternative transport if possible.

76 Tackle your driving – less accelerator, less brakes.

77 Consider what you throw away – promote recycling in the family, and see how long you can put 'nothing' into the grey waste bin.

78 Tackle your health – take exercise, moderate excesses in your diet.

79 Tackle your community – offer to help in local events or community programs e.g. Neighbourhood Watch.

80 Tackle your work – Plan to work nearer to home, or from home, in the future.

Health and safety at work

81 Comply with the law on health, safety and welfare. If you operate in more than one country, apply common standards based on the highest requirements. And if there's no legal requirement in your territory, look to the United Kingdom – it's been regulating health and safety successfully for over 200 years!

82 Undertake assessments to confirm that workplace risks have been reduced to acceptable levels.

83 Support consultation through safety representatives. Make joint inspections of the workplace, and investigate every incident and near miss reported. Deal promptly with the issues that come up.

84 Manage contractors as though they were your own staff. Never subcontract 'hazardous work' for only that reason.

85 50,000 drivers die on the roads of Europe each year, and thousands more elsewhere. Promote road safety, including the use of mobile telephones, and provide enhanced training and safe, well-maintained vehicles to drivers.

86 Consider behavioral safety programs – a positive and inclusive way to reduce accidents.

87 Encourage employees to 'take health and safety home' – e.g. initiatives to promote safe DIY.

88 Promote healthy eating. If you have a works canteen, offer healthy options on every menu.

89 AIDS and other sexually transmitted diseases are prevalent in many parts of the world. Make sure staff are aware of the risks when they travel.

90 Develop a rehabilitation program to promote and maintain work wellness, and to help sick or injured employees to return to work. Stress (in particular) is on the increase, and employers should be prepared.

General

91 Be informed. Re-read this book, and use the contacts and links within it. Use the internet to research your subject – it changes rapidly, and it pays to keep up to date.

92 Get active. Join a group that promotes something you believe in. It could be a wildlife charity, an environmental pressure group or a political party.

93 Publicly promote CSR and your values, write articles, give speeches and pass on the word – explain the benefits to others.

94 Consider benchmarking/comparing your organization against others like yours to see if your standards meet up to best practice.

95 Get involved in your sector's trade association working group on CSR. If there isn't one, consider setting one up.

96 Develop a register for your legal requirements for employment, health and safety and environmental law, and regularly review compliance.

97 Review the feasibility of becoming accredited to the Investor in People standard.

98 Consider using the SEDEX supplier database for international suppliers to verify standards and minimize their administrative burden – www.sedex.org.uk.

99 Review your process for investing in new projects. Consider the CSR implications at the earliest stage – it's more cost effective.

100 Start today by completing Test Your Thinking Exercise 20. Have the confidence . . . and don't give up!

Test your thinking 20

Review all of these 100 example actions, and write down your top 10 which you will start to implement today.

1

2

3

4

5

6

7

8

9

10

Appendix 2
Sample CSR policy

Every organization's context and CSR issues will vary and, of course, the policy and strategy adopted by your own management board should reflect these. Your CSR policy should demonstrate the commitment of senior management, clarify the main issues that the organization is to tackle and provide a platform for implementation, checking and review.

This sample policy, developed in alignment with the DTRT Model, will help you to make a flying start.

Sample CSR policy

Our organization recognizes that it operates in a community, society and world that we all share. We are committed to improving our operations and performance to minimize our risks and maximize our positive effects on the communities we interact with. We believe that our corporate social responsibility policy plays a vital role in the success of our operations. To this end we will:

1 Comply with all relevant national laws and international agreements applicable to the countries we operate in, including challenge bribery and corruption.
2 Minimize risk to our workforce, those who use our products and/or services, and the communities who may be affected by our operations.
3 Develop the life cycle of our products and services to minimize their impact on the environment and support sustainable development.
4 Drive ethical trading principles throughout our organization and value chain.
5 Treat our workforce with respect, upholding labor rights and actively supporting human rights throughout our supply chain.
6 Engage with our stakeholders, support the communities we operate in, listen to their concerns and strive to eliminate or mitigate our adverse community effects.

We have developed a corporate social responsibility strategy to embed these principles into our organization, and have implemented a management framework to regularly verify, improve and report upon our progress, to drive change and challenge convention. This policy will be communicated to all of our stakeholders and will be followed by our staff and all of those who work on our behalf.

Signed:
Position:
Date:

References

AccountAbility. (2007) *The State of Responsible Competiveness 2007.* [Online] Available from: http://www.accountability.org/research/responsible-competitiveness/index.html. [Accessed: 15th October 2015].

An Inconvenient Truth. (2006) Documentary. Directed by Davis Guggenheim and Al Gore. [DVD] USA: Paramount Pictures.

Archaeologyinfo. (2015) *Australopithecus Africanus.* [Online] Available from: http://archaeologyinfo.com/australopithecus-africanus. [Accessed: 29th April 2015].

Asbury, S. (2005) A risk-based approach to auditing. *The Environmentalist.* June 2005, p.29.

Asbury, S. (2013) *Health and Safety, Environment and Quality Audits – A Risk-based Approach.* Abingdon: Taylor & Francis.

Asbury, S. and Ball, R. (2009) *Do the Right Thing – The Practical, Jargon-free Guide to Corporate Social Responsibility.* Abingdon: Taylor & Francis, with the Institution of Occupational Safety and Health (IOSH).

BAA. (2002) *Sustainable Construction at Terminal 5.* Plymouth: Business in the Community.

Bailhii. (1932). M'Alister or Donoghue (Pauper) Appellant v. Stevenson Respondent. [Online] Available from: https://www.uni-trier.de/fileadmin/fb5/FFA/KURSUNTER LAGEN/Anglo-Amerikanisches_Recht/Law_of_Torts/Siry-SS-2012/Donoghue_v_Stevenson__1932__UKHL_100__26_May_1932_.pdf. [Accessed: 20th October 2015].

Baldacci, D. (2011) *The Whole Truth.* London: Pan Macmillan.

Bennett, A.W. and Bonnie, K.B. (2001) *The World of Caffeine – The Science and Culture of the World's Most Popular Drug.* London: Routledge.

Bernstein, P. (1998). *Against the Gods – The Remarkable Story of Risk.* New York: Wiley.

BITC. (2015) *Business in the Community CSR Toolkit.* [Online] Available from: www.bitc.org.uk. [Accessed: 6th October 2015].

Bhopal Medical Appeal. (2012) *Bhopal Marathon.* Brighton: Bhopal Medical Appeal.

Body Shop. (2005) *The Body Shop Values Report 2005.* [Online] Available from: http://www.yuswohady.com/wpcontent/uploads/2008/11/bodyshop_valuesreport_2005.pdf. [Accessed 16th October 2015].

Boyle, T. (2002). *Health and Safety – Risk Management.* Leicester: The Institution of Occupational Safety and Health.

BP. (2015a) *Gulf of Mexico Restoration.* [Online] Available from: www.bp.com/en/global/corporate/gulf-of-mexico-restoration.html. [Accessed: 19th June 2015].

BP. (2015b) *Sustainability*. [Online] Available from: http://www.bp.com/en/global/corporate/sustainability.html. [Accessed 8th October 2015].

British Sea Fishing. (2015) *The Collapse of the Grand Banks Cod Fishery*. [Online] Available from: http://britishseafishing.co.uk/the-collapse-of-the-grand-banks-cod-fishery/. [Accessed: 5th June 2015].

Browning, J.B. (1993) *Union Carbide – Disaster at Bhopal*. [Online] Available from: http://storage.dow.com.edgesuite.net/dow.com/Bhopal/browning.pdf. [Accessed: 19th June 2015].

Brundtland G.H. (1987) *Our Common Future – Report of the World Commission on Environment and Development*. Geneva: United Nations World Commission on Environment and Development.

BSi. (2007) *Occupational Health & Safety Management Systems – Specification*. BS OHSAS 18001:2007.

BSi. (2015) *ISO 26000 Guidance on Social Responsibility*. [Online] Available from: http://www.bsigroup.com/en-GB/ISO-26000-Social-Responsibility/. [Accessed: 22nd June 2015].

Burn-Callander, R. (2015). *Unilever Boss Paul Polman Slams Capitalist Obsession with Profit*. [Online] Available from: www.telegraph.co.uk/finance/newsbysector/epic/ulvr/11372550/Unilever-boss-Paul-Polman-slams-capitalist-obsession-with-profit.html. [Accessed: 19th June 2015].

Cadbury. (2015) *The History of Chocolate*. [Online] Available from: www.cadbury.co.uk/the-story. [Accessed: 19th June 2015].

Campbell, A. (2004) *Family Resources Survey – Annual Technical Report: 2002/2003. 2002/03*. Norwich: Office for National Statistics.

Cancer Research UK. (2015) *Can Cancer be Prevented?* [Online] Available from: http://www.cancerresearchuk.org/about-cancer/causes-of-cancer/can-cancer-be-prevented. [Accessed: 19th June 2015].

Carbon Disclosure Project. (2014) *Global Forests Report*. [Online] Available from: https://www.cdp.net/en-US/Programmes/Pages/forests-timber.aspx. [Accessed: 19th June 2015].

Carbonfund. (2015) *Corporate Risk Systems*. [Online] Available from: http://www.carbonfund.org/partners/item/corporate-risk-systems. [Accessed: 29th April 2015].

Change.Gov. (2009) *President-elect Barack Obama to Deliver Taped Greeting to Bi-partisan Governors Climate Summit*. [Online] available from: http://change.gov/newsroom/entry/president_elect_barack_obama_to_deliver_taped_greeting_to_bi_partisan_gover/. [Accessed: 14th June 2015].

Churchill, W. S. (1936) Speech in the House of Commons, November 12, 1936 "Debate on the Address". [Online] Available from: http://www.goodreads.com/quotes/33180-the-era-of-procrastination-of-half-measures-of-soothing-and-baffling. [Accessed 13th October 2015].

CITES. (2015) [Online] Available from: www.cites.org/eng/. [Accessed: 19th June 2015].

Clarke, A.C. (1962) *Profiles of the Future: An Inquiry Into the Limits of the Possible*. London: Indigo.

CNN. (2010) *BP Chief to Gulf Residents: 'I'm Sorry'*. [Online] Available from: http://edition.cnn.com/2010/US/05/30/gulf.oil.spill/. [Accessed 13th October 2015].

Coca-Cola. (2015) *2013/2014 Sustainability Report*. [Online] Available from: http://assets.coca-colacompany.com/77/4c/2a44a5234a3ca65d449d174a0ded/2013-2014-coca-cola-sustainability-report-pdf.pdf. [Accessed: 19th June 2015].

Companies Act. (2006) *Section 417*. London: The Stationery Office.

CorporateRegister.com. (2015) [Online] Available from: http://www.corporateregister. com/. [Accessed 6th October 2015].

Corporate Watch. (2005) *Checkout Chuckout: 3 – Building Your Case*. [Online] Available from: https://corporatewatch.org/content/checkout-chuckout-3-building-your-case-0. [Accessed: 15th October 2015].

Corporate Watch. (2015) *What's Wrong with Corporate Social Responsibility? – The Arguments Against CSR*. [Online] Available from: https://corporatewatch. org/content/whats-wrong-corporate-social-responsibility-arguments-against-csr. [Accessed: 19th June 2015].

COSO. (2015a) *Integrated Framework of Internal Control*. [Online] Available from: http://www.sox-online.com/coso_cobit_coso_framework.html. [Accessed 13th October 2015].

COSO. (2015b) *Enterprise Risk Management – Integrated Framework*. [Online] Available from: http://www.coso.org/documents/coso_erm_executivesummary. pdf. [Accessed 13th October 2015].

Covey, S. (2015) *PSEL*. [Online] Available from: http://www.personal.psu.edu/mrr18/ blogs/psel/2012/04/effective-leadership-is-putting-first-things-first-effective-management-is-discipline-carrying-it-ou.html. [Accessed: 29th April 2015].

Darwin, C. (1859) *On the Origin of Species by Means of Natural Selection, or the Preservation of Favoured Races in the Struggle for Life*. London: Murray.

DeGeorge, R.T. (2010) *Business Ethics*. Upper Saddle River: Pearson Education, Inc.

Deming, W.E. (2000a) *Out of the Crisis*. Cambridge, MA: MIT Press.

Deming, W.E. (2000b) *The New Economics for Industry, Government, Education*. Cambridge, MA: MIT Press.

Department for Food, the Environment and Rural Affairs. (2007) *Taking Forward the UK Climate Change Bill – The Government Response to Pre-legislative Scrutiny and Public Consultation*. Norwich: The Stationery Office.

Department for Work and Pensions. (2008) *Family Resources Survey*. [Online] Available from: www.dwp.gov.uk/asd/frs. [Accessed: 19th June 2015].

Department for Work and Pensions (2014). *Disability Facts and Figures*. [Online] Available from: www.gov.uk/government/publications/disability-facts-and-figures/ disability-facts-and-figures#fnref:1. [Accessed: 19th June 2015].

DestinAsian. (2012) *Trivia Time: How Many Hotel Rooms Are in the World?* [Online] Available from: http://www.destinasian.com/blog/news-briefs/total-hotel-rooms-in-world-str-global/. [Accessed: 24th June 2015].

Devalia, A. and Instone, A. (2008) *Personal Social Responsibility: A Powerful Workbook for Being Socially Responsible in Business*. London: Nirvana Publishing.

Disraeli, B. (1998) *Sybil*. Oxford: Oxford University Press.

Donovan, J. (2015) *Retired Shell Engineer Played Central Role*. [Online] Available from: http://royaldutchshellplc.com/2012/08/30/retired-shell-engineer-played-central-role-in-reserves-scandal/. [Accessed: 29th April 2015].

Dow Chemicals. (2015) Chronology. [Online] Available from: www.bhopal.com/. [Accessed: 19th June 2015].

Economist. (2009) *Triple Bottom Line*. [Online] Available from: http://www.economist. com/node/14301663. [Accessed: 9th June 2015].

Eichenwald, K. (2005) *Conspiracy of Fools: A True Story*. London: Random House.

Elkington, J. (1997) *Cannibals with Forks – The Triple Bottom Line of 21st Century Business*. Oxford: Capstone.

Environment Agency. (2003) *Strategy Development and Supplier Questionnaire and Assessment from Sustainable Procurement Guide*. Bristol: Environment Agency.

Environmental Law Reporter. (1988). Bush, G. (1988) *George Bush on the Environment*. [Online] available from: http://elr.info/sites/default/files/articles/18.10293.htm. [Accessed: 14th October 2015].

Ernst & Young. (2013). Impact report commissioned by Formula E Holdings. Based on a low scenario using the period 2015–2040.

ESPN. (2014) *Schools Eye Beer Sales For Help*. [Online] Available from: http://espn.go.com/college-football/story/_/id/11392186/colleges-turning-beer-sales-stadiums-alternative-revenue-stream. [Accessed 14th October 2015].

ESPN. (2015) [Online] Available from: http://scores.espn.go.com/ncf/boxscore?gameId=400610325. [Accessed: 19th June 2015].

Ethical Performance. (2015) [Online] Available from: www.ethicalperformance.com. [Accessed: 21st June 2015].

Ethical Trading Initiative. (2015) *ETI Base Code*. [Online] Available from: http://www.ethicaltrade.org/eti-base-code. [Accessed: 6th October 2015].

EU. (2015) [Online] Available from: http://ec.europa.eu/index_en.htm. [Accessed: 22nd June 2015].

EU Delegation to the UN. (2015) *Second Anniversary of the Rana Plaza Disaster in Bangladesh*. [Online] Available from: eu-un.europa.eu/articles/en/article_16361_en.htm. [Accessed: 19th June 2015].

European Commission. (2011) *A Renewed EU Strategy 2011–14 for Corporate Social Responsibility*. EU Brussels, 25.10.2011 COM(2011), p.681.

European Commission. (2013) *Staying Engaged: A Sustainability Compact for Continuous Improvements in Labour Rights and Factory Safety in the Ready-Made Garment and Knitwear Industry in Bangladesh*. [Online] Available from: http://trade.ec.europa.eu/doclib/docs/2013/july/tradoc_151601.pdf.[Accessed 15th October 2015].

Eves, D. and Gummer, J. (2005) *Questioning Performance – The Director's Essential Guide to Health, Safety and the Environment*. Leicester: IOSH Service Ltd.

Fairtrade Organization. (2015) *What is Fairtrade?* [Online] Available from: http://www.fairtrade.org.uk/en/what-is-fairtrade. [Accessed: 19th June 2015].

Forbes. (2015) *The World's Biggest Oil and Gas Companies – 2015*. [Online] Available from: http://www.forbes.com/sites/christopherhelman/2015/03/19/the-worlds-biggest-oil-and-gas-companies/. [Accessed 15th October 2015].

Forest Stewardship Council. (2015) [Online] Available from: www.fsc-uk.org/. [Accessed: 12th June 2015].

FT. (2010) Big oil, bigger oil. *Financial Times*. 24th February 2010.

Fuller, C.W. and Vassie, L.H. (2004) *Health and Safety Management – Principles and Best Practice*. London: Prentice Hall.

Furguson, L. (2015) *Beer Sales at Football Games will be a New Challenge to Administrators*. [Online] Available from: http://www.dailytexanonline.com/2015/06/21/beer-sales-at-football-games-will-be-a-new-challenge-to-administrators. [Accessed 14th October 2015].

Gardner, D. (2009). *Risk*. London: Virgin Books.

Global Reporting Initiative. (2013) *G4 Sustainability Reporting Guidelines.* Amsterdam: Global Reporting Initiative.

Gov.uk. (2015) *Human Trafficking: Tough Sentences to Help End Modern Slavery.* [Online] Available from: https://www.gov.uk/government/news/human-trafficking-tough-sentences-to-help-end-modern-slavery. [Accessed 13th October 2015].

Grimsby Telegraph. (2015) *Workers Urged to Donate A Day in Aid of Good Causes.* [Online] Available from: http://www.grimsbytelegraph.co.uk/Workers-urged-Donate-Day/story-26651667-detail/story.html#ixzz3dOmctl1k. [Accessed: 13th October 2015].

Guardian. (2010) *BP Oil Spill – An Interactive Timeline.* [Online] Available from: www.theguardian.com/environment/interactive/2010/jul/08/bp-oil-spill-timeline-interactive. [Accessed: 9th June 2015].

Guardian. (2013a) *Bangladesh Factory Collapse Blamed on Swampy Ground and Heavy Machinery.* [Online] Available from: www.theguardian.com/world/2013/may/23/bangladesh-factory-collapse-rana-plaza. [Accessed: 19th May 2015].

Guardian. (2013b). *Qatar World Cup Construction 'Will Leave 4,000 Migrant Workers Dead'.* [Online] Available from: http://www.theguardian.com/global-development/2013/sep/26/qatar-world-cup-migrant-workers-dead. [Accessed: 25th June 2015].

Guardian. (2014) *US and China Strike Deal on Carbon Cuts in Push for Global Climate Change Pact.* [Online] available from: http://www.theguardian.com/environment/2014/nov/12/china-and-us-make-carbon-pledge. [Accessed: 14th October 2015].

Handy, C. (1994) *The Empty Raincoat.* London: Arrow Books.

Hawken, P. (2015) BrainyQuote. [Online] Available from: http://www.brainyquote.com/quotes/quotes/p/paulhawken402032.html. [Accessed: 29th April 2015].

Health and Safety At Work, etc. Act. (1974) *(Commencement No.1) Order 1974, 1974/1439.* London: The Stationery Office.

Health and Safety Executive. (1997a) *Successful Health & Safety Management.* HSG65. Suffolk: HSE Books.

Health and Safety Executive. (1997b) *The Costs of Accidents at Work.* HSG96. Suffolk: HSE Books.

Health and Safety Executive. (2013) *Managing for Health & Safety.* HSG65. Suffolk: HSE Books.

Health and Safety Executive. (2015) *Research Reveals Secrets of Olympics Safety Success.* [Online] Available from: www.hse.gov.uk/press/2012/hse-olympics-research.htm. [Accessed: 19th April 2015].

Hirsch, T. (2002) *Cod's Warning From Newfoundland.* [Online] Available from:http://news.bbc.co.uk/1/hi/sci/tech/2580733.stm. [Accessed 16th October 2015].

History. (2015) Lord Leverhulme. [Online] Available from: www.history.co.uk/biographies/lord-leverhulme. [Accessed: 19th April 2015].

Hitchcock D. and Willard M. (2006) *The Business Guide to Sustainability: Practical Strategies and Tools for Organizations.* Oxford: Earthscan.

Holmes R. and Watts P. (2000) *Making Good Business Sense.* Geneva: World Business Council for Sustainable Development.

Huang, K. and Dixon, M.A. (2013) Examining the financial impact of alcohol sales on football game days – a case study of a major football program. *Journal of Sport Management: Official Journal of NASSM.* 27, p.207–216.

ILO. (2001). *Guidelines on Occupational Safety and Health. ILO-OSH, 2001.* Geneva: International Labour Organization.

The Institute of Employment Rights. (2015) *Modern Slavery Bill Debated in Lords.* [Online] Available from: http://www.ier.org.uk/news/modern-slavery-bill-debated-lords. [Accessed 13th October 2015].

Institute of Environmental Management & Assessment. (2007) *UK Legislation: Taking the Climate Change Bill Forward.* [Online] Available from: http://www.iema.net/news/uk-legislation-taking-climate-change-bill-forward. [Accessed: 14th October 2015].

International Coffee Organization. (2015a) *The Current State of the Global Coffee Trade.* [Online] Available from: http://www.ico.org/monthly_coffee_trade_stats.asp. [Accessed: 19th March 2015].

International Coffee Organization. (2015b) *International Coffee Organization: 1963–2013.* [Online] Available from: http://dev.ico.org/documents/cy2012-13/history-ico-50-years-e.pdf. [Accessed: 19th March 2015].

International Coffee Organization. (2015c) *Executive Summary.* [Online] Available from: http://dev.ico.org/libser/executive%20summary.pdf. [Accessed: 19th March 2015].

International Organization for Standardization. (2009). *Principles and General Guidelines on Risk Management. ISO 31000:2009 and Risk Management Vocabulary. ISO Guide 73.* Geneva: International Standards Organization.

International Organization for Standardization. (2010) *ISO 26000: Guidance on Corporate Responsibility.* [Online] Available from: http://www.iso.org/iso/iso26000. [Accessed 14th October 2015].

International Organization for Standardization. (2012) *Annex SL (Previously ISO Guide 83), Consolidated ISO Supplement of the ISO/IEC Directives.* Geneva: International Standards Organization.

International Organization for Standardization. (2015) *BS EN ISO 14001: Environmental Management Systems – Requirements With Guidance for Use.* London: BSI.

International Finance Corporation. (2008) *Stakeholder Engagement: A Good Practice Handbook for Companies Doing Business in Emerging Markets.* Washington, D.C.: World Bank Group.

International Olympic Committee. (2007) *Olympic Charter.* Switzerland: International Olympic Committee.

International Olympic Committee. (2015) *Ancient Olympic Games.* [Online] Available from: http://www.olympic.org/ancient-olympic-games. [Accessed 15th October 2015].

Ipsos MORI. (2000) *Winning with Integrity.* The report of a survey by MORI.

Ipsos MORI. (2015) *Consumers Vote With Their Feet on Corporate Tax Avoidance.* [Online] Available from: https://www.ipsos-mori.com/researchpublications/researcharchive/3529/Consumers-vote-with-their-feet-on-corporate-tax-avoidance.aspx. [Accessed: 11th June 2015].

Kemp, N. (2014) *Why Kenco is Taking on Gang Culture.* [Online] Available from: http://www.marketingmagazine.co.uk/article/1307805/why-kenco-taking-gang-culture. [Accessed: 15th October 2015].

Kenco. (2015) [Online] Available from: www.mykenco.com. [Accessed: 23rd March 2015].

Keys, T., Malnight, T.W. and van der Graaf, K. (2009). *Making the Most of Corporate Social Responsibility.* [Online] Available from: http://www.mckinsey.

com/insights/corporate_social_responsibility/making_the_most_of_corporate_
social_responsibility. [Accessed: 11th June 2015].

King, L.W. (2004) *The Code of Hammurabi*. Whitefish, MT: Kessinger Publishing.

Klein, N. (2000). *No Logo*. New York: Picador.

Krushhali Bank Limited. (2015) [Online] Available from: http://www.khushhalibank.
com.pk/special_initiatve/csr.php. [Accessed: 9th June 2015].

Lacocca, L. (2015) BrainyQuote. [Online] Available from: http://www.brainyquote.
com/quotes/quotes/l/leeiacocca383758.html. [Accessed: 29th April 2015].

Lean, G. (2011) *The Telegraph*. [Online] Available from: http://www.telegraph.
co.uk/culture/hay-festival/8537896/Hay-Festival-2011-Geoffrey-Lean-on-the-
future-of-fish.html. [Accessed: 18th May 2015].

Lee, S. and Ditko, S. (1962). *Amazing Fantasy*. (No. 15). New York: Marvel Comics.

Lemahieu, J. and Me, A. (2013) *Global Study on Homicide 2013 United Nations
Office on Drugs and Crime*. Vienna: United Nations Office on Drugs and
Crime.

Lippman, W. (1914) *Drift and Mastery*. Madison: University of Wisconsin Press.

LOCOG. (2009) *Towards a One Planet 2012*. Second Edition. London: London
2012.

LOCOG. (2012) *London 2012 Post Games Sustainability Report – A Legacy of
Change*. [Online] Available from: http://learninglegacy.independent.gov.uk/themes/
sustainability/london-2012-sustainability-plan-and-reports.php.   [Accessed   15th
October 2015].

Lyall, S. (2010) In BP's Record, a History of Boldness and Costly Blunders. *New York
Times*. July, 2010.

Mallenbaker.net. (2015a) *UK: Most FTSE Companies Produce CSR Reports*. [Online]
Available   from: http://www.mallenbaker.net/csr/page.php?Story_ID=1200.
[Accessed: 9th June 2015].

Mallenbaker.net (2015b) *Reply to the Case against CSR – The Latest Version*.
[Online] Available from: www.mallenbaker.net/csr/post.php?id=360. [Accessed:
14th April 2015].

Marriott. (2015) *Corporate Responsibility*. [Online] Available from: http://www.
marriott.com/corporate-social-responsibility/corporate-responsibility.mi.
[Accessed: 25th June 2015].

McSpotlight. [Online] Available from: http://www.mcspotlight.org/index.shtml.
[Accessed 13th October 2015].

Merritt, C. (2005) *Statement for the BP Independent Safety Review Panel*. [Online]
Available from: http://www.csb.gov/assets/1/19/Carolyn_Statement_3.pdf. [Accessed:
20th October 2015].

The Modern Slavery Act. (2015) London: The Stationery Office.

MIT. (2012) Sustainability nears a tipping point. *MIT Sloan Management Review*.
Winter 2012, 53 (2). pp.69–74.

Mondelez International. (2014) *Mondelez International Achieves 100 Percent Palm
Oil Sustainability Milestone Two Years Early*. [Online] Available from: http://
ir.mondelezinternational.com/releasedetail.cfm?releaseid=819677. [Accessed 14th
October 2015].

National Commission on the BP Deepwater Horizon Oil Spill and Offshore Drilling.
(2011) *Deep Water –The Gulf Oil Disaster and the Future of Offshore Drilling:
Report to the President*. [Online] Available from: http://www.gpo.gov/fdsys/

pkg/GPO-OILCOMMISSION/pdf/GPO-OILCOMMISSION.pdf. [Accessed 8th October 2015].

Nestlé. (2006) *The Nestlé Concept of Corporate Social Responsibility– As Implemented in Latin America*. [Online] Available from: https://www.unglobalcompact.org/system/attachments/196/original/COP.pdf?1262614174. [Accessed 8th October 2015].

Parker, G. (1997). *The Times Atlas of World History*. London: Times Books.

Philanthrocapitalism. (2015) [Online] Available from: www.philanthrocapitalism.net. [Accessed: 11th April 2015].

Pope Francis. (2015) [Online] Available from: http://www.cafod.org.uk/News/UK-news/pope-francis-first-encyclical. [Accessed: 19th October 2015].

Primark. (2015) *Rana Plaza*. [Online] Available from: www.primark.com/en/our-ethics/news/rana-plaza. [Accessed: 9th February 2015].

Pringle, H. (1997) *Cabot, Cod and the Colonists*. [Online] Available from: http://www.canadiangeographic.ca/wildlife-nature/articles/pdfs/atlantic-cod-cabot-cod-and-the-colonists.pdf. [Accessed: 19th October 2015].

Programme for the Endorsement of Forest Certification. (2015) *What Makes PEFC Unique?* [Online] Available from: www.pefc.co.uk/about-us/what-makes-pefc-unique. [Accessed: 19th March 2015].

Real Business. (2013) *Six Companies that Avoid Paying their Taxes*. [Online] Available from: http://realbusiness.co.uk/article/25034-six-companies-that-avoid-paying-their-taxes. [Accessed: 25th June 2015].

Reich, R.B. (2008) The case against corporate social responsibility. *Goldman School of Public Policy Working Paper*. No. GSPP08-003.

Rose, G. (1997) *The Collapse of the Grand Banks Cod Fishery*. [Online] Available from http://britishseafishing.co.uk/the-collapse-of-the-grand-banks-cod-fishery/ [Accessed: 16th October 2015].

The Royal Society for the Prevention of Accidents. (2014) (RoSPA) *Safety Express*. November/December. p.4.

Santayana, G. (1905) *Life of Reason*. [Online] Available from: http://www.brainyquote.com/quotes/quotes/g/georgesant101521.html. [Accessed 13th October 2015].

Saturday Down South. (2014) *Should SEC Football Stadiums Sell Alcohol?* [Online] Available from: http://www.saturdaydownsouth.com/2014/should-sec-football-stadiums-sell-alcohol/. [Accessed 14th October 2015].

Schanberg, S.H. (1996). On the playgrounds of America, every kid's goal is to score. In Pakistan, where children stitch soccer balls for six cents an hour, the goal is to survive. *Life Magazine*. June 1996: pp.38–48.

Shell Global. (2007) *Responsible Energy – The Shell Sustainability Review 2007*, [Online] Available from: http://reports.shell.com/sustainability-report/2014/servicepages/previous/files/shell_sustainability_review_2007.pdf. [Accessed 13th October 2015].

Social Accountability International. (2008) *SA8000: 2008*. [Online] Available from: http://www.sa-intl.org/index.cfm?fuseaction=Page.ViewPage&PageID=937. [Accessed 13th October 2015].

Spodek, H. (2001) *The World's History: Combined Volume*. Upper Saddle River, NJ: Prentice Hall.

Sreenivasan, J. (2009) *Poverty and the Government in America: A Historical Encyclopedia*. (Vol. 1). California: ABC-Clio.

Task Force on Incomes and Adjustment in the Atlantic Fishery. (1993) *Charting a New Course: Towards the Fishery of the Future*. Available from: http://www.dfo-mpo.gc.ca/Library/149033.pdf. [Accessed 20th October 2015].

Tnooz. (2014) *How Many Hotels in the World are there Anyway? Booking.com Keeps Adding Them*. [Online] Available from: http://www.tnooz.com/article/how-many-hotels-in-the-world-are-there-anyway-booking-com-keeps-adding-them/. [Accessed 15th October 2015].

Toone, B. (2004) *Protect Your People – And Your Business*. Leicester: IOSH Services Limited.

Tyler-Rubenstein, I. (2015) *How Much Do Companies Listen to NGOs?* [Online] Available from: https://www.ipsos-mori.com/newsevents/blogs/makingsenseofsociety/1656/How-much-do-companies-listen-to-NGOs.aspx. [Accessed: 11th June 2015].

Tzu, S. (2009) *The Art of War*. Trans. Lionel Giles. [1910] Pax Librorum.

UK Automobile Association. (2015) *Eco-driving Advice*. [Online] Available from: http://www.theaa.com/motoring_advice/fuels-and-environment/drive-smart.html. [Accessed 15th October 2015].

UN. (1948) *UN Declaration of Human Rights*. [Online] Available from: http://www.un.org/en/documents/udhr/. [Accessed 15th October 2015].

UN. (2005) *Global Forest Resources Assessment 2005*. [Online] Available from: http://www.fao.org/forestry/fra/fra2005/en/. [Accessed 13th October 2015].

UNEP. (2011) *REDDY Set Grow*. Geneva: UNEP Finance Initiative.

UNEP. (2015) *The Vienna Convention for the Protection of the Ozone Layer*. [Online] Available from: http://ozone.unep.org/en/treaties-and-decisions. [Accessed 13th October 2015].

Unilever. (2015) *Making Sustainable Living Commonplace*. [Online] Available from: https://brightfuture.unilever.co.uk/. [Accessed: 16th May 2015].

United States of America v. BP Exploration & Production, Inc., et al. (2015) *Findings of Fact and Conclusions of Law*. [Online] Available from: www.laed.uscourts.gov/OilSpill/Orders/9042014FindingsofFactandConclusionsofLaw.pdf. [Accessed: 8th May 2015].

U.S House Committee on Science and Technology. (1986). Investigation of the Challenger Accident; Report of the Committee on Science and Technology, House of Representatives. Washington: US Government Printing Office.

USA Today. (2015). *The 10 Oldest Company Logos in the World*. [Online] Available from http://www.usatoday.com/story/money/business/2014/06/21/oldest-company-logos/11052039/. [Accessed: 9th June 2015].

van Poll, B. (2012) *How Many Hotels Are There in the World?* [Online] Available from: http://www.spottedbylocals.com/blog/booking-com-and-the-race-towards-offering-all-hotels/. [Accessed: 24th June 2015].

War on Want. (2015) *Coca-Cola – The Alternative Report*. (Published March 2006). [Online] Available from: http://www.waronwant.org/resources/coca-cola-alternative-report. [Accessed: 19th June 2015].

Washington Post. (2015) (UPDATED) *The Toll of Human Casualities in Qatar*. [Online] Available from: http://www.washingtonpost.com/blogs/wonkblog/wp/2015/05/27/a-body-count-in-qatar-illustrates-the-consequences-of-fifa-corruption/. [Accessed: 23rd June 2015].

Wells, H.G. (1920) *Outline of History*. (Vol. 1). New York: Macmillan.

Westminster Biodiversity Partnership. (2007) *Local Biodiversity Action Plan*. [Online] Available from: http://www3.westminster.gov.uk/docstores/publications_store/Westminster_Biodiversity_Action_Plan_Adopted_2007.pdf. [Accessed: 6th October 2015].

Wikipedia. (2015a) *Risk*. [Online] Available from: http://en.wikipedia.org/wiki/Risk. [Accessed: 8th May 2015].

Wikipedia. (2015b) *BP*. [Online] Available from: https://en.wikipedia.org/wiki/BP. [Accessed 8th October 2015].

Wilson, E.O. (2002) *The Future of Life*. New York: Little, Brown and Company.

Wolken, D. (2014) *Colleges, Seeking Revenue, Consider Beer Sales at Stadiums*. USA TODAY. [Online] Available from: http://www.usatoday.com/story/sports/college/2014/06/22/beer-sales-college-football-basketball-games-campuses/10276865/. [Accessed: 6th October 2015].

World Bank. (2013) *India: Corporate Social Responsibility*. [Online] Available from: http://www.worldbank.org/en/news/feature/2013/08/27/india-corporate-social-responsibility. [Accessed: 19th May 2015].

Wordsworth, W. (1798) *Lines Composed a Few Miles Above Tintern Abbey, On Revisiting the Banks of the Wye During a Tour, July 13, 1798*. Lines 121–134. Illinois: Adams Press.

World Conservation Union. *Convention on International Trade in Endangered Species of Wild Fauna and Flora, 1979*. [Online] Available from: www.cites.org/eng/disc/species. [Accessed: 15th October 2015].

World Commission on Environment and Development. (1987) *Our Common Future*. Oxford: Oxford University Press.

Worldometers. (2015) *Current World Population*. [Online] Available from: http://www.worldometers.info/world-population/. [Accessed: 29th April 2015].

WWF. (2015a) *Threats: Deforestation*. [Online] Available from: https://www.worldwildlife.org/threats/deforestation. [Accessed: 29th April 2015].

WWF. (2015b) *Amazon Region Protected Areas Programme*. [Online] Available from: http://wwf.panda.org/what_we_do/where_we_work/amazon/vision_amazon/models/amazon_protected_areas/financing/arpa/. [Accessed: 29th April 2015].

Glossary of Acronyms

CITES	Convention on International Trade in Endangered Species of Wild Fauna and Flora
COSO	Committee of Sponsoring Organizations of the Treadway Commission
CSR	Corporate Social Responsibility
DBL	Double Bottom Line
DMA	Describing Material Aspects
DTRT	Do The Right Thing
EMS	Environmental Management System
ESIA	Environmental and Social Impact Assessment
FIA	Fédération Internationale de l'Automobile (effectively, International Automobile Federation)
GRI	Global Report Initiative
ILO	International Labour Organization
IPCC	Intergovernmental Panel on Climate Change
IOC	International Olympic Committee
IOSH	Institution of Occupational Safety and Health
ISO	International Organization for Standardization (NB. as ISO would have different acronyms in different languages (e.g. IOS in English), the founders decided to give it the short form ISO. ISO is derived from the Greek 'isos', meaning equal)
LOCOG	London Organising Committee of the Olympic and Paralympic Games
MSS	Management System Standard
ODA	Olympic Delivery Authority
PDCA	Plan, Do, Check, Act
PSR	Personal Social Responsibility
QBL	Quadruple Bottom Line
TBL	Triple Bottom Line
UNFCCC	United Nations Framework Convention on Climate Change

Index

AA 1000 series of standards 72,
    134–135
abuse 140, 145–146
accessibility 222, 225, 234, 241
accidents 41, 118, 119; Bhopal disaster
    208–216; BP Deepwater Horizon
    disaster 160, 161–162, 163–168;
    FIFA World Cups 245–246; London
    Olympics 244; Rani Plaza disaster
    171–175; road accidents 157, 254
accountability 19, 134, 156
AccountAbility 135
accounting 18, 19
accreditation 134, 183, 202
action plans 123–124, 249
added value 108, 194
Adidas 81
advertising 110, 160
Agenda 21 55, 112, 195
agricultural standards 199
Aire and Calder Project 112
ALARP (As Low As Reasonably
    Practical) 38, 40
alcohol 88–91
Alexander, Meredith 208–209
Amazon 129
Amazon Region Protected Areas
    (ARPA) campaign 142
American college football 86–91
Anderson, Warren 210–211, 215, 216
Annan, Kofi 59
Annex SL 8, 10, 12–13, 21, 22, 24
Apple 16–17, 129
Approved Carbon Managed Supplier
    (ACaMS) programme 180–182

Aramco 155–159
arms suppliers 117
Armstrong, Neil 248
The Art of War (Sun Tzu) 4, 5
Asbury, Stephen 14, 15, 42, 77, 145
Asda 66, 225
assets 32, 156
Association of British Insurers (ABI) 73
assurance 134, 135
auditing 19, 124, 145–148

Babylon 46
BAe Systems 117
Baldacci, David 126
Ball, R. 14, 15
Bangladesh 171–175
banking 72–73
Bass Ale 79
Behind the Brands Scorecard 65
Benetton 173
Bernstein, Peter 35–36
Bhopal disaster 152, 208–216
Bierce, Ambrose 84
Bin Laden, Osama 190
biodiversity 196, 198, 224, 251; four
    ideas 232–233; gardens 253; London
    Olympics 222, 227–228, 242;
    SA8000 standard 133
'Black Swans' 37
Blatter, Sepp 245
Body Shop 80–81, 82–83, 117
bonded labour 148n1, 170, 252
Booking.com 98
Bourneville 49–50
boycotts 130

Boyle, T. 34
BP 38, 159–168
branding 79–82, 183
Branson, Richard 235
Brazil 194
British Airports Authority (BAA)
    112–113
British American Tobacco 135
British Empire 46
Brokenshire, James 132
Browning, Jackson 216
Brundtland Report 55
BS 5750 standard 135
BS 7750 standard 135
BS OHSAS 18001 standard 11, 15, 21,
    72, 77, 79, 136–137
BT 243
Bush, George H.W. 55
Bush, George W. 56
business control 4–31, 42; Deming
    5–10; DTRT Model 22–23;
    evolution of management thinking 6;
    information for management 17–18;
    internal control frameworks 20–22;
    standards 10–15; Sun Tzu 4–5; see
    also management
business environment 23, 24–29, 32, 41
Business in the Community Toolkit
    (BITC) 109
business partners 22
Business Reviews 126–127

Cadbury 47, 49–51, 52, 247
Café Direct 183
Cameron, David 166
Cancer Research UK 207
capitalism 151, 152–153, 170
car sharing 250
car use 204–206, 217, 251, 253, 254
carbon dioxide emissions 1–2, 56–59,
    65, 229–230; benefits of minimizing
    223; Cadbury 50; Heathrow Airport
    Terminal 5 113; London Olympics
    222; reducing your carbon footprint
    250; supply chains 180–182; see also
    climate change
Carbon Disclosure Project 141, 144
Carbon Trust 229, 230

CarbonFix Foundation 180–182
Carson, Rachel 53
Catcher Technologies 16–17
CDP 65
certification 183, 249; CarbonFix
    Foundation 181–182; forests
    140–144, 201–202; organic products
    198–199; Rainforest Alliance 199;
    SA8000 standard 133, 134
change 190–191, 218
charity 49, 73–75, 106–107, 111, 153,
    185, 207, 250
Chernobyl disaster 1
child labour 45, 47, 251; ETI Base Code
    138; Nike 146, 147; personal social
    responsibility 189; SA8000 standard
    133; UN Global Compact 178;
    Universal Declaration of Human
    Rights 60
China 16–17, 59, 83, 134, 146
Churchill, Winston 148
Clarke, A.C. 83
Clean Air Act (1956) 53
climate change 55–59, 179–180, 223;
    forest certification 143; London
    Olympics 227; personal social
    responsibility 192, 203–204, 253;
    SA8000 standard 133; ten ideas 229;
    Unilever 63; see also carbon dioxide
    emissions
Clinton, Hillary 166
Coca-Cola 120–123, 135, 183, 243
coffee 192–197
collective bargaining 60, 138
Committee of Sponsoring
    Organizations of the Treadway
    Commission (COSO) 18–20
communication 41, 43, 44, 123, 156
community 15, 23, 44, 109, 110–111,
    250; BP 160; Henderson Insurance
    Brokers Limited 74; involvement of
    the 223, 226; ISO 26000 standard
    137; Marriott 102; mixed-use
    communities 222, 224; personal
    social responsibility 207–208,
    217, 253; Rainforest Alliance 199;
    reporting 127; risk assessment
    154; sample CSR policy 256; Saudi

Aramco 156; small and medium-sized enterprises 108; supermarkets 67–68; *see also* DTRT Model
Companies Act (1985/2006) 126, 127
compensation 53, 60, 174, 211–214
competitive advantage 71, 151, 183, 225
consultation 94, 95, 105, 111
context 24–29, 42–43, 44, 117
continuous improvement 156
contracts 170, 178
Convention on International Trade in Endangered Species of Wild Fauna and Flora (CITES) 54, 232, 251
Copenhagen Accord 57
corporate governance 18–20, 21
Corporate Risk Systems Limited 2, 77
corporate social responsibility (CSR): action plan 123–124; appetite for 73–75; benefits of 248; branding 79–82; case against 149–168; definitions of 68–69; facts and figures about 107–108; history of 45–60; management system standards 14–15; Olympic Games 219, 220, 247; as an opportunity 106; promoting 254; PSR influence on 216–218; reporting on 126–132, 145; sample policy 256–257; stakeholders 84; transparency 42
Corporate Watch 154
corporation tax 128–130
corruption 18, 178, 245, 246, 251, 256
costs 40, 118–119, 167, 183
Covey, Steven 4
customers 21–22, 85, 93; boycotts by 130; changing values 154; customer service 169; ethical trading 110; London Olympics 243; losing out on 151; loyalty 107, 150; materiality assessment 103; mirroring the customer base 119; objectives 91; purchasing decisions 108, 189; super-capitalism 153; value chain benefits of CSR 195

Dallara 237
Darwin, Charles 51

Deepwater Horizon disaster (BP) 38, 160, 161–162, 163–168
deforestation 63, 64, 144
Deming, William Edwards 5–10, 11
Deming Wheel 8–9, 10, 15, 22, 136
dialogue 92
Diderot, Denis 149
disabled people 225, 234, 252
disciplinary practices 60
discrimination 120, 151, 154, 251, 252; disability 225; ETI Base Code 138, 139; Olympic principles 220; personal social responsibility 207; SA8000 standard 133; UN Global Compact 178; Universal Declaration of Human Rights 60
Disraeli, Benjamin 52
Ditko, S. 169
diversity 119
Dixon, M.A. 90
Donne, John 189
Donovan, J. 10
double bottom line (DBL) 72–73
Dow Chemical 209
Dow Jones Sustainability Index (DJSI) 65
driving 204–206, 217, 253
DTRT (Do The Right Thing) Model 22–23, 42–44, 109, 227; American college football 87; Apple's suppliers in China 16; Bhopal disaster 208; Cadbury 48; carbon management 179; Coca-Cola 122–123; coffee 193; FIFA World Cup 245; forests 140; Formula E 235; Grand Banks Fisheries 25; Heathrow Airport Terminal 5 113; Henderson Insurance Brokers Limited 74; hotels 99; opportunities 124–125; Pearson 76; Rani Plaza disaster 172–173; risk 36, 154; Saudi Aramco 155; tax avoidance 128; triple bottom line 71–72; Unilever 62
Dubos, René 45
due diligence 132, 230

eBay 129
The Economist 70

efficiency 107
Egyptians 4
Eichenwald, Kurt 10
electric cars 235–241
electrical appliances 201
Elkington, John 70
emergency preparedness 156
employees 21, 85, 93, 110, 118–120,
    252; Bangladesh labour rights 175;
    Cadbury 49–50; Coca-Cola 122;
    discrimination against 151, 154;
    ETI Base Code 137–140; health and
    safety actions 254; Health and Safety
    at Work etc. Act 53; healthy lifestyles
    226, 233–234; inclusion 234; loyalty
    107, 108; materiality assessment
    103; Nike 145–146; objectives 91;
    Pearson 75–76; personal social
    responsibility 217–218; reporting
    127; risk assessment 32, 41; sample
    CSR policy 256; sustainable
    procurement 184, 186; UN Global
    Compact 178; unfair dismissal 153;
    Unilever 62; see also workforce rights
employment opportunities 223, 225
endangered species 54, 232, 251
energy: BP 160; energy efficiency
    58–59, 114, 183, 187, 192, 223, 229,
    252; energy labels 203, 204, 250;
    London Olympics 227; Marriott
    102; overhead reduction 150;
    personal social responsibility 217,
    253; SA8000 standard 133; Saudi
    Aramco 159
Enron Corporation 10
Environment Agency 184
environmental and social impact
    assessment (ESIA) 110–111
environmental issues 1–2, 15, 109,
    111–112, 153, 248, 250–251;
    AA 1000 series of standards 134;
    Body Shop 82–83; BP Deepwater
    Horizon disaster 160, 165,
    167–168; Brundtland Report 55;
    Cadbury 'Purple Goes Green'
    strategy 50–51; coffee 195; DTRT
    Model 23, 44; endangered species
    54; environmentally responsible

materials 222, 224–225; forests
    140–144; Formula E 241; Grand
    Banks Fisheries 25–28; Heathrow
    Airport Terminal 5 112–113; hotels
    100, 101, 102; ISO 14001 standard
    135; ISO 26000 standard 137;
    London Olympics 221, 222,
    227–228, 242; organic products
    198–199; personal social
    responsibility 192, 217; Pope Francis
    on 3; Rainforest Alliance 199–200;
    reporting 127; risk assessment 32;
    SA8000 standard 133–134; sample
    CSR policy 256; Saudi Aramco
    158–159; sustainable procurement
    183; UN Global Compact 178;
    Unilever's 'Sustainable Living Plan'
    63–65; see also climate change;
    energy; pollution; sustainability; waste
Environmental Protection Act (1990)
    112
ERIC (Eliminate, Reduce, Isolate,
    Control) 40
ethical trading 15, 110, 150, 208; Body
    Shop 81, 83; DTRT Model 23, 44;
    risk assessment 154; sample CSR
    policy 256; sustainable procurement
    183; see also DTRT Model
Ethical Trading Initiative (ETI) Base
    Code 47, 72, 137–140
ethics 22, 60, 109, 251; accounting
    19; human relationships 114–115;
    purchasing decisions 108, 189;
    sustainable procurement 183
Ethiopian famines 54–55
European Union (EU) 57, 58–59, 152,
    175, 194, 223
excellence 159, 184, 186–187
exploitation 45, 46

Facebook 129
Facility Environmental Performance
    Index (FEPI) 158–159
Factory Act (1833) 46–47
fair trade 116, 192, 193, 195–196,
    197–198, 208
fairness 46, 63
Falklands War 9

famines 54–55
farmers 176
fear 10
FedEx 71
Fibonacci (Leonardo Pisano) 35
FIFA World Cup 244–247
financial burden of CSR 151, 153–154
financial sector crisis 131
fire safety 158, 174, 175
fisheries 25–28
Food Legacy Pledge 243
food safety 195
football 244–247
forced labour 148n1, 170; ETI Base
    Code 137; SA8000 standard 133;
    UN Global Compact 178; Universal
    Declaration of Human Rights 60
Foreign Corrupt Practices Act (1977)
    18
Forestry Stewardship Certification
    (FSC) 141, 142–143, 201–202, 232
forests 140–144, 201–202
Formula E 235–241
4Ts of risk 36–37, 40
Foxconn 17
Francis, Mary 73
freedom of association 60, 116, 138, 178
FTSE4Good Index 65
Fuller, C.W. 34

Gandhi, Mahatma 190
Gardner, D. 33
Gates, Bill 190
Geldof, Bob 190
Global Corporate Sustainability
    Leaders 65
Global Reporting Initiative 69, 70–71,
    72, 103–104
Google 129
Gore, Al 56
government 14–15, 92, 93, 97, 153
Grand Banks Fisheries, Canada 25–28
Green America 16–17
green dot symbol 202–203
greenhouse gas emissions 56–59, 144,
    229–230; see also carbon dioxide
    emissions
Greenpeace 81

greenwashing 80, 83
grievance management 94, 95, 98,
    251
Gulf of Mexico disaster (BP) 38, 160,
    161–162, 163–168

habitats 133
Hackitt, Judith 33
Halliburton 163, 165–166, 167
Hammurabi Codex 46
Handy, C. 170
harassment 140, 145–146
harm 36
Hawken, Paul 4
Hayward, Tony 38, 162, 165, 166
hazards 36, 119, 138
health: healthy eating 254; healthy
    lifestyles 223, 226, 233–234; London
    Olympics 227, 228, 242; personal
    social responsibility 206–207, 253;
    Unilever 64
health and safety 15, 118, 153, 188,
    233, 253–254; Apple's suppliers in
    China 16–17; Bangladesh 174–175;
    DTRT Model 23, 44; ETI Base
    Code 138; ILO-OSH 2001 standard
    11–12; London Olympics 244;
    management plans 111; OHSAS
    18001 standard 21, 136; origins
    of 46; Pearson 76–79; Rainforest
    Alliance 199; return on investment
    152; risk assessment 33, 104; Saudi
    Aramco 156–158; 3W approach
    246–247; Universal Declaration of
    Human Rights 60; see also DTRT
    Model
Health and Safety at Work etc. Act
    (1974) 53, 111, 120
Health and Safety Executive 34, 118
Heathrow Airport Terminal 5 112–113,
    234
Heinz 30
Henderson Insurance Brokers Limited
    (HIBL) 73–75
Hewland 237
Hitler, Adolf 190
Holmes, R. 69
Hon Hai Precision Industry Co., Ltd 17

Honduras 196
hotels 98–102
Huang, K. 90
human rights 60, 68, 109, 115–116,
    252; BP 160; Coca-Cola 122;
    Olympic principles 220; SA8000
    standard 133; sample CSR policy
    256; UN Global Compact 178
human trafficking 131–132, 170

Iacocca, Lee 6
ignorance of the law 20
ILO-OSH 2001 standard 11–12, 15
improvement 43, 44
incident reporting 156
inclusion 227, 228, 234, 241
India 183, 208–216
information: Business Reviews 127;
    stakeholder engagement 92, 94, 95,
    97, 105
Innocent Smoothies 183
innovation 71
Innovation Group Plc. 179–181
inputs 114
integrity 19
Intergovernmental Panel on Climate
    Change (IPCC) 55
internal control 18, 19, 20–22
International Bill of Human Rights
    115–116
International Coffee Agreement 194
International Finance Corporation 85,
    95, 96
International Labour Organization
    (ILO) 11–12, 15, 60, 133;
    Bangladesh 175, 175; ETI Base Code
    137–140
International Olympic Committee
    (IOC) 220
International Organization for
    Standardization (ISO) 8, 10–13,
    59–60, 68, 72, 85, 137; see also ISO
    standards
International Register of Certificated
    Auditors (IRCA) 145
Investor in People 254
investors 21, 103

ISO 14001 standard 8, 11, 13, 15, 21,
    59–60, 72, 135–136, 158, 176–177,
    183, 188n1, 208, 226–227
ISO 20121 standard 243
ISO 26000 standard 59–60, 68, 72, 85,
    137
ISO 45001 standard 11, 13, 15, 21, 72,
    136
ISO 9001 standard 8, 10–11, 13, 15, 21
Italy 134

Japan 6
JCB 30
Johnson, Lyndon B. 55
Juran, Joseph 6

Kenco 152, 193, 196–197
key performance indicators (KPIs) 10,
    28, 124, 127, 208, 249
Keys, T. 106
Khushhali Bank Limited 72–73
Klein, Naomi 81
knowledge exchange workshops 187
Korea 146
Kyoto Protocol 56, 57–58

labelling 197–203, 250, 251
labour practices see employees
Lamy, Pascal 247–248
leadership 4, 156
Leadership in Energy and
    Environmental Design (LEED) 101
Leahy, Terry 66
Lee, S. 169
legal requirements 22, 23, 42, 44, 68;
    compensation claims 53; health
    and safety 253; register of 254; risk
    assessment 32; sample CSR policy
    256; stakeholder engagement 93, 96;
    see also DTRT Model
legislation: Clean Air Act 53;
    Companies Act 126, 127;
    environmental protection 112;
    Factory Act 46–47; Grand Banks
    Fisheries 26; Health and Safety at
    Work etc. Act 53, 111, 120; Modern
    Slavery Act 131–132; National

Minimum Wage Act 120; Victorian era 51; worker protection 119–120; Working Time Regulations 120
Lego 135
Lever Brothers 52
Leverhulme, Lord 52, 62
Lippman, Walter 218
Live Aid 54, 55
living wages 139
Lloyds Bank 47, 247
lobbying 150, 153
logos 79–80
London Olympics (2012) 219–228, 234, 241–244, 247
London smog 53
Low, Mike 137
loyalty: customers 107, 150; employees 107, 108; suppliers 183
Lyall, S. 161–162

Malnight, T.W. 106
management 4, 249; Deming 5–10; DTRT Model 22–23; evolution of management thinking 6; information for 17–18; risk 32, 41–42; sample CSR policy 257; stakeholder engagement 93, 94, 95, 98; standards 10–15; Sun Tzu 4–5; sustainable procurement 183; see also senior management
Management of Health and Safety at Work Regulations 111, 120
management system standards (MSS) 12–13, 14–15, 132–140, 208
Mandela, Nelson 190
market responsibility 116–117
market share 107, 150
marketing 110, 152, 184, 185, 196-197
Marks and Spencer 152
Marriott International, Inc. 99–102
Matalan 172
materiality 102–104, 123, 152
McAllister, Peter 174
McDonald's 80–81
McKie, Peter 118
McLaren Electronics Systems 237
media 84, 92, 97, 132, 151

Merritt, Carolyn W. 41
Mesopotamia 46
Mexico 146
Michelin 237, 240
microfinance 72
mind mapping 85
minimum wage 120
mission 28–29, 38, 39
MIT 71–72
mitigated risk 35
Möbius loop 200
Modern Slavery Act (2015) 131–132
Mondelēz International 50–51, 195–196
monitoring 94, 95, 98, 111, 249
Monsoon 172
Morrison's 66
Mother Teresa 190

National Minimum Wage Act (1998) 120
National Society for the Prevention of Cruelty to Children (NSPCC) 49
negligence 52
negotiation 94, 95
'neighbour principle' 52
Nestlé 193, 194, 195
Nike 71, 145–148
nongovernmental organizations (NGOs) 92, 93, 97, 152

Obama, Barack 56, 59, 165, 166
objectives 23, 28–31, 32, 43, 44, 91–92
occupational safety and health see health and safety
OHSAS 18001 standard 11, 15, 21, 72, 77, 79, 136–137
oil companies 155–168
Olympic Delivery Authority (ODA) 221–222, 226–227
Olympic Games 219–228, 234, 241–244, 247
Operating and Financial Review (OFR) 126
Operational Excellence (OE) 159
opportunities 33, 34, 106–107, 117, 124–125

organic products 198–199
outputs 114
overtime 133, 139
Oxfam 65
ozone depletion 55

packaging: Cadbury 50; ethical trading
    110; labelling 197–203; returnable
    183, 187, 232; Unilever 64, 65; waste
    policy 231
Packard, Ben 186
Pakistan 72–73, 134, 146, 147, 148n1
palm oil 51, 65
partnerships 94, 95, 106–107, 187
Pearson plc. 75–79
performance: reporting 126–127, 208;
    SA8000 standard 133; Saudi Aramco
    158
personal social responsibility (PSR)
    55, 189–218, 248, 253; labelling
    197–203; personal actions 203–208,
    216–217; seven steps to change
    190–191
philanthropists 47, 49
physical abuse 140
Piper Alpha disaster 152
Pisano, Leonardo (Fibonacci) 35
Plan-Do-Check-Act (PDCA) 8–9, 11,
    12, 15, 22, 136
plans 31
politicians 150, 153
pollution 25, 45, 151, 154, 225,
    233; Bhopal disaster 215; ISO
    14001 standard 21; landfill 224;
    London smog 53; personal social
    responsibility 189, 204; prevention
    of 250; SA8000 standard 133; Soil
    Association 198; Victorian Britain 47
Polman, Paul 64
Pope Francis 3
Port Sunlight 62
positive thinking 190
prices 176, 197–198
Primark 172, 174
processes 114
procurement 169, 178, 182–187, 195,
    242, 250, 251; see also suppliers
productivity 11, 47–48, 107, 118, 226

profit 60, 70, 71, 118, 149, 150,
    151–152, 176
Programme for the Endorsement of
    Forest Certification (PEFC) 142, 143,
    201–202
Project Catalyst 112
project monitoring 94, 95, 98
Project Sunlight 64–65
Puma 70
purchasing see procurement
purchasing decisions, consumers 108,
    189
'Purple Goes Green' strategy 50–51

quadruple bottom line (QBL) 73
Quaker Principles 49, 50, 52, 62
quality management 21

racism 252
Rainforest Alliance 193, 199–200
Rani Plaza disaster 152, 171–175
recycling 114, 198, 224, 250; council
    costs 149; labels 200–201, 202;
    London Olympics 221, 222, 227,
    243; personal social responsibility
    206, 217, 253; ten ideas 230, 231,
    232; value chain 177
regular employment 139–140
Reich, R.B. 152–153
relationships 114
Renault 237, 239
reporting 126–132, 208; AA 1000 series
    of standards 134; Business Reviews
    126–127; G4 reporting standards
    69, 70–71, 103; Modern Slavery Act
    131–132; public register of reports
    145; to stakeholders 19, 94, 95, 98,
    123
reputation 32, 71, 107, 150
resources: SA8000 standard 133;
    Soil Association 198; stakeholder
    engagement 94, 97; sustainable
    procurement 184
return on investment 152, 154
risk 6, 32–42, 150; 4Ts 36–37, 40;
    'Black Swans' 37; BP Deepwater
    Horizon disaster 164; brief history
    of 35–36; Business Reviews 127;

definitions of 33–34; deforestation 144; DTRT Model 23, 43, 44; hazard and 36; human factor 41; inherent or residual 34–35; management and 41–42; risk assessment 32, 33, 104, 144, 154, 156; risk matrix 33, 38, 40, 41; risk-reward balance 151, 152, 168; sample CSR policy 256; sustainable procurement 183, 184; understanding 37–38
road accidents 157, 254
Romania 134
Rowntree 47, 49, 52, 247
Royal Dutch Shell *see* Shell
Royal Society for the Prevention of Accidents (RoSPA) 77, 79
Royal Society for the Prevention of Cruelty to Animals (RSPCA) 49
Rudd, Nigel 33

SA8000 standard 72, 133–134, 208
safety 41, 118; Bangladesh 175; BP 161; FIFA World Cups 245–247; London Olympics 241–242; mixed-use communities 224; Rani Plaza disaster 174; Saudi Aramco 156–158; value chain benefits of CSR 195; *see also* health and safety
Sainsbury's 66
sales 107, 152, 169, 176
Santayana, George 3
Saudi Arabian Oil Company (Saudi Aramco) 155–159
schools 157
SEDEX supplier database 254
senior management 11, 249; business context 28–29; commitment to CSR 123; corporate governance 19–20; lack of guidance for 18; tone at the top 41
service sector 179
sexual harassment 140, 146
shareholders 29, 60, 68, 85, 93; Body Shop 82; communication of performance to 75; objectives 91; profit for 149, 150, 151–152; sustainable procurement 183
Shell 10, 30, 70, 135

Shewhart, Walter 8
slavery 46, 131–132, 170, 252
Smith, E.J. 37
smog 53
social capital 111
social justice 69
social media 59, 84, 102
social responsibility 137, 154
society 22, 45, 60, 85, 93, 248; definition of 69n2; expectations 84; objectives 92; opportunities 107, 124–125
Soil Association 198
Spark Racing Technology 237
stakeholders 15, 19, 21–22, 68, 69, 84–105, 248; AA 1000 series of standards 134, 135; communication with 75, 123; dealing with concerns of 149; definition of 85; engagement 92–98, 134, 135, 208; forest protection 143; identification of 94, 249; inclusiveness 103–104; materiality 102–104; needs of 107; objectives 91–92; PEFC 202; risk evaluation 42; sample CSR policy 256, 257; sustainable procurement 184; triple bottom line 71; Unilever 63
standards: accounting 19; forest protection 143; G4 reporting standards 69, 70–71, 103; health and safety 77, 79; Rainforest Alliance 199; triple bottom line 72; verification 132–148; worker protection 119–120; *see also* BS standards; ISO standards
Starbucks 129–130, 193
Steen, Anthony 132
Stella Artois 79
strategy 5, 32, 184
stress 254
Sun Tzu 4–5
super-capitalism 152–153
supermarkets 66–68, 176
suppliers 51, 85, 107, 249, 251; Body Shop 83; carbon management 180; choosing 177–178; Coca-Cola 122; contracts 170; developing nations

47; energy efficiency 229; ethical trading 110; London Olympics 242; materiality assessment 103; Nike 146; objectives 91; packaging 232; practices 179; Rani Plaza disaster 174; Saudi Aramco 156; SEDEX database 254; sustainable procurement 182–187; Tesco 176; Unilever 63–64; value chain benefits of CSR 195; *see also* procurement

supply chains 169–188; coffee 194; ethical trading 150; Modern Slavery Act 131, 132; personal social responsibility 189; promotion of CSR 249; supply chain management 152, 171, 208; supply chain reviews 124; sustainable procurement 182–187

sustainability: AA 1000 series of standards 134, 135; Coca-Cola 120–121; forest protection 142, 143; Formula E 235, 237, 241; ISO 14001 standard 226–227; ISO 26000 standard 137; London Olympics 221–222, 226–227, 241, 243; PEFC 202; personal social responsibility 192, 217; quadruple bottom line 73; service sector 179; three pillars of 70; Unilever 62–65; *see also* DTRT Model

SustainAbility 65, 70

Sustainability Compact 175

sustainable development 68, 73, 217, 256

sustainable procurement 182–187

System of Profound Knowledge 9

Taiwan 146

Tao Te Ching 1

targets 31, 123, 208; deforestation 144; ISO 14001 standard 135; realistic 190, 191

tax avoidance 128–130, 131

Technical Management Board (TMB) 13

Tesco 66, 71, 176, 225

threats 33, 117

3Ps 70, 71

3W approach 246–247

time management 104

tobacco 117

Toyota 9

trade unions 133, 138

traffic safety 157

training: knowledge exchange workshops 187; Saudi Aramco 156; sustainable procurement 184; waste management 232

Transocean 163, 165–166, 167

transparency 19, 42; Coffee vs. Gangs programme 196; FSC scheme 143; Unilever 63

transport: car sharing 250; car use 204–206, 217, 251, 253, 254; company policy 251; electric cars 235–241; environmental protection 112; public 221, 222, 224, 227, 242, 252; road accidents 157, 254; SA8000 standard 134

triple bottom line (TBL) 70–72

trust, lack of 130–131

Tyler-Rubenstein, I. 106

uncertainty 23, 32, 34

Unilever 52, 61–65

Union Carbide 208–216

United Kingdom: best practice guidance 15; carbon management 179–182; climate change 56; Environment Agency 184; environmental protection 112; history of CSR 46–53; insured and uninsured costs 118; Modern Slavery Act 131–132; organic products 198; tax avoidance 129–130; worker protection 119, 120

United Nations Global Compact 59, 72, 152, 177, 178, 183

United States (US): climate change 56, 59; coffee dispute with Brazil 194; college football 86–91; corporate governance 20; Foreign Corrupt Practices Act 18; tax avoidance 129; worker protection 119

Universal Declaration of Human Rights 60, 115, 116, 133, 170

unmitigated risk 35

value: price and 176; shared 68, 194; value creation and protection 34
value chain concept 176–177
value chain management 140, 142
values 30, 41, 45, 154, 184
Van der Graaf, K. 106
Vassie, L.H. 34
verification 43, 44, 132–148
Victorian era 47–50, 51–52
vision 28–31, 38, 39, 63
Vodafone 135
volunteering 207, 250

wages: ETI Base Code 139; minimum wage 120; Nike 146, 147; SA8000 standard 133
Walmart 66, 172, 225
War on Want 121–122
waste 109, 112, 114, 224; duty of care for 177; Heathrow Airport Terminal 5 113; London Olympics 222, 227, 243; minimization of 152; personal social responsibility 206; Rainforest Alliance 199; SA8000 standard 134; shared waste minimization programmes 187; Soil Association 198; sustainable procurement 183; ten ideas 230–232; Unilever 63, 65; *see also* recycling
Waste and Resources Action Programme (WRAP) 232, 243

water 223, 225; Cadbury 50; Coca-Cola 121, 122; Heathrow Airport Terminal 5 113; leaks 251; London Olympics 222; Marriott 102; personal social responsibility 204, 217, 253; Rainforest Alliance 199; SA8000 standard 133, 134; Unilever 63; Water Resources Act 112
Water Resources Act (1991) 112
Watts, P. 69
well-being 64, 121
wilful blindness 20
Williams Advanced Engineering 237
win-win situations 154, 185
Wolken, Dan 90–91
women 63, 121
Wordsworth, William 83
workforce rights 15, 23, 44, 154; *see also* DTRT Model; employees
working conditions 45, 48; Apple's suppliers in China 16–17; ETI Base Code 47, 137–140; fair trade 197; Nike 145–146; personal social responsibility 189; Rainforest Alliance 199; SA8000 standard 133; Soil Association 199
working hours 45, 47, 60, 120, 133, 139, 252
Working Time Regulations (1998) 120
World Bank 69, 85, 96
World Wide Fund for Nature (WWF) 80–81, 142